Philip Matyszak

T0328083

# FORGOTTEN
# PEOPLES
## OF THE
# ANCIENT
# WORLD

With 186 illustrations

*Previous pages* Anthropoid sarcophagi from the cemetery at Deir el-Balah, Late Canaanite period, thirteenth–fourteenth century BC.

*Following pages* Mada'in Saleh in Saudi Arabia was the second largest Nabataean settlement after Petra, and includes this monumental tomb carved from a rock outcrop.

# Introduction
# **Resurrecting a Forgotten World**

They are called 'the mists of time' for a reason. Both as individuals and as a culture we only really take notice of people and events close to our own era. In 2013, *Time* magazine compiled a list of 'the 100 most significant figures in history'. Around 40 per cent of those on the list had lived in the last 150 years, and the majority of the rest in the past 500. Sargon the Great of Akkad, founder of the world's first empire (r. *c.* 2334–2279 BC), was not considered sufficiently significant to qualify. On the other hand, the 22nd (and 24th) US President, Grover Cleveland, who died in 1908, did make the list. The further away other people are from us in space and time, it seems, the less they impinge on our consciousness.

It is not just personalities but entire ancient peoples who have faded from our collective memory. While it is true that some of the more significant forms are visible in the mists – the Romans, the Assyrians and the Egyptians are unlikely soon to vanish from view – other peoples and tribes who rocked civilizations and changed the ethnic pattern of humanity are now only dimly recalled, even when they are remembered at all. Some once great peoples have altogether disappeared except as names to intrigue ethnographers and archaeologists: the Luwians, Orniaci and hundreds of others.

More intriguing are those peoples whom we still glimpse occasionally, who have survived through some quirk of language or culture. Today we think we know the Aborigines, yet the first Aborigines were believed to have lived in central Italy, as described by the historian Dionysius of Halicarnassus. It seemed to the Romans that this ancient tribe had been there forever; consequently, by the modern era, the word 'Aboriginal' has come to describe the native inhabitants of a place, even if that place is somewhere far distant from the original Aborigines.

This book is about such peoples who, though largely forgotten, have directly or indirectly affected us today. Or they are peoples about whom we remember just one thing while the rest is lost. What do we know of the Bactrians, apart from their two-humped camels? Or of the Samaritans, other than that one of them was good? We call an uncultured lout a Philistine, but were the Philistines philistines, and come to that, were the Vandals vandals?

There are very many such peoples, and to describe them all is beyond the scope of this single book, which is concerned with the lost peoples of one region of the ancient world. It is intended to give a picture of the busy, brawling, multicultural mass of humanity which occupied the ancient Middle East, Mediterranean and parts of Europe. One purpose of gathering together these obscure peoples is to remind ourselves that civilization is a collective human project. It is not the 'great' civilizations alone that made our modern world.

Egypt, Babylonia and Assyria dominate the pre-Classical era, just as the Hebrews, Romans and Greeks crowd others out of sight in the centuries that followed. Yet none of these great civilizations would have taken shape without the contributions, major and minor, of the peoples who lived on their peripheries. The Phrygians contributed, as did the Chaldeans and the Epirots – and without these peoples we would not have, respectively, the Liberty cap of the French revolutionaries, idiomatic 'feet of clay' or Pyrrhic victories.

In a way, the story of these different, often idiosyncratic, forgotten peoples is the story of Western civilization from a different perspective. Instead of looking at later Classical history as a narrative of the expanding power of Rome, this book examines what that expansion meant for peoples such as the Celtiberians or Nabataeans – for whom Rome brought at best radical cultural change and, at worst, extinction. Yet even as they faded, these peoples influenced their conquerors, so that the Rome of late antiquity was far different from the Rome of the early Republic.

Over the centuries the focus of this text moves westwards, from the world's first city, Uruk, by the River Euphrates, in ancient Sumeria, to the tribal heartlands of the Iceni in the Fens of eastern Britain. This is not because civilization also moved west – Babylonia and Egypt managed to remain a lot more civilized than Britain throughout the ancient era. But civilization certainly expanded westwards, and a large part of our story comes from how peoples and cultures already established in the west coped with that expansion.

**Note:** The dates given for each people are approximations which indicate the main period during which these peoples or civilizations were present on the stage of history. While in some cases any given date might be open to debate, the times or periods chosen are mostly based either on known significant events (such as decisive battles) or on the first or last mentions in ancient sources. The *Oxford Classical Dictionary*, edited by Simon Hornblower and Antony Spawforth (4th ed., 2012), and other Oxford resources have been used as a reference point wherever possible.

# Part One
# **The First Civilizations**
# Early States in Mesopotamia and Egypt

What exactly is civilization? Essentially it's where we find large-scale societies, often cities and states organized hierarchically, with rulers (usually together with priests and a warrior caste) controlling labourers and craftsmen to direct the flow of wealth, establishing inequality. Civilization is certainly about decent roads and sewers, but it is also about taxation and social order, advances in technology – critically weaponry – and, more often than not, the moving of 'lesser peoples' out of the way of 'progress'.

This story begins when humans in Mesopotamia first learned to live together in large numbers. It is on the whole their ideas which spread westwards, changing and being changed by the peoples encountered along the way. Our story ends with waves of migratory peoples invading Europe from the north and east. Yet these invaders did not destroy civilization. Instead they were absorbed into it, just as the first empire-builders were absorbed into Sumeria all those thousands of years ago.

When we look at the early history of Mesopotamia – in ancient Greek literally the land 'between two rivers' and covering modern-day Iraq and parts of Syria – and the Levant, the first impression is of confusion and chaos. Cities seem to rise and fall in a heartbeat, and people with strange names briefly flicker on and off the stage of history. It is hard to keep track of even major civilizations, let alone peripheral tribes and nations.

There are two reasons for this. First, in these early days Mesopotamia was a confusing place, and the lands to the north and west of it even more so. Cities were brand new, and civilization was just beginning to get to grips with urbanism. Basic principles such as administration, law codes and record-keeping were being developed from scratch. Nor were the innovators in these early cities allowed to get on with their work without disturbance. Large settlements attracted waves of migrants, mostly from the north. Newcomers, whether arriving peacefully or as armed invaders, had to be integrated into the already complex mix of cultures existing in the region.

The second reason why this period seems so chaotic is because of the 'telescoping' perception of history. 'Ancient history' happened long ago, and we tend to imagine that it all happened more or less at once.

Even people who are familiar with the ancient Greek historian Herodotus (*c.* 484–425 BC) may be surprised to learn that when he saw the pyramids at Giza in Egypt, they were already half as old as they are now. Herodotus also describes the city of Babylon. One of its kings had a passion for archaeology. It takes a moment to adjust to the fact that the ruler of a civilization so old that archaeologists today are delighted to discover any relics of its existence was himself interested in digging up evidence of earlier civilizations. The artefacts he unearthed were even more ancient when he found them than the ruins of his own civilization are today.

Finally, our understanding of the first civilizations is constantly evolving as archaeologists and scientists make new discoveries. Textbooks published just a few decades ago are already in need of substantial revision. So it's no wonder that ancient Mesopotamia can seem such a perplexing place. And even in ancient Egypt, where we seem to have a more focused picture of the trajectory of civilization, there are still interludes of relative chaos that historians call 'intermediate periods' – a technical term for 'times when we have no clue what was going on'. Therefore, in this earliest era, it is even more necessary than usual to establish our forgotten peoples in a framework of time and place.

It is no accident that civilization first emerged along the Tigris and Euphrates rivers in Mesopotamia, and a short time later along the Nile in Egypt. In Mesopotamia crops only flourished thanks to irrigation, a project which required large numbers of people to work together. Such organized efforts not only fed the labourers who created and maintained the irrigation canals, but also generated an agricultural surplus that could feed the hungry mouths in the first cities. Likewise in Egypt, labour was centrally organized to exploit the soils enriched by the annual flooding of the Nile.

Thus in both Egypt and Mesopotamia, geographical circumstances allowed dominating elites to harness the power of collective activity, propelling the growth of the first cities, states and empires. Climate change seems to have been a trigger too: a steep decline in sea levels after 3500 BC reduced the flow of the great rivers, forcing an intensification of canal building. The cities best able to exploit scarce resources came out on top through a combination of strength and sophistication. Uruk, well-positioned beside the Euphrates in southern Mesopotamia, became the first known city in the world in around 3500 BC. At its height, Uruk, capital of the Sumerian civilization, occupied an area twice the size of Classical Athens, and as many as 50,000 people may have lived within its walls.

To manage an increasingly complex economy, the Sumerians invented the world's first writing system. This was cuneiform – a script of wedge-shaped symbols produced by pressing a stylus cut from reed into soft clay tablets. Archaeologists are eternally grateful for the fact that these clay tablets are almost indestructible, particularly when baked hard in one of the many conflagrations that plagued early cities. As a result, tens of thousands of records covering thousands of years have survived, documenting the details of the successive states and empires of the Middle East.

A Semitic-speaking people, the **Akkadians** established the world's first empire, which they ruled from the lost city of Akkad. The Akkadians dominated not just the Sumerian city-states in the south but all of Mesopotamia for 150 years, before fading from view around 2190 BC.

Thereafter the main pattern of Mesopotamian power politics is one of rivalry between two new centres of authority. Babylon (originally an Akkadian stronghold) in the south and Assyria in the north established competing empires after 1800 BC. It was a little-known, semi-nomadic people from Syria, the **Amorites**, who put Babylon on the road to empire, particularly under Hammurabi, the city's famous law-giver.

By now new centres of power had emerged at the western and eastern peripheries of the Middle East. The **Hittites** in Anatolia became strong enough to sack Babylon in 1595 BC, while the **Elamites** of the western Iranian highlands were a constant thorn in the side of the lowland Mesopotamians. (They also took a turn at conquering Babylon, briefly, in 694 BC.)

By comparison with the often bewildering flux of states and empires in Mesopotamia, the waxing and waning of Egyptian civilization to the south seems deceptively straightforward. The unification of Upper and Lower Egypt after 3100 BC resulted some 600 years later, during the Old Kingdom, in the building of the pyramids of Giza – a spectacular manifestation of the power of a highly centralized state. Yet the Egyptians were not immune to disruption from invaders. Around 1650 BC they were almost overwhelmed from the north by the mysterious **Hyksos**, and suffered the ignominy of foreign domination for the next century. The Egyptians eventually threw the invaders out, but sensibly retained their innovations in agriculture and weaponry.

The new Egyptian royal dynasty established the New Kingdom around 1550 BC. This became a fully-fledged empire, launching regular campaigns north into the Levant and south into Nubia to expand Egypt's borders. This military exercise brought the Egyptians, led by Ramesses the Great, into conflict with the Hittites, most notably at the so-called 'first battle in history' at Qadesh in Syria, around 1274 BC. It appears that the Egyptians came second in this confrontation – though that was not how Ramesses recorded it, carving monumental images of his glorious victories on temple walls across the country.

The lands these powers fought over in the Levant had been occupied by the **Canaanites** for millennia. But, with what historians know as the Bronze Age collapse of around 1200 BC, it was the elusive **Sea Peoples** who extinguished the Hittites and threw Egypt into chaos. The battles between Sea Peoples and the communities they targeted were more savage but no less intense than the debates among modern scholars who attempt to determine where the Sea Peoples came from, or what drove them.

What is certain is that the Sea Peoples were the harbingers of a so-called Dark Age that endured for 300 years, until the states and empires of the new Iron Age emerged, transforming humanity once more.

# *c.* 2334 BC – 2190 BC
# **The Akkadians**
## The First Empire Builders

*Naram-sin, mighty king, the king of Akkad,*
*  king of the four corners of the earth*
*Who glorifies Ishtar and Amunitum....*
*Whose ancestor Sargon defeated Uruk,*
*  and freed the people of Kish*
*Shaving off the hairstyles [of slaves] and*
*  breaking their shackles.*

Tablet of Naram-Sin

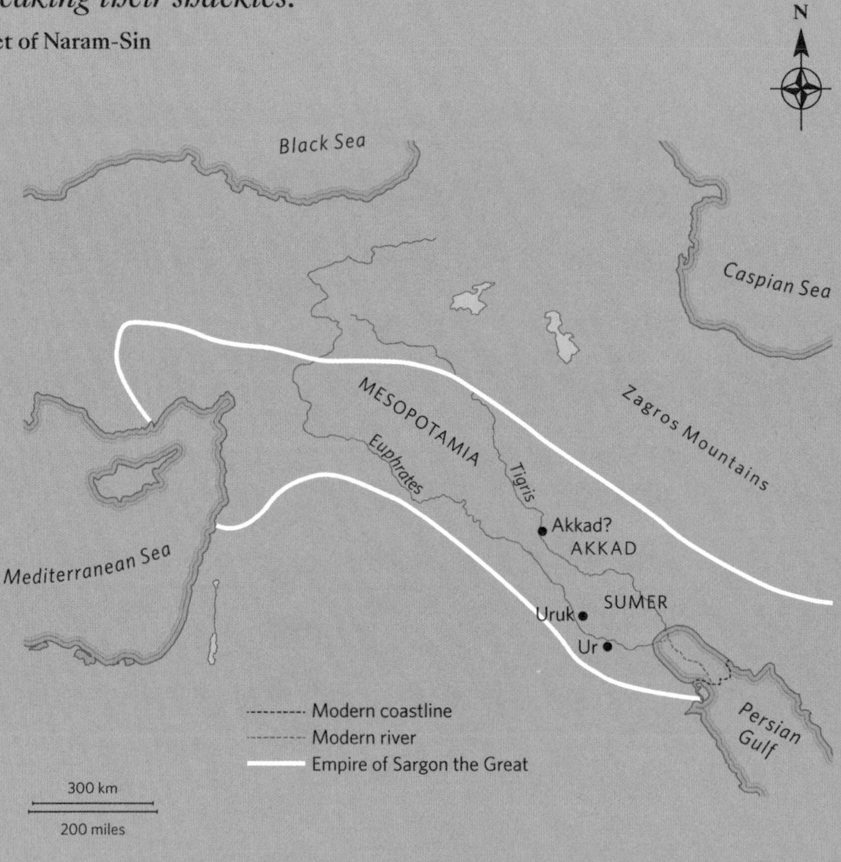

N

Black Sea

Caspian Sea

MESOPOTAMIA

Zagros Mountains

Euphrates

Tigris

Akkad?
AKKAD

SUMER

Uruk

Ur

Mediterranean Sea

Persian Gulf

- - - - - - Modern coastline
- - - - - - Modern river
———— Empire of Sargon the Great

300 km

200 miles

The Akkadians achieved a series of firsts that set the template for the great states that were to follow. They founded the world's first empire, ruled over by the first god-king, and established the first professional military force.

## Sargon, founder of the first empire

The people called the Akkadians were one obscure tribe among many in the huge and diverse melting pot that was Upper Mesopotamia in the third millennium BC. But Akkadian history really begins with a king called Sargon the Great (r. *c.* 2334–2279 BC). How Sargon transformed these obscure peoples into rulers of an empire that stretched from the headwaters of the Euphrates to the Persian Gulf is uncertain. Sargon's origins are – literally – the stuff of myth. It is claimed that his mother was a priestess, and when Sargon was born she placed him in a basket and cast it into a river. The resemblance to the much later tale of Romulus and Remus (one of Sargon's sons was called Rimush) is unmistakable, though apparently Sargon grew up as a gardener while the founders of Rome began their careers as shepherds.

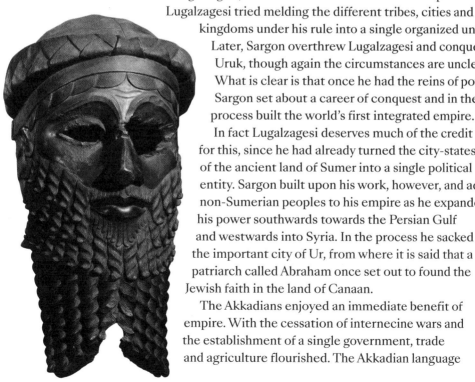

A bronze head of Sargon the Great. It is probable that the head was mutilated in antiquity when it fell into the hands of enemies of the Akkadians.

During Sargon's youth, the region was under the control of a king called Lugalzagesi, who ruled from Uruk. In a novel experiment, Lugalzagesi tried melding the different tribes, cities and kingdoms under his rule into a single organized unit. Later, Sargon overthrew Lugalzagesi and conquered Uruk, though again the circumstances are unclear. What is clear is that once he had the reins of power, Sargon set about a career of conquest and in the process built the world's first integrated empire.

In fact Lugalzagesi deserves much of the credit for this, since he had already turned the city-states of the ancient land of Sumer into a single political entity. Sargon built upon his work, however, and added non-Sumerian peoples to his empire as he expanded his power southwards towards the Persian Gulf and westwards into Syria. In the process he sacked the important city of Ur, from where it is said that a patriarch called Abraham once set out to found the Jewish faith in the land of Canaan.

The Akkadians enjoyed an immediate benefit of empire. With the cessation of internecine wars and the establishment of a single government, trade and agriculture flourished. The Akkadian language was adapted to the ubiquitous cuneiform script of the region, and clay tablets have been discovered from which we learn of Akkad's commercial interactions with peoples as far away as Cyprus, Egypt and the Indus Valley.

## Ruling as god-kings

It is not known whether Sargon founded the city of Akkad or whether it already existed. Its exact location eludes archaeologists, though it is now thought to have been somewhere on the Tigris. Sargon himself alleges he came from the otherwise unknown city of Azurpiranu. Certainly Akkad was either born or reborn under his rule, and for the next century this city was the political centre of Mesopotamia. The Akkadian system of government became the standard that was later imitated throughout the region. Essentially this was a palace culture in which the emperor, in another social innovation, became a god-king.

Both Sargon and the most illustrious of his successors, Naram-Sin (2261–2224 BC), had the good fortune of having highly capable daughters whom they appointed to priestly functions. This greatly eased the transition to the perception of kings as gods, as at this time temples were not only religious but also administrative centres. Other daughters were married to governors in distant but important provinces to ensure the loyalty of these administrators. These measures later became standard practice, but as no one had ever governed an empire like theirs before, the Akkadian kings were making it up as they went along.

From *c.* 2334 BC for fifty-five years Sargon ruled what he doubtless considered most of the world ('the four corners of the universe' as he put it). However, despite having some benefits, his long reign did not reconcile those he ruled over to the new concept of empire. As soon as Sargon died, many of his subjects rebelled in a bid to regain their independence. Until the final fall of Akkad, such rebellions took place after the death of each of the empire's seven kings.

## Economy and culture

One aspect that greatly helped the Akkadians in the maintenance of their empire was that the most important part – Sumer – was almost entirely dependent on irrigation to sustain agriculture. If carried out properly, irrigation combined with abundant sunlight produces outstanding crops, but this requires a large degree of social co-operation and organization. This made the Sumerians more

reliant on a proper administration than were – for example – the nomadic and rebellious Amorite herdsmen on the empire's fringes.

Furthermore, while the vast majority of the population of Akkad worked the land, the efficiency of the agricultural system generated a surplus that could be used to sustain clerks, priests, merchants and administrators. Surplus grain also helped to maintain a field army. It is believed that the palace guard of Sargon was one of the first professional military forces in known history. This was a trained group, probably no larger than a thousand strong, but which was nevertheless highly influential on the battlefield against poorly trained militias.

Akkadian warfare was still relatively primitive. For example the Akkadian 'cavalry chariot' was a donkey-drawn cart. (Horses bred large enough to carry riders were still a millennium away.) Sargon improved the Akkadian military by putting his phalanx – armed with copper-tipped spears and wooden shields – into a deeper formation and using serried blocks of archers to destroy particular targets, especially chariots. The aim of most Akkadian military expeditions was to secure the trade routes of the empire. For all their abundance of grain, the Akkadians needed to trade for timber and minerals.

The rise of Akkad meant that Akkadian became the common language of the region, making it the first Semitic language to compete with native Sumerian. This linguistic change is recorded in inscribed clay tablets. The majority of Akkadian texts we have today are preserved on such tablets, mostly from a later period than the Akkadian empire, as Akkadian was also used by a number of successor states such as the Neo-Assyrians. Surviving contemporary texts indicate an interest in omens and a fear of witchcraft and demons.

Akkadian sculpture was used for propaganda purposes, showing the Akkadian king conquering his enemies or consorting with the gods. Unsurprisingly, Akkad's enemies and former conquered peoples were none too fond of such depictions, and with the fall of Akkad many of these sculptures were destroyed. A famous surviving bust of Sargon has the eyes gouged out and the ears cut off – punishments sometimes inflicted on disobedient slaves.

A clay tablet inscribed in Akkadian cuneiform now in the British Museum. This appears to have been a school practice tablet which contains parts of the birth legend of Sargon the Great.

## The fall of the Akkadians

Shar-Kali-Sharri, the last major Akkadian king, came to power in troubled times. There are indications that climatic change brought drought, which disrupted the irrigation systems on which the Akkadians depended. So severe was this drought that it appears from the archaeological record that some cities were abandoned altogether. Akkadian weakness then encouraged raiders, such as the Gutian people of southwestern Iran, who were gathering on Akkad's frontiers, while the expense of fighting off these threats increased taxes to the point at which vassal states rebelled.

Around 2193 BC, the Akkadian empire buckled, ushering in an era of anarchy and chaos in the region. So comprehensive was the Akkadian fall that Akkad, the capital, was abandoned and was buried by time. The rediscovery of this lost city is something of a holy grail for archaeologists looking for clues about the many mysteries surrounding Akkad, and also for hints as to the origins of the later civilizations of Ur and Assyria.

## Future Echoes

Naram-Sin was the grandson of Sargon and ruled Akkad when the state was at its greatest. One surviving record of his achievements is a large carved stele recording his victory over the Lullubi of the central Zagros Mountains. It is often speculated that Naram-Sin is Nimrod, 'the mighty hunter' of the Bible. Scholars have noted that the era and the extent of Nimrod's domains roughly correspond, and there is a linguistic and phonological similarity in the names.

If so, the name of Naram-Sin has since been associated with a famous piece of music by Edward Elgar, the ship for one of Ernest Shackleton's Antarctic expeditions and an aeroplane. In a less illustrious fashion (thanks to Bugs Bunny and his incompetent hunter), and mostly in the United States, 'Nimrod' today refers to someone who bungles the simplest of tasks.

Naram-Sin victorious over his enemies: this depiction of the king was carved around 2250 BC on a stele of limestone almost 2 m (6 ft) high and now in the Louvre Museum, Paris.

## *c.* 2000 BC – 1595 BC
# **The Amorites**
## 'Founders' of Babylon

*Those once terrible giants the Rephaim were
replaced by the Amorites. These are an evil
people more wicked than any other who still
exist today, who no longer measure out their
lives upon this earth.*

Pseudo-Genesis 29:10–12

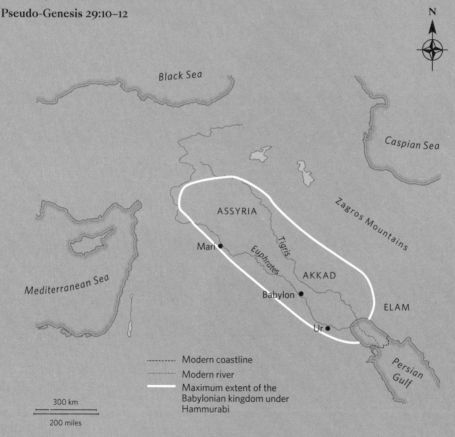

Modern coastline
Modern river
Maximum extent of the
Babylonian kingdom under
Hammurabi

300 km

200 miles

B abylon is one of the best-known cities of antiquity, capital of two empires at different times and famous for its Hanging Gardens, as well as notorious for the Babylonian captivity of the Jews. Founded in the pre-Amorite era during the late third millennium BC, the Akkadian town of Babylon was nothing special until it fell into the hands of the Amorites. It was they who created the Babylonian city-state and went on to make the city itself the largest and most populous in the world.

The Akkadians would have considered the Amorites unlikely founders of one of the great centres of Mesopotamian civilization, for they regarded them as barely civilized. An early text of a legend called 'The Marriage of Martu' contains an unflattering description, referring to the Amorites as 'monkey-men' and accusing them of eating raw meat and having no house while alive and no proper burial when dead.

## Who were the Amorites?

'The Worshipper of Larsa': an anonymous citizen dedicated this statuette to the god Amurru that he might safeguard Hammurabi's life.

In fact, at this time the term 'Amorite' may not have referred to a specific people at all, but was instead a generalized insult used by the agricultural Mesopotamians to refer to the raiding tribesmen on their borders during the late third millennium BC. Regrettably – from the Akkadian point of view at least – the nomadic Amorites were better able to cope with the period of severe drought that seems to have hit the region at the start of the second millennium BC. The Akkadians fared badly, and as their irrigation systems failed, the Amorites began a piecemeal occupation of their land, sometimes by conquest and sometimes by simply occupying abandoned fields.

Although the timing is far from certain, it appears that long after the Amorites moved into Mesopotamia from the northwest, their relatives were driven out of the land of Canaan by an expansionist people called the Israelites, as described in Deuteronomy (3:6–8):

And we utterly destroyed them ... the men, women, and children, of every city. But all the cattle, and the spoil of the cities, we took for a prey to ourselves. And we took at that time out of the hand of the two kings of the Amorites the land that was on this side of Jordan, from the river of Arnon unto mount Hermon.

In Mesopotamia, the Amorites quickly developed a taste for city life, and as a tribe soon merged with the native Sumerian population. Amorite kings took over the important city of Mari on the Euphrates and had already conquered Babylon by 1990 BC, quickly turning this unassuming town into a major city-state.

## The lawgiver

At the end of the next century, a man called Ammurapi was born and later came to be king in Babylon. By now the Amorites of Babylon worshipped Sumerian gods and appear to have despised their own nomadic kin as heartily as the Akkadians had once done. So integrated had the urban Amorites become with the native population that Ammurapi was better known by the Akkadian form of his name, Hammurabi.

Hammurabi began his royal career as a conqueror, devastating the rival city of Mari and forcing the once-mighty Assyrians into vassal status. He also turned on the Elamites – a fellow nomadic people who had made a substantial contribution to the downfall of Akkad. With the conquest of Elam, Hammurabi was master of most of Mesopotamia. However, this first period of Babylonian ascendancy was short-lived, and Hammurabi's promising empire fell apart during the reign of his son and successor.

This brief hegemony nevertheless had deep and lasting effects on the region – so much so that for the rest of antiquity this southern part of Mesopotamia is known as Babylonia. For one thing, the Amorites broke the temple monopoly on civic administration, which now became a secular rather than a religious affair. Perhaps the most famous aspect of this is in the field of law. Until the time of the Amorite kings the 'law' been interpreted by priests as an expression of divine will. Hammurabi was not the first to set out a codex which defined criminal acts and prescribed punishments for them, but his was the first law code to have a serious impact.

This is in part because Hammurabi ensured that his laws – all 282 of them – were not kept as obscure temple records, but were inscribed on a stele and put on public display. The laws were written in Akkadian, still the common tongue of the region despite the Amorite supremacy. It is doubtful whether more than a fraction of the population were literate enough to read them, but the laws were there, literally written in stone, for all to see.

Incredibly, this is still the case. The black stone stele on which Hammurabi had his laws inscribed is a monolithic four-tonne block of a tough stone called diorite. Since the laws were so influential, the stele itself was revered. So much so that when the Elamites later enjoyed a period of dominance they removed the stone from

*Opposite* The stele bearing the Law Code of Hammurabi was admired and preserved in antiquity. It has survived through the ages and can still be consulted today in the Louvre Museum in Paris.

The remains of the royal palace of Zimri-Lim at Mari. This was one of the greatest palaces in contemporary Mesopotamia, though the turbulent times meant that the king's stay there was seldom comfortable.

Babylon and transported it to their capital at Susa, in modern Iran (along with the stele of Naram-Sin). There it remained, as the ancient city slowly crumbled into ruins. In 1901 a French archaeological expedition rediscovered the stele, and that same stone which once revealed the laws of Hammurabi to the Babylonians is again on public display, in the Louvre Museum in Paris, though legal codes by the hundred have come and gone in the intervening centuries.

## The Amorite era

The years 2000 BC to 1600 BC are sometimes called the 'Amorite era' of Mesopotamian history. While the social and economic changes the Amorites had made to Sumerian culture were to endure, the Amorites themselves did not. Already under pressure from the Israelites in Canaan, the Amorites were now also expelled from northern Mesopotamia by a freshly resurgent Assyria. Meanwhile, just to the north of the former Amorite heartlands, the Hittites began raiding deep into Mesopotamia.

For all its size as a city, Babylon shrank in power until it dominated little more than the lands immediately around it. Here the Amorite kings held on until 1595 BC, when the Hittites sacked the city. Despite the disaster, Babylon was to endure for more than another thousand years. Excavations show that people with Amorite names still lived there, but as a separate ethnic group the Amorites had vanished from Mesopotamia.

It is uncertain whether the Amorites remained for another century or two in southern Anatolia as a subject race to the Hittites, or whether 'Amorite' had again become a derogatory term for 'nomad'. (This would seem to be how it is used in the later books of the Bible.) Either way, after the huge disruptions which ended the Bronze Age around 1200 BC, the Amorites disappear from history, a forgotten people until modern archaeologists began to take an interest in them once more.

# Future Echoes

Hammurabi's underlying intention in his laws – 'The duty of government is that justice should prevail so that the strong shall not harm the weak' – remains one of the fundamental principles of the law today. Another remarkable stipulation of Hammurabi was something resembling a 'minimum wage' for some agricultural workers. Nevertheless, the Amorites were not completely progressive. If a man struck a woman and caused her to miscarry and die, he was punished by the execution of one of his daughters (Law 210).

The Laws of Hammurabi were significant in two enduring ways. First, whereas earlier legal systems stressed compensation for injury, Hammurabi was more focused on punishing the offender. He introduced the concept later referred to as the *lex talionis*, known colloquially as 'an eye for an eye and a tooth for a tooth'. This is literally what Hammurabi's law code says, but it is more famous for being repeated in the Bible in the books of Exodus (21:23–25) and Leviticus (24:19–21).

Another legal precedent set by Hammurabi was that he was the first to make the presumption of innocence a foundation of legal proceedings – a person should be considered innocent of a crime until proven guilty. However, if found guilty Hammurabi's often draconian punishments came into full effect – the concept of mitigating circumstances being still unknown.

Because Mesopotamian society laid the foundations of civilization, we tend to think that their choices were inevitable. That priests should be in charge of land use, taxation and other civic functions seems strange to those in civilizations today accustomed to some degree of separation between church and state. Yet until this happened under the Amorites, neither an aristocratic landowning class nor a merchant class could develop. Each of these groups was to play a major part in future world history.

# *c.* 2000 BC – 700 BC
# **The Canaanites**
# Israel Before the Israelites

*Canaan [the son of Ham] saw that the Land of
Lebanon to the river of Egypt was very good.
Therefore ... he dwelled in that land east and
west of the Jordan, to the border of the sea....
And he dwelled in that land of Lebanon from
Hamath to the gates of Egypt, he and his sons
even until now, and for that reason the land is
called Canaan.*

Pseudo-Genesis 10:29–31

A bronze Canaanite deity of the fourteenth–thirteenth century BC, still partly covered in gold foil but missing the throne on which he once sat. Measuring 12.7 cm (5 in.) tall, the figurine is now in the Metropolitan Museum of Art, New York.

The Land of Canaan occupied what is today one of the most disputed and politically complex regions of the planet. Canaan consisted of the area from roughly north of the Sea of Galilee down to the Dead Sea in the south, extending westwards from the River Jordan to the sea, and about the same distance to the east. Today this encompasses much of Syria, the Lebanon, the Golan Heights and the homelands of the Palestinians and Israelis.

During the late Bronze Age (1550–1200 BC) the people of Canaan likewise lived in interesting times, as their homeland lay within the overlapping spheres of influence of the Egyptian, Hittite and Assyrian empires. Canaan was thus a favoured international battleground, while the Canaanites made things worse by simultaneously waging a number of vicious wars among themselves.

This was in part because the land of Canaan was rich in cultural and ethnic diversity. Archaeology shows that Canaanites in later times encompassed Hebrew, Philistine and Phoenician peoples, each with different burial rites, traditions and religious opinions. Nevertheless, modern studies make it increasingly clear that most of these differences represent diverging societies which developed from the same ethnic stock of Semitic peoples, with additions from others migrating there from elsewhere, such as Amorites. The peoples of Canaan had so much in common that even ancient sources refer to the occupants of the area collectively as 'Canaanites'.

## Ancient origins

Canaanites had been in the land for a very long time. The city of Jericho in AD 2018 had a population of some 20,000 inhabitants. This is probably close to what its population was in 2018 BC, when Jericho was a medium-rank but prosperous Canaanite city that was already around 7,000 years old. (By comparison the 'eternal city' of Rome has yet to reach its 2,800th birthday.)

Our first record of the Canaanites being grouped together under that name comes from a famous letter written in the early second millennium BC by a military official to Shamshi-Adad I, king of the Amorite city of Mari. The letter refers to a violent bout of conflict in a town called Rahisum, describing the participants as 'robbers and Canaanites'. It seems this reputation continued – a later people of Canaan called the 'Habiru' have the same name as the Akkadian word for 'robber', though whether the Habiru gave their name to the word, or vice versa, is uncertain.

These early Canaanites were already divided between those who lived in small kingdoms, mostly based on city-states, nomadic tribes and shepherd peoples who regularly shifted their flocks between summer and winter pastures. Although these three groups had strong and very different opinions on land rights and usage, they also sometimes co-operated to take advantage of the rich trading opportunities created by their position between empires possessed of different resources.

The land of Canaan also benefited from a unique asset of its own. On the coast was found a small species of snail that, when carefully boiled, yielded a purple liquid which was the only colour-fast dye known to antiquity. For much of the Bronze Age the word 'Canaan' seems to have described both the purple colour of the dye and the land it came from. Roman emperors later donned the 'imperial purple', signifying how prestigious this unique dye remained down the centuries.

## Canaanites abroad

The Canaanites appear to have come close to building an empire of their own during the years after 1800 BC, when they expanded southwards into Egypt. Taking advantage of a period of violent instability in that country, the Canaanites set themselves up as an independent people in the eastern part of the Nile Delta. Their rulers are known to Egyptologists as the Fourteenth Dynasty.

The Fourteenth Dynasty is poorly recorded, and it was speedily replaced by the incoming Hyksos people. However, it is interesting because at the same time that archaeology suggests one Canaanite group was settling in Egypt, other Canaanites were forcefully differentiating themselves from their fellows. These people were the Hebrews. According to the Bible, the Hebrews had been oppressed in Egypt for generations, but at the beginning of the second millennium BC they made a determined exit from that country.

## The Israelites

The Bible says that Yahweh informed Moses that he would lead the Israelites to a 'land of milk and honey, the home of the Canaanites, Hittites and Amorites' (Exodus 3:8). The Hebrews therefore set about acquiring their divinely endowed land in a series of violent conquests. The first Canaanite city to fall was Jericho, famously after the Hebrews, led by Joshua, had marched around it blowing trumpets.

In this version of events, Jericho was then subject to the process of *herem*, a term alluding to the 'making harmless anything

The fall of Jericho shown in a seventeenth-century Russian church fresco. Archaeology has revealed that Jericho was already in ruins before Joshua's trumpets sounded.

threatening the religion of the Hebrews'. Contemporary Israelites would have interpreted this innocuous-sounding phrase as requiring the extirpation of every living thing within the walls of the city, and the burning of material which would otherwise be taken as plunder. The process was repeated with other Canaanite cities as the Hebrews conquered them.

An alternative interpretation of the Hebrew seizure of Canaan disputes whether the Exodus had such a major effect on the land. This approach suggests instead that the Canaanites had already begun the process of differentiating themselves into Hebrews and Phoenicians (among others). The turbulent conditions prevailing in Egypt may well have resulted in large numbers of Hebrews returning to Canaan, which tipped the ethnic balance in some cities. But that, claim the revisionists, is all that happened.

Such scholars flatly deny that a violent conquest ever took place. They point out that archaeological evidence and contemporary texts give flimsy to non-existent support for the murderous activities described in the Book of Exodus. For example, the walls of Jericho were indeed flattened and the city abandoned for a while thereafter, but the culprits appear to have been the Egyptians. Radiocarbon dating of the destruction layer suggests that Jericho would already have been in ruins when the Hebrew general Joshua is said to have arrived and taken the city.

The Egyptians, the Assyrians and later the Babylonians all campaigned extensively in Canaan, adding to the general chaos in the region. The biblical reports of systematic depopulation of non-Jews in conquered areas remain unsubstantiated in any of the available sources.

## Foreign affairs

Whatever the power structure in late Bronze Age Canaan, it is evident that the Canaanites were still regarded as subordinate peoples by the kingdoms of the Mitanni in northern Syria and (once they had stabilized their affairs) the Egyptians. In fact, around 1350 BC the Babylonian king Burra-Buriyas wrote to the Egyptian pharaoh Akhenaten complaining that '[Canaanite] men killed my merchants and took away their money ... Canaan is your country and its kings are your servants. Bring these men to book, and make compensation' (Amarna Letter EA 8). This is a clear indication that the Canaanites were not regarded as a fully independent people, though the Hittites would have strongly disagreed that Canaan was the pharaoh's country.

In fact the Hittites became an increasingly aggressive presence on the northern borders of Canaan, and during the later Bronze Age they succeeded in supplanting the Egyptian hegemony over much of the land. Hittite dominance was promptly challenged by the Assyrians, who remained paramount in the region thereafter. The famous episode in the second Book of Kings (18–19) in which – as the poet Byron later put it – 'The Assyrian came down like the wolf on the fold/And his cohorts were gleaming in purple and gold', relates to the later attack on Jerusalem by the Assyrian king Sennacherib in 701 BC.

By this point Canaan had already ceased to exist as a cultural entity. It now comprised the Hebrew kingdoms of Judah and Israel, and the land of Phoenicia, with much of the remainder subsumed into the empires of Egypt and Assyria. The people no longer referred to themselves as Canaanites, though their origins were not forgotten. For example the Greek geographer Hecataeus later remarked, 'In the common language of Attica it [the region] is called "Canna" as Phoenicia was formerly known.'

## Future Echoes

The 'Return to Canaan' has been a theme of many painters over the centuries, an example being *Return of Jacob with His Family* by Bassano (Jacopo da Ponte), a subject he first painted in 1560 and revisited several times.

The idea of Canaan as 'Reaching the Promised Land' has passed into modern English terminology as an expression meaning 'the state of having achieved a difficult objective'. As such, we find Canaan in Connecticut, USA, where grateful settlers arrived in 1739.

Canaan was described as 'the Land of Milk and Honey' to Moses, and this evocative phrase has since seen considerable use in other contexts. It has been the title of books, films and even a Broadway musical in 1961. Over half a dozen modern musicians have released tracks with that title. More recently, Israel's Milk & Honey Distillery has been producing single-malt whisky since 2016.

*Return of Jacob with His Family*, by Bassano (Jacopo da Ponte), *c*.1580. The Return to the Promised Land was a favoured theme of Renaissance painters.

# c. 2700 BC – 646 BC
# **The Elamites**
# The Empire Before Persia

*The wicked Elamite, who cared not for what is worthy ... in war his onslaught was swift. He devastated the dwelling-places and made them ruins, he carried off the gods, he destroyed the shrines.*

Babylonian Legend of Enmeduranki

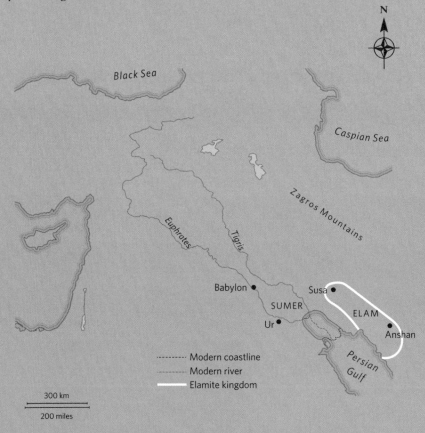

Black Sea

N

Caspian Sea

Zagros Mountains

Euphrates

Tigris

Babylon

Susa

SUMER

ELAM

Ur

Anshan

Persian Gulf

--------- Modern coastline
--------- Modern river
——— Elamite kingdom

300 km

200 miles

Around 3100 BC proto-Iranian tribesmen living on the plateau to the northeast of the Persian Gulf began to coalesce into a nation. They called themselves 'Highlanders', or, in their unique language, *Heltam-ti*. The Akkadians translated this name as *Elamtu*.

The writers of the Bible named them 'Elamites', believing that this people were descended from Elam, the grandson of Noah. Since the Elamite language bears little resemblance to the family of Semitic languages, there is a counter-argument that the biblical Elam gets his name from the Elamites rather than the other way round. Interestingly, Elam is said to have had a daughter called Susan. In the Classical era, the land of Elam was sometimes called Susiana after the later capital of Susa.

## The rise of Elam

Elamite history proper begins around 2700 BC, when the Elamites came into violent contact with the record-keeping Sumerians. Elam was briefly reduced to a vassal state, but this mountain people had an indomitable streak which made it impossible to keep them subdued for long. As soon as Sumerian rule faltered, the Elamites went on the offensive and conquered parts of Mesopotamia.

This set the stage for a period of back-and-forth warfare, diplomacy and trade, during which the Elamite Awan dynasty of kings conquered Sumer, were then crushed by Sargon of Akkad, regained control of southern Mesopotamia and were finally defeated by the kings of the resurgent city of Ur.

By the time the dust settled around 1500 BC, the Elamites were a recognized nation who had now begun to use their own written language in place of Akkadian. They had also expanded into the lowlands south of the Zagros Mountains, and there taken over

A clay tablet in proto-Elamite script, which appears to be an accounting record. Proto-Elamite remains undeciphered, though some elements are recognizable from later, known cuneiform texts.

the city of Susa. This ancient city was at one stage under Akkadian control and was then occupied by the expansionist power of Ur. Once the Elamites had dealt with that aggressive city, Susa became Elamite.

Elamite kings took to calling themselves 'King of Anshan [the Highlands of Elam] and Susa', while the archaeological record shows a steady increase in the use of the Elamite language in the surrounding area. Another sign of cultural domination is that by around 1300 BC Elamite mountain gods were also being worshipped in the lowlands of Susiana.

## Empire and collapse

Elamite civilization flourished at the end of the Bronze Age. An Elamite king called Shutruk-Nahhunte (*c.* 1185–1155 BC) took advantage of Assyrian attacks on Babylon, which had weakened the city. After the Assyrians had withdrawn, the Elamites conquered Babylon themselves, carrying away the famous stele inscribed with the Laws of Hammurabi.

Shutruk-Nahhunte gained sufficient prestige from his conquests to be succeeded by his son. This seems an unusual event among Elamite rulers, who had – as far as we can discern from the scanty evidence – previously shared the throne between the aristocratic landowning families which dominated the social and political life of the kingdom. The Shutrukid dynasty lasted for three generations and came to exert control over most of Mesopotamia and

Made from mud brick, the impressive Elamite ziggurat at Chogha Zanbil was originally over 50 m (160 ft) tall and is now a UNESCO World Heritage Site in Khuzestan, Iran.

the borderlands between it and Elam. At this time Elamite armies campaigned as far north as Arrapha, not far from the modern city of Kirkuk.

The far north of Mesopotamia was the Assyrian heartland, and the Assyrian kings now turned their serious attention on Elam. By then Elam was in some disarray, and there are hints of a dynastic struggle. The king Hutelutush-Inshushinak appears to have simultaneously been his predecessor's son and grandson, as a result of that monarch's incestuous relationship with his daughter.

Elsewhere, Babylon was now under the rule of king Nebuchadnezzar I (*c.* 1125–1104 BC), who took the disorganized city-state firmly in hand and led the Babylonian army in an invasion of Elam. The Elamites were taken by surprise, but mustered their army for a defence on the banks of their holy river of Ulaya, near Susa. They were utterly defeated and Susa was sacked, with the Babylonians triumphantly reclaiming their statue of the god Marduk that the Elamites had carried away in an earlier conquest. With the fall of Susa, the Elamite empire descended into a period of anarchy. In fact much of the region was experiencing immense disorder at this time, the result of what is known as the Bronze Age collapse.

Historians still argue about the cause of this cataclysmic event. However, if its origins are unknown, the results are not. Mycenaean Greece, the Hittite empire and dozens of minor civilizations fell into a dark age of warfare and serious decline, which came close to bringing down even mighty Egypt. As it was, Egypt lost all the lands it held in Syria and Canaan. Of Elam, almost nothing is known for the next three centuries.

## Later Elam

One feature of the turmoil at the end of the Bronze Age was the migration of previously unknown peoples. In Greece, for example, the newcomers were the people who became known as the Dorians. In the east, the newcomers were an Iranian people known collectively as 'Medes'. The Medes pushed the Elamites out of their highland home, so that the territory around Susa now became the Elam of the Bible and the Classical era. The reason that very little is known of Elam in this early Iron Age period is because the Elamites had not yet started writing texts again. It is notable that one Babylonian king seems to have an Elamite name, and the Babylonians record that they fought alongside the Elamites against the Assyrians around 815 BC.

As Babylonian texts become more common in the centuries following the Bronze Age collapse, it is possible to keep track of the Elamites through occasional mentions by their neighbour. Thus we know that the Elamites tried to maintain a delicate balancing act by supporting the Babylonians against the Assyrians, while simultaneously also trying to get on with the Assyrians.

However, once Babylon had fallen to the Assyrians in 700 BC relations with Assyria went downhill fast. The Elamites feared, rightly, that they were to be the next target of Assyrian aggression. In true Elamite style, they did not wait to be attacked. Instead they went on the offensive under their king, Urtak. The attack failed and Urtak was killed. This triggered a prolonged bout of dynastic instability that might have led to the immediate fall of Elam had the Assyrians not had dynastic problems of their own, coupled with the arrival of further warlike migrants on Assyria's northern borders.

Eventually the Assyrian king Ashurbanipal (669–c. 631 BC) asserted his grip on affairs. The Elamites fought long and hard, but were comprehensively defeated. What happened in 646 BC Ashurbanipal relates in his own words, later found inscribed on a tablet in his capital Nineveh:

I conquered their holy city, great Susa, the home of their mysteries, the dwelling place of their gods. I captured their palaces, and broke open the storerooms of gold, silver and other treasures.... The temples of Elam were no more, their gods and goddesses mere voices in the wind. I poured sunlight into the tombs of their kings, both old and new, and carried the bones to Assyria. The lands of Elam I devastated, and in their fields I sowed salt.

In keeping with contemporary practice, Ashurbanipal distributed as exiles around his empire those Elamite peoples whom he did not massacre wholesale. A shadow of the Elamite people remained in their homeland, but, scattered and defenceless, the last of the Elamites were soon defeated and absorbed by the Iranian peoples to the south.

## Future Echoes

Much of what we know of the Elamites comes from studying the remarkable number of statuettes and sculptures they left behind. Not only striking and elegant in itself, Elamite art was highly influential on the later artistic development of the region.

Students of the Old Testament will also be familiar with the Elamites, who are allegedly descended from Noah's son Shem. Isaiah describes them as a land of bowmen (Isaiah 22:6), and Jeremiah, in his usual convivial manner, says they shall be forced to drink the cup of divine wrath for their ungodly ways (Jeremiah 25:25). According to the Acts of the Apostles (2:9), Elamites were among those who were present in Jerusalem at Pentecost.

This 24-cm (10-in.) high carved head of an Elamite, now in the Louvre, Paris, was probably used in the man's funerary rites and gives us a remarkably clear idea of what the ancient Elamites looked like.

# *c.* 1700 BC – 1200 BC
# **The Hittites**
## Masters of Anatolia

*I wish good friendship to exist between you
and me. I have expressed a wish to your father.
We certainly shall make it come true between us.*

**Letter from the Hittite king Suppiluliuma to Akhenaten,
Amarna Letters, EA 41**

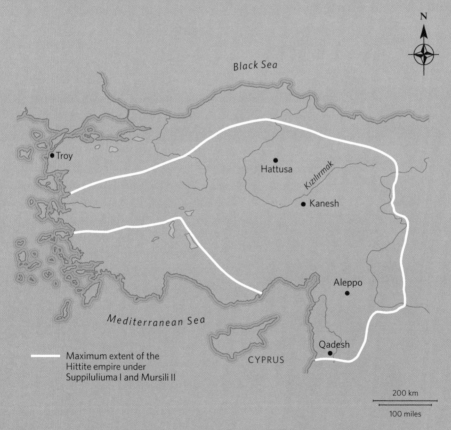

N

Black Sea

Troy

Hattusa

Kızılırmak

Kanesh

Aleppo

Qadesh

CYPRUS

Mediterranean Sea

Maximum extent of the
Hittite empire under
Suppiluliuma I and Mursili II

200 km

100 miles

Had someone asked about the Hittites 150 years ago, the answer they would have received is that they were an obscure people living somewhere north of Israel, with members of their ethnic group dwelling in the land of Canaan. The two most famous Hittites were Uriah – a man cuckolded, betrayed and killed by King David – and Heth, the great-grandson of Noah, who allegedly founded the Hittite race.

This summary would have come as a surprise to the people who called themselves the Nesumna. They were masters of most of Anatolia, rivals of Egypt and feared raiders in Mesopotamia. Yet even today they are known as Hittites, as this is what the Hebrews called them. This powerful and influential people would have been completely forgotten by history if it were not for their occasional mention in the Old Testament – and even that gives the completely wrong impression that the Hittites consisted of a smattering of minor kingdoms rather than a great empire.

The Egyptians called them the 'Khetti' and the Akkadian-writing peoples of Mesopotamia called them the 'Hatti' – perhaps as a reference to the even more obscure Hattian people whom the Hittites replaced. Only in modern times, and after the full decipherment by 1960 of Hittite inscriptions written in the Luwian language, have scholars realized that all these different names refer to the same vanished people.

An exquisitely crafted tiny Hittite goddess made of gold, which was probably worn as an amulet. If the disc-shaped headdress represents the sun, this would be the solar goddess Arinna.

## Unknown origins

Even now, there is much that remains mysterious about the Hittites. For example, where did they come from? This is an important and controversial question because the Hittites were among the earliest users of a language in the Indo-European group. The peoples who spoke Indo-European languages have since spread across Europe and as far as India. For example 'pad' (Vedic Sanskrit), 'peda' (Hittite), 'pod' (Greek) and 'pedal' (English) are all derived from the same prehistoric word for foot. The Hittites were also expert horsemen who took chariot warfare to new levels, and their word for horse, 'ekku', is the root of the English word equine.

Once it had become clear that the Hittites were an early Indo-European people, it was hoped that they might provide clues as to the whereabouts of the as-yet undiscovered 'Indo-European homeland'. Did the Hittites sweep down from the north, possibly from the Caucasus region of eastern Europe? Or were they, as some less romantic modern scholars are inclined to believe, a native people of Anatolia who flourished and rose to prominence for reasons still unclear?

In either case, it is now plain that the Hittites replaced the earlier Hattian people, and took over their capital city of Hattusa. This city sprawled across a series of rocky crags in a loop of what is now the Kızılırmak (the ancient Halys) river in north-central Turkey. Excavations have found palace, temple and barrack complexes, and, most importantly, baked clay tablets comprising entire sets of royal archives, which tell us almost all of what we know today about the Hittites.

## Hittites rising

Rather typically, given the obscurity which still surrounds them, the history of the Hittites is divided into either two or three periods, depending on which historian you ask. There is a general consensus about the Old Kingdom (approximately 1700–1500 BC) and the New Kingdom (1400–1200 BC), but disagreement as to whether the century between the two counts as a Middle Kingdom or merely as a period of wild anarchy during which the Hittite kingdom in effect ceased to exist.

The Old Kingdom Hittites became an Anatolian power under a warrior king called Hattusili (c. 1650–1625 BC), who re-founded Hattusa after it had been razed by people from the city of Kanesh (who also formally laid a curse on the ruins). Like many a conqueror, Hattusili had to deal with violent rebellions among the peoples whom he brought into the empire, and it is possible these rebellious 'servants' (as they are named in ancient texts) also included his sons. On his deathbed, Hattusili designated as his heir not a son, but a grandson called Mursili (c. 1625–1595 BC).

Mursili was just as proficient a conqueror as Hattusili, and after extensive campaigns in Syria he brought the city of Aleppo under Hittite control. However, Mursili is most famous for taking his army on a 2,000-km (1,245-mile) route march to Mesopotamia, ending with the sack of Babylon in 1595 BC which saw the Amorite kings fall from power in that city. (To confuse matters, an alternative chronology based on Babylonian texts dates this raid to 1531 BC, which shows how much tidying up historians still have to do for this era.)

If the 'when' of Mursili's raid is still debated, the 'why' is even more inexplicable. Certainly there was no possibility of outright conquest – in an era of poor communications Babylon was simply too distant. Evidently the Hittite aristocracy also took a dim view of the raid, for on his return Mursili was assassinated in a coup by

Sphinxes guard a gateway in the ruins of the Hittite capital of Hattusa on the bend of the River Kızılırmak in modern Turkey.

his brother-in-law. The family precedent thus set, the new king was eventually assassinated by his son-in-law. Each new king was less competent than his predecessor, and a mixture of ineptitude and inefficiency, perhaps exacerbated by climate change, led to the Old Kingdom falling apart by 1490 BC.

## Hittite renaissance

Around a century later a king called Tudhaliya restored order, only for the Hittite kingdom to descend into chaos once more on his death. However, Tudhaliya did make some important innovations.

Most significantly, he transformed the king from first among equals, as the Old Kingdom rulers had been, into a demi-god who was the conduit for relationships between the Hittites and their divinities (most of whom seem to have been adopted wholesale from the religion of the Hattians who had gone before).

So it was as a god-king that Suppiluliuma I took over in about 1345 BC. Fortunately for him, an aggressive Assyria was wreaking havoc to the east, thus weakening many Hittite rivals. Between them, Assyria and Suppiluliuma made short work of the last of the Hurrians in northern Mesopotamia, and consequently Hittite power again expanded into Syria. This brought the Hittites into direct conflict with Egypt, which had its own interests in the region. Suppiluliuma and the Egyptian pharaoh managed to remain polite to each other through diplomatic correspondence – some of which, written on clay tablets, has miraculously survived. However, the relationship eventually broke down. The new Egyptian ruler was Ramesses II ('the Great', r. 1279–1213 BC), one of the most remarkable pharaohs in that nation's long history. It was fortunate for the Hittites that they now had a highly competent leader of their own, Muwatalli II (c. 1295–1272 BC), grandson of Suppiluliuma.

The Egyptians and Hittites clashed in an epic confrontation in northern Syria. The battle of Qadesh (c. 1274 BC) was a confused affair, and both sides claimed victory. Once the dust settled, negotiators worked out a peace. Peace was necessary, not least because the Hittites were having increasing difficulty in staving off Assyrian aggression.

The Hittites lost ground to the Assyrians but held out until the entire region was rocked by the mysterious cataclysm of the Bronze Age collapse of the twelfth century BC. Among the civilizations obliterated were the Minoans of Crete, the Mycenaeans of Greece – and the Hittites of Anatolia. In 1190 BC the Hittite capital Hattusa became the latest in a series of cities wiped out by pillaging invaders.

On this bas-relief from Hattusa, a line of mysterious figures – possibly gods – marches to an unknown destination.

This silver stag, now in the Metropolitan Museum of Art, New York, is actually a Hittite drinking horn, carefully forged from separate pieces and hammered together.

The highly organized Assyrians pounced on the remains of the Hittite empire, and within a few generations the Hittites were no longer even a memory.

## Future Echoes

After the inconclusive battle of Qadesh, Hittite and Egyptian diplomats negotiated a peace settlement. This agreement is generally considered to be the world's first peace treaty. Remarkably we have both sides' versions – carved on temple walls in Egypt and inscribed on clay tablets preserved at Hattusa.

Another first came a generation later, when Hittite power probed westwards, trading and skirmishing with both Troy and Mycenaean Greece. Cyprus was at this time a sea power, and in 1210 BC the Hittites challenged that power in the world's first recorded sea battle (and won).

## *c.* 1670 BC – 1550 BC
# The Hyksos
## Invaders of Egypt

*Men of an obscure tribe came from the east, completely unexpectedly. They dared to invade our land [of Egypt] and easily conquered it, for we could not face them in battle. They subdued our kings, razed our cities and destroyed the temples of our gods. Our people were cruelly mistreated. Men were killed, and the women and children enslaved.*

From Manetho's *Aegyptiaca* quoted in Josephus, *Against Apion* 1.73

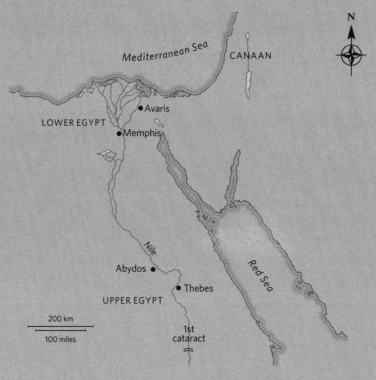

The 'obscure tribe', whom the Roman-Jewish historian Josephus (wrongly) called the 'Shepherd Kings', were the Hyksos. It was once believed that these people swept over Egypt like a human tsunami, spreading devastation and death in their wake, before eventually settling down to tyrannize the ruined lands they had conquered. According to this version of history, the Egyptians were completely unable to prevent the invasion because the country was wracked by plague and roiled by dynastic conflicts. Furthermore, the Hyksos had chariots – heretofore unheard of in Egypt – composite bows, scale armour and superior bronze weapons. Small wonder that Egypt succumbed so quickly, to languish under foreign occupation for the next two hundred years.

History, as the saying goes, is written by the victors. The Egyptians, under a series of warrior kings, eventually succeeded in expelling the Hyksos from their lands. Once they had accomplished that, the pharaohs set about writing the history of the Hyksos invasion as in the version given above to maximize their achievement – a version generally accepted by historians until the twenty-first century.

## Rewriting history

The first indication that Josephus might have been mistaken in taking as his source the now lost *Aegyptiaca* of Manetho was the discovery that Hyksos does not mean 'Shepherd Kings'. Instead it comes from the Egyptian term *heqa khasut* meaning 'rulers from foreign lands'. Note the plural 'lands'. These rulers seem to have been a mixed group. While most have names that suggest Canaanite, or at least Semitic, origins, others may have been Hurrian.

When a city is razed, a 'destruction layer' is formed – a thin crust of ash, broken mud brick and other debris which allows archaeologists using modern scientific techniques such as thermoluminescence and radiocarbon dating to determine almost exactly when the destruction took place. Rather confusingly, while the Hyksos were allegedly rampaging across Egypt, burning cities to the ground as they went, they unaccountably failed to leave a detectable destruction layer in the cities they conquered.

Sceptical Egyptologists then took a closer look at contemporary papyri relating to Hyksos dominion in Lower Egypt (roughly the Nile delta region). What they found were clear indications that the Hyksos kings were rather efficient rulers whose Egyptian subjects seemed not to have minded them at all. Furthermore, Upper Egypt, centred

A 'duckbill' axe-head of the type wielded by Hyksos invaders. The Egyptians would have found this example of superior Hyksos weaponry particularly fearsome as their soldiers had no protective helmets.

Pharaoh Tutankhamun rides out in his chariot to crush Egypt's enemies on this well-preserved painted casket found in his tomb. The chariot was one of the advances the Egyptians learned from the Hyksos.

on Thebes (Luxor), remained under native rule, and for at least a century, the Egyptian and Hyksos parts of Egypt got along amicably.

As a result, the 'Hyksos invasion' has been extensively re-thought. Though subject to future revision and currently mired in considerable controversy, the provisional history of the Hyksos is as follows. By the seventeenth century BC, the Egyptian Thirteenth Dynasty of the Middle Kingdom was in decline. At the time, the Middle East as a whole was suffering a period of disruption resulting from the migration of large numbers of Indo-European groups from the north and east. Peoples from the lands north of Canaan were displaced, and many of these moved south and settled in the city of Avaris in the Nile Delta. At the time, the Egyptian pharaoh had enough to contend with without starting a war with a well-armed and numerous enemy, so the migration was largely peaceful.

In any case, the early Hyksos expansion did not so much occupy Egyptian territory as elbow aside and absorb these earlier Canaanite settlers in Lower Egypt. It also helped that the new arrivals were not looking for trouble. Archaeology shows that some Egyptians held

A seal bearing the name of a Hyksos king called Apophis, c. 1581–1541 BC. Found in the eastern Nile Delta, it is now in the Metropolitan Museum, New York.

high-ranking positions in the Hyksos administration in Avaris, and the newcomers worked hard to integrate themselves into Egyptian life. Their gods were the usual Semitic deities of Baal and Anat, but after scanning through the Egyptian pantheon for a suitable candidate, the Hyksos decided that Baal was the Egyptian god Set, and worshipped him in that guise. They also carefully copied and preserved old papyrus documents, and today many of these valuable records only exist as Hyksos copies.

## Hyksos advances

The Hyksos also brought with them many advances, including new crop varieties, and better ways of exploiting those already present. Improved irrigation led to greater harvests, and the Hyksos introduced the vertical loom, which led to linens that were as superior to the Egyptian equivalent as the new ceramics produced by imported firing techniques were to native pots. In short, the Hyksos came as something of a shock to a culture

Nubians travel down the Nile in this Egyptian wall painting of a papyrus boat of the fourteenth century BC. It is uncertain whether the men are traders or captives.

already over two thousand years old and which had become insular and introverted. The outside world had been developing and innovating while the Egyptians were not looking, and the Hyksos forcibly injected these latest developments directly into the mainstream of Egyptian life.

Many scholars now believe that the Hyksos spread their rule through 'creeping conquest'. On some occasions they may have migrated to Egyptian cities as not unwelcome craftsmen, merchants and mercenaries. Their numbers fuelled by arrivals from abroad, the newcomers gradually overwhelmed the native peoples, who either moved elsewhere or simply lived alongside them. While there was doubtless the occasional minor skirmish, there is simply no evidence for the whirlwind of destruction described in later Egyptian texts.

## Rise and fall

If the pharaohs of Upper Egypt did have trouble with the dynamism of the new arrivals, they were in any case otherwise occupied fending off pressure from the Nubians in the south. As a result they sought ways to accommodate the Hyksos to their north. They may even have paid them tribute – something the proud and nationalistic Egyptians would not have enjoyed at all.

The name 'Hyksos' properly refers to the kings of Lower Egypt at this time. Who precisely those kings were we are not sure. Josephus, via his source Manetho, gives us a series of six kings whose names bear no relation to any inscription found in Egypt itself. The ethnic origin of the kings and their manner of succession is as unknown as the ethnic make-up of the people they ruled. It is highly probable that the latter were a mixture of peoples from western Mesopotamia and lower Anatolia – emigrants to a new land of opportunity.

For a while, new and old co-existed in Egypt. The government in Thebes negotiated passage through Hyksos lands so that their merchants could reach the Mediterranean. On their northward voyages, these traders would pass Hyksos ships heading upstream to trade with the Nubians.

But the peace could not last. Eventually both plague and the dynastic disruption that had embroiled Egypt died down, and the Theban pharaohs set about ridding Lower Egypt of the invaders. The first pharaoh to attempt this died in the process, but his son Kamose (r. *c.* 1555–1550 BC) had greater success before he (probably) also fell in battle.

The Egyptians had been learning well, and had assimilated the Hyksos military improvements into their own army. A new dynasty (the Eighteenth) made the ejection of the Hyksos into a crusade to 'cleanse the land of Asiatics'. Under Ahmose I (r. *c.* 1549–1525 BC) they succeeded, destroying the Hyksos capital of Avaris in the process. Just as the origins of the Hyksos are uncertain, likewise no one knows where they went once they had been driven out. Certainly there was no point in asking the Egyptians. They set about busily purging Egypt of every trace of the former immigrants, and as we have seen, they also set about rewriting the history of the 'conquest' to make their triumph look greater.

## Future Echoes

While they used their revisionist version of history to stir up nationalist sentiment, the pharaohs were not so reactionary as to give up the innovations the Hyksos had brought with them.

The chariot and the composite bow became essential components of the Egyptian military machine, just as the new crops and techniques introduced by the Hyksos galvanized the Egyptian economy. Without the Hyksos occupation, Egypt would probably never have expanded into the Levant or become a Mediterranean power with a great empire under later kings such as Ramesses II.

# *c.* 1200 BC – 1178 BC
# The Sea Peoples
## Riders of the Storm

*See, oh my father! The enemy ships came, they burned ... and did evil things in our land ... the country is abandoned.... I tell you, my father: the enemy that came here did much damage to us.*

Letter sent by King Ammurapi of Ugarit

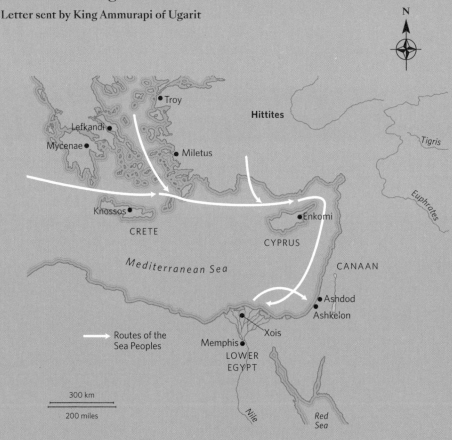

The 'Enkomi god': this statuette, around 50 cm (20 in.) high, of a Sea Peoples' divinity wears a helmet with bull's horns, which was often used to depict gods in Bronze Age art.

A desperate appeal from one king to another is one of the few surviving records of the devastating collapse of civilization that ended the Bronze Age. That the letter was excavated from burned-out ruins indicates that help was probably not forthcoming – most likely because everyone else was in just as much trouble. Who were these people in 'enemy ships'? Where did they come from and, after the crisis, where did they go?

All we know of the 'Sea Peoples' comes from the cultures that met them. And for most of those who did, the encounter ended in the same way. Not much survived. We do not know what gods the invaders worshipped; whether they were nomadic seafarers or raided in ships from a fixed base; whether they shared a single culture or were a confederation of different tribes. Most of what we do know of the Sea Peoples comes from the one civilization that managed to fend them off – the Egyptians.

## The Egyptian experience

One of the most interesting things about Egyptian accounts of the Sea Peoples is what they do not say – there is no mention of either their identity or their origins. The implication is that the Egyptians already knew, and assumed that anyone who read their reports would know too. The slightly startled and offended tone of the early inscriptions suggests that the Sea Peoples were regarded as a friendly and mostly harmless folk who had suddenly turned upon the Egyptians and savaged them.

'They came from the sea and none could withstand them', declared Ramesses II. The pharaohs had a tendency to talk up their enemies, as with the Hyksos, to make their own victories seem even more dramatic and impressive. Nevertheless, it seems clear that in the Sea Peoples, Egypt's ancient civilization faced a true existential threat – as the recently extinct Mycenaeans and Hittites could testify. Whoever the Sea Peoples were, they were organized, numerous and highly skilled at fighting.

Ramesses actually did a very good job of withstanding the invaders. He fought a kind of guerrilla war, launching ambushes from hidden tributaries of the Nile Delta, his troops raining arrows down upon the hostile fleets. Later, he defeated one of the Sea Peoples, the Sherden, in a major sea battle.

## Raiders of the apocalypse

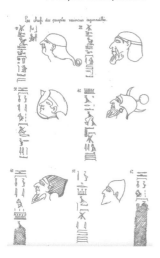

A drawing of different tribes of Sea Peoples with an accompanying description carved on a fortified gate at Medinet Habu, Egypt, sketched by Jean-François Champollion.

One of the many problems of identifying the Sea Peoples is that this name comes not from contemporary records, but from nineteenth-century historians. They studied Egyptian and Hittite records and concluded that the same people were responsible for much of the chaos surrounding the Bronze Age collapse. Modern scholars have reconsidered this evidence with a more critical eye. It is now generally believed that the Sea Peoples were as much a symptom as a cause of the collapse, and they may well have been made up of several different peoples and even entirely different cultures.

There is strong evidence of migratory pressures outside the boundaries of developed states at this time, and some of the Sea Peoples might have been barbarian tribes on the move. It is quite probable that such peoples took to the seas during the general collapse and pillaged the lands of more settled folk. There is a parallel 1,500 years later in the crisis that faced the Roman empire in the third century AD. Then a migratory people called the Goths – land-locked steppe warriors who had never seen the open sea – managed within a few decades to develop a huge pirate fleet which terrorized the coast of Asia Minor.

The Egyptians reported that women, children and livestock accompanied the Sea Peoples' army, suggesting that they had been

Ramesses III smites the Sea Peoples in this self-aggrandizing wall carving from Medinet Habu. Note the Egyptian bows and the large shields carried by some of the Sea Peoples.

displaced from their own homes and were seeking somewhere new to settle. It seems that, like the Goths, the Sea Peoples were victims of the crisis, and their invasions simply passed on to others the suffering they had experienced themselves. But until we can establish where their original homes were, this must remain a hypothesis.

## Waves of invaders

Some historians have suggested that certain groups among the Sea Peoples were not barbarian invaders at all. They may have been Minoans fleeing from the devastation of Crete, or, in one romantic but improbable theory, Trojans seeking refuge after the sack of their city by the Greeks. The idea that at least some of the Sea Peoples were established Mediterranean peoples is certainly suggested by the fact that the Egyptians seemed to know their attackers, and even differentiated between them, giving no fewer than nine names to their foes.

The peoples named in the Egyptian records have been conjectured to be proto-Etruscans (Teresh), Sardinians (Sherden) and Philistines (Peleset), among others. And these invaders came in waves – even after Ramesses confidently claimed to have defeated the Sherden (and took the survivors into his army), his successor Merneptah (r. 1213–1203 BC) faced the onslaught of the Shekelesh, Lukka, Ekwesh and others.

Although they would never admit it, the Egyptians quite possibly owed their survival to the Hyksos who had dominated their country until two centuries previously. Without the military innovations – including horse-drawn chariots and bronze weaponry – and economic developments by which the Hyksos had strengthened the country, Egypt might have fallen to this new wave of invaders. Merneptah's inscriptions make it plain that the invaders intended not just to raid, but also to take over and resettle Egypt.

Unlike Ramesses, Merneptah chose to face his attackers on land. The climactic battle was fought at the unidentified site of Pi-yer in the Nile Delta, and his decisive victory secured Egypt's frontiers for a generation. But even then the Sea Peoples were not entirely vanquished. They descended on the Amorite kingdom of Amurru, in modern-day Syria, and left it 'as desolate as though the people and the land had never been', according to a contemporary Egyptian inscription of Ramesses III (r. 1186–1155 BC), the next pharaoh to take them on.

Despite the claims of Ramesses III's predecessors that they had ended the threat of the Sea Peoples once and for all, it is clear in fact they had not. The unfortunate Ramesses III spent his entire reign fighting off the invaders in a series of campaigns that demoralized his people and emptied the treasury.

Ramesses III was more proactive than his predecessors and seems to have taken the fight to the enemy in Canaan. When the Sea Peoples then formed a confederated fleet and attempted to swarm Egypt's coast in 1178 BC, Ramesses III responded by luring the enemy close to land, near the Delta city of Xois. There, a horde of shore-based archers unleashed their arrows on the densely packed ships, and grappling hooks hauled the enemy craft against pikemen waiting in stockades. The battle seems to have finally eliminated the Sea Peoples, but the cost was high.

Egypt was left bankrupt, and as his reward for saving the land, Ramesses was assassinated in a conspiracy of courtiers who took advantage of popular unrest. The Sea Peoples themselves seem never to have regrouped as an organized force. Piracy and raids remained a feature of Mediterranean life, but as the Classical era dawned such attacks became less frequent. Where the wandering of the Sea Peoples finally ended is probably now impossible to tell, but this has not stopped historians from speculating.

## Future Echoes

Ramesses III tried hard to rebuild an economy damaged by the strain of fighting the Sea Peoples, but his government simply did not have enough money to maintain the basic functions of the state. As a result, in 1159 BC the necropolis workers at Deir el-Medina, near the city of Thebes, unpaid and disgruntled, downed tools. They marched into Thebes and staged a sit-in in the temple of the priests in charge of overseeing their payment. When they received what was due they left, but resumed their strike when no further wages arrived. The matter was never resolved and was eventually folded into the general chaos surrounding the assassination of Ramesses III. Nevertheless, the Sea Peoples remain indirectly responsible for the first organized labour strike in recorded history.

Egyptian craftsmen at work creating funerary objects in a wall painting from the tomb of Nebamun and Ipuky at Thebes, c. 1390–1349 BC.

# Part Two
# **From Assyria to Alexander**
## Recovering from the Great Collapse

Necessity, they say, is the mother of invention. Perhaps so, but desperation is an even more productive parent. The Bronze Age collapse of around 1200 BC ruptured trade routes which had been painstakingly established over millennia and which by that time stretched right across the Mediterranean world. Timber, pottery and slaves moved along these routes, but nothing was more important than tin.

Tin is not naturally available in much of Mesopotamia or the eastern Mediterranean, and so was imported from as far afield as Britain. Without tin, blacksmiths could not forge bronze, the material so important that an entire era was later named for it. Something had to be done urgently, for bronze was essential for everything from weapons to ploughs to cooking vessels. People were forced to find an alternative and began to smelt ore to obtain iron – which has a much higher melting point than tin or copper and requires more complex methods to produce.

A wonderful discovery was made: working iron ore in a charcoal fire made the metal become both tough and flexible. This is because carbon from the charcoal infuses iron to make steel, though no one knew that at the time. All they were aware of was that humans had been gifted with a metal vastly superior to bronze, and, being humans, they promptly crafted this wonderful new material into weapons and enthusiastically used them to kill other humans.

Early acquisition of ironworking technology allowed peoples and tribes to punch above their weight. The allegedly illiterate **Philistines** were able to hold off the more numerous and sophisticated Israelites through their possession of superior weaponry. (Though the Bible assures us that a talent for treachery and subversion was also helpful.)

New peoples rose to prominence as those innovative and adaptable enough to adjust to a changed world quickly filled the void left by the great collapse. Often these newcomers were pastoralists or nomads, such as the **Arameans**, who had been on the periphery of the former Bronze Age states. These peoples were less committed to the old world order, and were better at adapting to new circumstances.

For with the destruction of the old world, traditional ways of doing things no longer applied. The complex symbols of cuneiform and hieroglyphics looked cumbersome alongside a new style of writing that reproduced not images of the things described but the sounds used for them in speech – the first alphabetic script, pioneered by the Phoenicians. And as trade developed again, writing became more common, for now clay tablets had been replaced by an Egyptian technology: papyrus. This thinner, more flexible material was made from the pith of reeds growing along the Nile. It is the ancestor of the English word 'paper' (a material now being replaced by the tablet). The Phoenicians also made a number of innovations in shipbuilding and would surely have gone on to dominate Mediterranean trade were it not for their northern neighbours, the Greeks.

The Greeks were now divided into different ethnic groups, the most important of which were the Ionians – possibly the survivors of the Mycenaean collapse – and the **Dorians**, who may have originally been barbarian invaders who became thoroughly Greek. Other barbarians to the north, such as the **Illyrians**, resisted the siren call of Greek culture and remained as wild as ever, until eventually they too were subdued by the Romans.

Greek colonies had proliferated during the Dark Ages, when the use of writing disappeared. When record-keeping began once more, those records were inscribed using the alphabet on papyrus in Greek cities on the coast of Spain, Italy, North Africa, Asia Minor and the Black Sea. If you could get there in a trireme, the Greeks had got there – and founded a colony.

Some of the most important Greek colonies were on the island of Sicily, where Syracuse swiftly became as large and powerful as any city on the Greek mainland. The Greeks of Sicily quickly came to terms with the native **Sicels**, though they feuded bitterly with the Carthaginians in the southwest of the island. Even today we are familiar with cities outside Greece that first had Greek names: Massalia (Marseille), Nea Polis (the 'New City' today called Naples), Syracuse and Tripoli (the 'Three Cities'). Technically speaking, none of these colonies can be called a metropolis, because 'metropolis' means 'mother city' (except in the case of the city actually called Metropolis, which was in Thessaly in northern Greece). The now vanished city of Emporium ('trading station') in Spain has countless descendants in the department-store 'Emporiums' of a generation ago.

Civilization now took root in the Mediterranean, but it had never left its heartlands in Egypt and Mesopotamia. Though the Egyptians considered their land a seething cauldron of political and social unrest, the rest of the world saw it as a timeless, unchanging civilization on the banks of the Nile. Much as the Greeks had learned from the Phoenicians, they also took inspiration from Egypt's religion, architecture and arts.

The Egyptians had maintained their supplies of tin from the African interior, and consequently continued to manufacture bronze for centuries after the rest of the developed world had switched to steel. It was exactly the opposite in Mesopotamia and the Levant – ironworking developed early in Anatolia and steel was quickly adopted throughout the region.

As might be expected, the militaristic Assyrians were among the first to appreciate the potential of steel weapons. Through the ninth to the seventh centuries BC the Assyrians brutally exploited their advantage and conquered Babylon, Elam, Lydia, Phoenicia and the Israelite kingdoms. It was the practice of the Assyrians to resettle entire defeated populations elsewhere, which is how the **Lost Tribes of Israel** were misplaced. The **Phrygians** in their mountain fastness held out under their king Mita, famed today in legend as Midas, the king with the golden touch.

Egypt discovered that centuries-old tactics and bronze weaponry quite literally could not cut it against steel armour. They were already struggling to quash Nubian invasions from Kush in the south. At one point both Egypt and Nubia were ruled by the **Kushites**. The Assyrians pushed over a regime that was already toppling. In 670 BC Egypt became an Assyrian possession – something the Egyptians never accepted, and rebelled against at every available opportunity.

But the art of maintaining empires was still under-developed, and it does not seem to have dawned on the Assyrians that ruling requires a degree of consent by the ruled. Military force and terror (the Assyrians were particularly fond of impaling and flaying their detractors alive) can only take an empire so far before the dammed-up hatred of centuries overwhelms it. When civil war weakened Assyria's grip, almost every one of the empire's subjects rose in rebellion. By 609 BC Assyria had fallen.

The empire's former vassals such as the **Medes** and Babylonians methodically levelled the Assyrian capitals of Assur and Nineveh to make absolutely sure that Assyria would never rise again. Power passed to the Babylonians, whose rulers came from the magic-wielding tribe of the **Chaldeans**. In turn Babylon was later forced to yield to the growing might of Persia. Persia's economic strength was in part based on the re-foundation of trade routes, in particular with China and the east. Another people that benefited from this trade were the **Bactrians**. Caravans of their famous double-humped camels were to become emblematic of what was later called the Silk Road.

In Asia Minor new opportunities allowed the rise of new kingdoms. None was richer than the kingdom of the **Lydians**, famed in Greek myth as a land of strange monsters and great wealth. The wealthiest of the Lydian kings was of course Croesus. He launched a doomed attempt to destroy the upstart Persian empire, and his defeat saw Asia Minor fall to Persian domination.

While these events were shaking the world's great civilizations, out on the uncultured outer edge of Carthaginian influence, a bunch of barbarian bandits had seized control of a hilltop in central Italy. The event barely excited more than local gossip, yet the foundation of Rome was profoundly to affect later ages.

# 722 BC – today
# The Lost Tribes of Israel
## Scattered Among All People?

*And the Lord shall scatter thee among all people, from the one end of the earth even unto the other; and there thou shalt serve other gods, which neither thou nor thy fathers have known, even wood and stone.*

*And among these nations shalt thou find no ease, neither shall the sole of thy foot have rest: but the Lord shall give thee there a trembling heart, and failing of eyes, and sorrow of mind.*

Deuteronomy 28:64–65

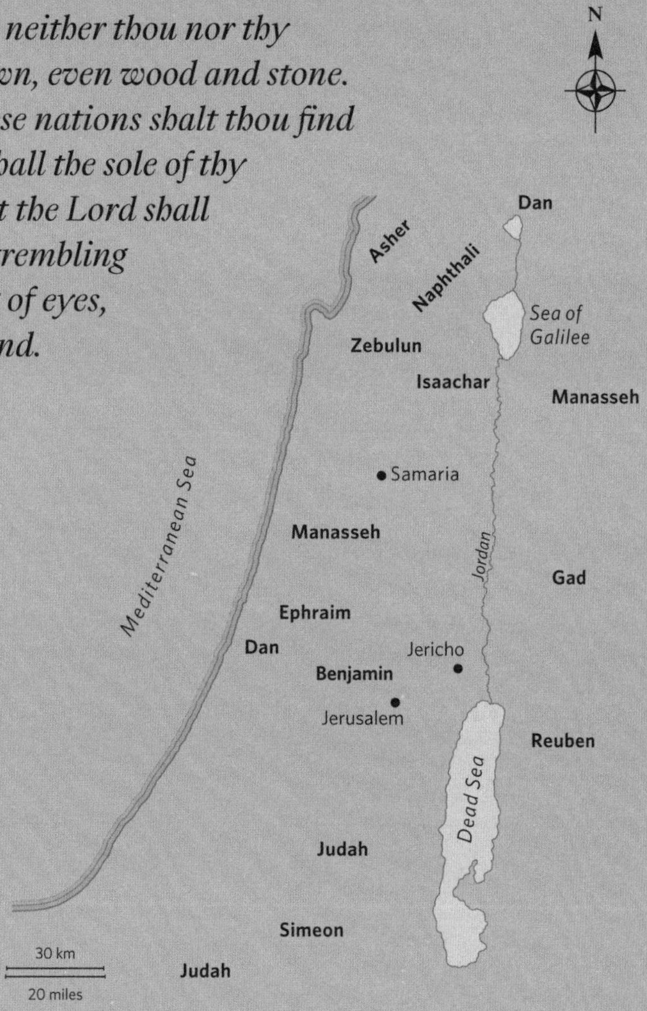

N

Asher

Dan

Naphthali

Sea of Galilee

Zebulun

Isaachar

Manasseh

Mediterranean Sea

• Samaria

Manasseh

Jordan

Ephraim

Gad

Dan

Jericho •

Benjamin

Jerusalem •

Reuben

Dead Sea

Judah

Simeon

30 km

20 miles

Judah

While most of the tribes of Israel are certainly not forgotten, they are utterly lost. In fact the people of Israel who are today called Jews derive that name from a single tribe – Judah. According to the biblical record, the patriarch Jacob allocated the land of Israel to twelve tribes. These were Asher, Benjamin, Dan, Ephraim, Gad, Issachar, Judah, Manasseh, Naphtali, Reuben, Simeon and Zebulun. The priestly tribe of Levi held no land, and its members were distributed across Israel. How and why Judah survived while ten others disappeared tells us much about the maelstrom of warfare and demographic upheaval in the Middle East during the eighth century BC.

Around the start of the Iron Age (*c.* 1050 BC) the kingdom of Israel was split between those tribes which recognized Rehoboam, the son of Solomon, as their king, and the ten tribes which did not. The major southern tribe was that of Judah, so although the tribe of Benjamin joined with it, the southern kingdom was known as the Kingdom of Judah.

There is much that is today controversial about this new kingdom, as modern scholars are less prepared to take on trust the Bible's assertion that Judah became sufficiently powerful to match the more populous Israelite state to the north. A distinct possibility is that Judah was something of a rump state, which only clung to a precarious existence because its kings held the near-impregnable fortress of Jerusalem – around which a small city was beginning to grow.

Tiglath-Pileser III, king of the Assyrians and a great warrior, who came down upon the Israelites 'like a wolf on the fold'.

## Enter the Assyrians

Israel and Judah developed as somewhat typical contemporary statelets. That is, they feuded between themselves and with their neighbours, the Arameans and Philistines, and were completely unprepared for the growing threat of the Assyrians. The catalyst for this threat was an Assyrian king called Tiglath-Pileser III (r. 744-727 BC). Despite being the third of that name, this Tiglath-Pileser represented dramatic change rather than continuity. He seized the Assyrian throne during a bout of civil war, and set about giving his new kingdom a complete makeover. Once the bureaucracy had been overhauled, Tiglath-Pileser reshaped the army, transforming it from a civil militia into a professional force.

Tiglath-Pileser quickly realized that the best way to pay for a full-time professional army was to use revenues from peoples whom that army had conquered, and he launched on a career of conquest and expansion that ended only with his death. By then he had conquered Babylon (as Assyrian kings did at every opportunity) and also the peoples of Urartu and the so-called Neo-Hittites. This left the Assyrians poised to sweep down on the kingdoms of Israel and Judah.

The Israelites in the north first attempted to buy Tiglath-Pileser off with a huge ransom of silver (2 Kings 15:19), but, realizing that this could not be sustained as a regular tribute, they attempted a military defence in alliance with their former enemies, the Arameans. According to the Bible, this godless alliance, combined with the Israelite tolerance of the worship of Baal and other abominations, was enough to bring down the wrath of the Almighty upon the northern kingdom. The final straw was when the Arameans and Israelites turned on Judah and demanded they join the anti-Assyrian alliance – or else.

Detail of a relief wall-panel from Nimrud, showing a procession of Assyrian soldiers carrying statues of their gods on their shoulders. Though oppressive rulers in many ways, the Assyrians do not seem to have attempted to force their faith on the monotheistic Hebrews.

Assyrian archers attack a city. As the siege engine moves up the ramp to attack the walls, the impaled victims in the background are a dire portent of the fate awaiting the city's defenders.

Working on the principle that 'my enemy's enemy is my friend', the king of Judah, Ahaz, appealed to Tiglath-Pileser, who responded to the call for help with great energy and enthusiasm. In around 734 BC the Assyrians attacked and destroyed Aramean Damascus, and the kingdom of Israel became a subject nation in the Assyrian empire. However, the northern Israelites clearly shared with their southern brethren that recalcitrant attitude which was to be so annoying to future conquerors, and before long they were scheming to regain their independence by playing the Assyrians off against the Egyptians.

### Exile and resettlement

The Assyrians, now ruled by Shalmaneser V (r. 727  722 BC), were unimpressed, and the Bible baldly reports the upshot. 'Then the king of Assyria came up throughout all the land, and went up to Samaria, and besieged it three years. In the ninth year of [the rule of the Israelite king] Hoshea, the king of Assyria took Samaria, and carried away Israel into Assyria, and placed them in Halah and in Habor by the river of Gozan, and in the cities of the Medes' (2 Kings 17:5–6).

Detail of an Assyrian wall relief from Nineveh showing the inhabitants of Lachish being taken into exile after their city had been captured by the Assyrian army.

Only the kingdom of Judah and the tribe of Benjamin remained. What happened to the ten tribes deported to Assyria has since been a matter of great and generally fruitless speculation. The whereabouts of Halah and Gozan are unknown, though if they are near the Habor, the river of Gozan, then this is a tributary which flows into the Euphrates, and so they would be somewhere in northern Syria. The 'cities of the Medes' were even further east, and were probably in lands once occupied by the Elamites.

The Assyrians were great believers in the wholesale resettlement of populations around their empire as a way of quelling unrest. The land emptied by the deportation of the ten tribes was refilled with imported peoples from Babylon and other conquests. It might be reasonable to suggest that, once dispersed and settled in a new environment, the lost tribes gradually blended with the native peoples. Within a few generations, intermarriage and adoption of the native religion and customs would have caused them to vanish entirely. But rational thinking was not a strong characteristic of those in later centuries who became obsessed by the fate of the lost tribes.

## Future Echoes

The experience from later diasporas of the Jewish people shows that in at least those cases the Jews were able to resist assimilation and preserve their cultural identity against all the odds. Therefore, for centuries the hope remained that the ten tribes were out there, somewhere. For example, there is a passing reference in the New Testament to one 'Anna ... of the Tribe of Asher' (Luke 2:36). Asher was one of the lost tribes, so how a woman from this tribe might have come to be living in Roman-controlled Judea seven centuries later has never been explained.

Nine hundred years later, a man called Eldad turned up in Tunisia and presented himself to the Jewish community there. He claimed to be of the tribe of Dan, living near the legendary River Sambatyon. This river was allegedly impassable six days of the week, but calm on the seventh. The seventh day was the Sabbath, which no god-fearing person could break by crossing the river, so the tribe remained cut off from the world. (Attempts have since been made to link the tribe of Dan with the Beta Israel people of Ethiopia, who have since been recognized as Jews by the modern state of Israel.)

Searches for the lost tribes have also found them in Afghanistan, where the Pashtuns are considered by some as possible former Israelites. Genetic testing has so far failed to turn up a conclusive link. This is also the case with 'lost tribesmen' in China and the Cherokee of North America, all of whose genes seem to disqualify them from being the missing Israelites. (In fact it would be fair to claim that modern science has removed more members of the ten lost tribes than Tiglath-Pileser ever did.) This also applies to the Igbo Jews of Nigeria, who nevertheless still believe that among their ancestors are members of at least five of the lost tribes.

Perhaps these tribes moved on further into pre-historic Africa, as other descendants have come forward from East Africa and Zimbabwe. Or possibly the roaming Israelites took a completely different turn, and in defiance of logic, geography and (as it turns out) genetic testing became the Japanese. This nineteenth-century theory was never based on credible evidence, and today is mentioned only in the context of romantic fantasies concerning the lost tribes.

On the other hand, if the last plausible reported whereabouts of the lost tribes are considered together with the other peoples who have been in the region since – including Greeks, Romans and Mongols – and added to this picture are the numbers of emigrants leaving those same lands for the west, it is probably safe to say that few communities in Europe, the Americas and the Middle East do not include descendants of the lost tribes of Israel.

## c. 1200 BC – today
# The Arameans
## Nomadic Conquerors in the Middle East

*I gathered my chariots and warriors in the service
of my Lord [the god] Ashur ... I went to the country
of the Aramaeans ... [whom] I smote. I slew their
warriors and carried off their goods, their wealth ...
I crossed the Euphrates after them ... I burnt them
with fire, destroyed and overthrew them.*
Inscription of the Assyrian king Tiglath Pileser I

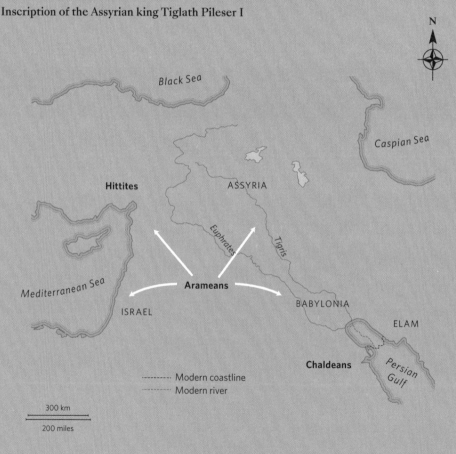

N

Black Sea

Caspian Sea

Hittites

ASSYRIA

Euphrates

Tigris

Mediterranean Sea

Arameans

ISRAEL

BABYLONIA

ELAM

Chaldeans

Persian Gulf

·········· Modern coastline
·········· Modern river

300 km

200 miles

W ho today has heard of the Arameans? Yet this remarkably adaptable and creative people not only developed one of the languages used in the Bible and by Jesus, they also still survive in scattered enclaves even now, thousands of years after their first appearance in the Middle East. What then is their story?

By most counts, the Bronze Age collapse of the twelfth century BC was apocalyptic. Trade foundered, cities and whole civilizations were wiped out and population numbers plunged. Cultures centred on city-dwellers producing sophisticated products were replaced by illiterate subsistence farmers making their own crude clay pots.

Yet even this desolation and destruction produced opportunities for some. One of the two main groups which benefited was the highly organized and adaptable Assyrians. They were quick to realize the potential of iron weapons that replaced bronze as the trade routes supplying the tin necessary to make bronze disappeared. With their neighbours in disarray, the Assyrians soon began to build a substantial empire. Their strongest opposition came from the other group that benefited most from the Bronze Age collapse – the Arameans.

Carved stone slabs bearing sculptures such as this were traditional decorations on the walls of Neo-Hittite palaces and temples. This winged human-headed lion is one of many excavated at Tell Halaf, an ancient Aramean site.

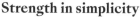

## Strength in simplicity

In some ways the Arameans lay at the other end of the spectrum from the centralized, organized Assyrians. While the Assyrian administrative machine was robust enough to withstand the shocks of the prevailing chaos, the Arameans bypassed the problem by having no administrative machinery to speak of. Assyria managed to keep its complex irrigation-based agricultural system going, while the Arameans – who were pastoral nomads – simply took over the fields of farmers who had failed to meet the new challenges.

Because archaeological evidence pointed to the nomadic Arameans moving into lands previously occupied by farmers, many historians of the nineteenth and twentieth centuries leapt to the conclusion that waves of Aramean invaders from the northeast had actually caused the Bronze Age collapse. However, more sophisticated analysis of the evidence shows that the lands were often already vacant, or that the

Arameans displaced peoples too weakened to defend themselves. The Arameans, like the Sea Peoples, were a symptom not a cause of the crisis.

Instead of arriving in a huge migration, it seems that the Arameans were always around, perhaps as a sub-group of a people the early Assyrians called the 'Aramu' (when they noticed them at all). Had the Bronze Age collapse not taken place, the Arameans might have been another of the many peoples who briefly appear in the record and then vanish forever. As it was, the Arameans had a culture and lifestyle well adapted to the new circumstances, and they thrived.

Rather like their Assyrian rivals, the key to Aramean success was adaptability. Where there was a power vacuum, the Arameans filled it. Where the peoples of depopulated areas needed newcomers to help with farming and defence, the Arameans became welcome neighbours. Where the Assyrians were determined to take land for their growing empire, the Arameans were stubborn fighters, their very disorganization making them all the harder to defeat.

The Assyrian state was organized under a sole autocratic king, but the Arameans had no single leader and had to be defeated tribe by tribe. And with no cities or permanent fields to defend, the Arameans often found it more convenient simply to move out of the way of Assyrian armies, and then flow back once those armies were needed elsewhere.

## Adapting to circumstances

As a result of such innate adaptability, by the time the dust had settled after the Bronze Age collapse, the new early Iron Age saw the Arameans occupying a broad swathe of the Middle East, from southern Anatolia to southern Mesopotamia and the northern borders of the Israelite kingdoms.

Settlement varied, depending on circumstances. In what is today north Syria, it appears that the struggling Neo-Hittite civilization made little attempt to oppose the Aramean newcomers. While clashes very probably did occur, the few surviving texts reveal only a steady increase of Aramean names among community leaders, suggesting not a violent displacement of the native population but a gradual assimilation, or at least a sort of symbiosis. (An earlier idea that farmers and herdsmen are natural enemies has recently been revised. Cultural studies have now shown that sometimes pastoral nomads and settled agriculturalists form complex relationships in which neither can do without the other.)

To the south, the Arameans expanded to the point where they bumped into the organized and somewhat xenophobic states of the Phoenicians and Israelites. Once a series of military clashes had made it plain that the current occupants would fight hard for their land, the Arameans contented themselves with settling along the northern and eastern borders. In usual Aramean fashion, there was no state of 'Aramea', but instead a rag-tag collection of minor kingdoms, which fought and feuded without discrimination against fellow Arameans, Israelites or Phoenicians.

## Arameans and Assyrians

Further inland, the Arameans had to contend with the Assyrians. Here the fortunes of the Arameans mirrored those of the Assyrians. When the Assyrians were weak, the Arameans expanded, when the Assyrians became organized under a competent king, Aramean territory contracted. The Assyrians could not ignore the Arameans, because their trade routes to the west lay across Aramean-occupied lands, and the highly diversified nature of the Aramean leadership made trade treaties almost impossible.

Instead, from around 1050 BC until approximately 700 BC the Assyrians tried persistently to bring the western Arameans under their control. The Assyrians eventually succeeded, in part because they recognized that, once the Arameans were conquered and absorbed into the empire, it was easier to leave them with their own cultural identity and language. Indeed, Aramean became one of the official languages of the Assyrian empire, a fact that led to Aramean gradually replacing Akkadian as the common tongue of the Middle East.

In southern Mesopotamia the situation was vastly more complex. Here the Arameans were simply another addition to a multicultural stew that already contained Babylonians, Assyrians, Sumerians and Elamite remnants. The Arameans were also jostling for elbow room with another recently arrived people, the Chaldeans. As far as historians are concerned, one

On this Neo-Hittite stele from the Aramean site of Sam'al dating to the eighth century BC, an elaborately dressed person sits in front of a table laden with food and drink, while a servant wafts a fan. A winged sun disc hovers above.

advantage of the Aramean incursion into this densely settled and long-civilized region is that there is a (relatively) well-documented account of how the locals reacted to the new arrivals.

The Arameans immediately involved themselves in local politics, which often meant supporting whichever local ruler was opposed to the Assyrians. They also made life harder for pro-Assyrian monarchs, while other rulers became pro-Assyrian simply in order to get Assyrian protection from Aramean raiders. While the Chaldeans showed a tendency to merge with the local peoples, the Arameans seem to have continued as a distinct group for longer, and they remained pastoralists as the Chaldeans happily became adjusted to urban life.

Even when they eventually became an accepted fact of life in southern Mesopotamia, the Arameans there were never particularly welcome. Conflicts were frequent over the succeeding centuries, until the Arameans, like the Babylonians and other residents of the region, were finally subsumed into the series of empires which dominated Mesopotamia for the rest of antiquity.

A funerary relief from a tomb at Palmyra, modern Syria, showing the deceased reclining on a couch while his family members stand behind. The inscription in Aramaic names the family along with what appears to be a list of five generations of ancestors.

Aramean influences are clear in this wall hanging in a chapel at Deyrulumur Monastery, Midyat, eastern Anatolia. It is probable that Jesus himself spoke Aramaic.

## Future Echoes

The adaptability of the Arameans meant that their culture tended to blend with that of any people they dwelt among. As a result, unlike other dominant languages such as Greek, Latin and English, the spread of Aramaic was not accompanied by many other obvious Aramean cultural influences.

The Assyrian adoption of Aramaic as one of the languages of their empire was in part a pragmatic means of accommodating their new and reluctant Aramean subjects, but also a recognition that the relatively simple alphabetic structure of Aramaic made administration much easier than using the complex languages of earlier record-keeping. The Arameans themselves derived the alphabet from the Phoenicians, but quickly adapted it. The spread of Aramaic is evident in its later use in the Bible (the Book of Daniel was originally written in Aramaic) and by its adoption in the later Persian empire.

Eventually many non-Aramean peoples, from Iraq to what is now Turkey, came to use Aramaic as their first language. An Aramaic dialect was spoken in Galilee at the time of the early Roman empire, and Jesus almost certainly gave his sermons and parables in that language. Variants of Aramaic still survive today, making it one of the oldest languages still in everyday use.

The ability of the Arameans to fit in while remaining distinct has allowed them to survive as a people for the past five thousand years. They have been Jewish (the Bible counted the conversion of the Aramaic king Namaan as a major coup), while others became Christian (many Christian communities in the Middle East identify as Aramaic) and others became Muslims.

The Arameans remain in scattered enclaves still today, both internationally and in the Middle East. As just one example of this remarkable people's continuing endurance, the Aramean Syriac Football Association (founded in Sweden) participates in international competitions and has a lively Facebook page.

## c. 1200 BC – 8th century BC
# The Philistines
## Strangers in a Strange Land

*Now the Philistines gathered together their armies to battle.... And Saul and the men of Israel were gathered together, and pitched by the valley of Elah, and set the battle in array against the Philistines.... And there went out a champion out of the camp of the Philistines, named Goliath, of Gath, whose height was six cubits and a span. And he had an helmet of brass upon his head, and he was armed with a coat of mail; and the weight of the coat was five thousand shekels of brass.*

1 Samuel 17:1–5

*Mediterranean Sea*

Sea of Galilee

*Jordan*

**N**

ISRAEL

Jerusalem

Ashdod
Ashkelon
**Philistines**
Ekron
Gath
JUDAH
Gaza

*Dead Sea*

30 km
20 miles

Delilah, lover of Samson, was probably a Philistine; the gigantic warrior Goliath certainly was, and every uncultured boor in the ages since has been called one. But who were the Philistines whom the ancient Israelites so loved to hate? How did they earn their unfavourable reputation, and did they deserve it? Where did they come from, and what ultimately became of them?

## From the Sea to Canaan

The Bronze Age collapse witnessed a series of mass migrations. As we have seen, the Egyptians struggled against several waves of migrants during this period. For the most part, where these would-be invaders came from is as much a mystery as where they ended up after the Egyptians had fought them off. There is, however, one exception.

In an inscription, the pharaoh Ramesses III boasts of his victory over a confederation of Sea Peoples in 1178 BC, one of whom is named as the 'Prst' or 'Plst'. Hieroglyphics do not include vowels, and so expanded with the presumed vowels inserted, this becomes the 'Peleset' – a name familiar to Bible scholars. The Hebrews apparently knew of the same people. They called them the Peleshet and the Bible paints them as the persistent enemies of the Israelites in Canaan. Modern translations follow the Greeks, who rendered the Hebrew word as 'Philistines'.

Philistine figurine from Tel Qasile, of around the tenth century BC, probably depicting a fertility goddess. Pottery and sculpture provide tantalizing clues as to the mysterious origins of the Philistines.

## The Cretan connection

So how did the Philistines go from fighting the Egyptians on boats to fighting the Hebrews inland in Canaan? And where did they come from in the first place? The Bible's Table of Nations offers one answer: 'Egypt was the father of the ... Kasluhites (from whom the Philistines came), and Caphtorites' (Genesis 10:13–14). This confirms an involvement with Egypt, but would be vastly more helpful if anyone knew who the Kasluhites were, or where Caphtor was. And to add to the confusion, Hebrew sources sometimes seem to use 'Philistine' simply to mean 'hostile strangers'.

Some scholars have suggested that 'Caphtor' might have been ancient Crete. Pottery resembling Cretan-style vessels has been found in Palestinian archaeological sites. But this compelling connection is less conclusive than it might at first seem. Pots got around in the ancient world – following the same logic based on pottery styles alone, concluding that the Philistines were Aegean would also tell us that the Egyptians were Athenian. More intriguing perhaps are the oval Philistine graves, a curious mode of burial that was also practised on Crete.

It seems clear from their material culture that the Philistines were not native Canaanites (they also eschewed the Semitic practice of circumcision). The theory goes that the Philistines originated in Crete, but were driven from there by the general chaos of the Bronze Age collapse. The Philistines then confederated with other displaced peoples in an attempt to force their way into Egypt. Rebuffed by Ramesses III, the Philistines ricocheted on to the coast of the Levant, and settled in the area around the ancient city of Ashkelon.

This is a beguiling theory, and recent DNA analysis of skeletons from Ashkelon seems to confirm migration at this time from southern Europe. This DNA signature soon disappears, however, possibly due to intermarriage or perhaps it could be the result of Assyrian mass deportation from Ashkelon. Also useful would be evidence of the language that the Philistines spoke. Occasional Philistine words preserved in the Bible suggest a non-Semitic tongue, and some Philistine names – such as that of the most famous Philistine, Goliath – are certainly not native to the Levant. The problem is that these names cannot be convincingly linked with anywhere else either. In fact, to contradict the Sea Peoples hypothesis, some of the closest relatives to the few words we know of the Philistine tongue are from a Neo-Hittite state on the other side of Syria, intriguingly called Palistin.

## Enemies of Israel

What is certain is that once the Philistines had arrived from wherever their homeland was, they settled down in eleventh-century BC Canaan. The heartland of their country was based around the five cities of Gaza, Ashkelon, Ashdod, Gath and Ekron, and they set about expanding. Their presence was bitterly resented by the Israelites, who had only recently established themselves as a people there. They were very clear in their own minds to whom the 'Promised Land' had been promised – and it was not to the Philistines. The Philistines spent the remainder of their time as a distinct people entrenched in frequent, bitter and generally inconclusive struggles with the Israelites.

Their formative military adventures in the Mediterranean had probably helped to familiarize the Philistines with the latest in

In this relief sculpture from Medinet Habu in Egypt lines of Philistine captives are shown wearing their distinctive headdresses. The Philistines eventually settled in less well-defended lands further north.

military tactics and technology. This included the new-fangled methods of iron-working, which the Philistines were careful not to share with their aggressive neighbours. 'Now there was no smith found throughout all the land of Israel: for the Philistines said, Lest the Israelites make them swords and spears', as the Bible remarks (1 Samuel 13:19). Archaeology confirms that although comparatively illiterate, even by the low standards of the time, the Philistines were nevertheless a hierarchical and well-organized people. Cities were ruled by commanders called *seranim*, and both cities and rural homesteads show evidence of competent arrangement. In fact, discipline and superior weaponry were no doubt necessary to their survival, as the Philistines probably never numbered more than 40,000 – about a third of the population of modern Oxford in England.

The lack of any of their texts means that the Philistines can never speak to us in their own words. Most of what we know of them, apart from archaeology, comes from the Bible. Over the years scholarship has swung from uncritical acceptance of its contents to the point where almost every word of the Old Testament is disputed. Did Samson indeed slaughter the Philistines with the jawbone of an ass, or is this an allegory for an Israelite triumph despite their inferior weaponry?

David and Goliath, as depicted on a silver plate of the Byzantine period. The Philistines were always outnumbered and surrounded by enemies, making them the underdogs in the struggle.

Another point of interest is Samson's relationship with the seductive Delilah. She was from the valley of Sorek, on the border of Israelite territory, and the implication is that she might have been a Philistine herself. Certainly the Philistines seem to have had little difficulty in contacting and bribing Delilah. Israelite–Philistine relations may not always have been as straightforwardly hostile as tradition represents them.

However, we cannot push the texts too far. Before we debate whether David's defeat of the giant Goliath was a real event or mere folklore, it should be noted that some modern scholars dispute whether there was an ancient 'kingdom of David' at all. (Non-biblical evidence for the kingdom is hard to come by, though recently a city dating to the time of David has been systematically excavated in the valley of Elah, where David fought Goliath according to the Bible.) What is certain is that the Philistines could not keep iron weaponry from their enemy forever, and it may have been about this time – the tenth century BC – that the Israelites finally overwhelmed the tiny Philistine statelet.

## Disappearance

The Philistines' defeat was not absolute, however. Their limited survival may have been due to the fact that soon after the final conflict, the Israelites split into the separate and rival kingdoms of Israel and Judah. With the Israelites consumed in internecine warfare, the Philistines were left to their own devices. Though they were never again an organized state, the five cities remained as independent Philistine entities that held their own against the Israelites in a series of disorganized border clashes.

Some of the last mentions of the Philistines come from the state that eventually swallowed them up. As the power of Assyria expanded into the Levant, we find references to the Philistines by Tiglath-Pileser III in the later eighth century BC, which make it plain that by then they were already Assyrian vassals. A century and a half later, the Neo-Babylonians under Nebuchadnezzar II (r. 605–c. 562 BC) conquered the region. It is uncertain whether there were by then any Philistines who called themselves such. Many may have merged with the local peoples, or – as Assyrian texts hint – been exiled for rebellion along with the mutinous King Sidqia of Ashkelon.

If the latter, the Philistines may have suffered the same fate as the Lost Tribes of Israel, who were deported at around the same time. Sadly for the lost Philistine people, no one has since tried as hard to find them again.

## Future Echoes

Just as the origins of the Philistines are a matter of debate, so is the origin of the name 'Palestine'. The word is ancient, being used by the Greek historian Herodotus around 450 BC, and probably comes from the Hebrew 'Peleshet'. It became controversial in the mid-second century AD when the Roman emperor Hadrian crushed a Jewish revolt and drove the Jews from their homeland. One theory is that the vindictive Hadrian gave the name 'Syria Palestina' to the former province of Judea to celebrate the ancient enemies of the Jews. It is grimly ironic, then, that the people who are now called the Palestinians dispute ownership of much of the region with the Israelis, just as the Philistines once did with the Israelites.

The Philistines were notorious for their illiteracy, and the Israelites found their culture so alien that they preferred to believe that the Philistines had no culture whatsoever. Ever since, 'philistine' has been used as a derogatory term describing a boor with no appreciation of the finer things in life. This may change. Archaeological investigations at various Philistine sites including Ashkelon, Ashdod and Ekron have produced evidence of a developed civilization.

# c. 1000 BC – c. 5th century AD
# **The Dorians**
# People of the Spear

*Even after the Trojan War, Hellas was still engaged in removing and settling [tribes], and thus lacked the tranquility which must precede growth.... After the Dorians became masters of the Peloponnese much had to be done and many years had to elapse before Hellas could attain to a durable peace undisturbed by migrations.*

Thucydides, *History of the Peloponnesian War* 1.12

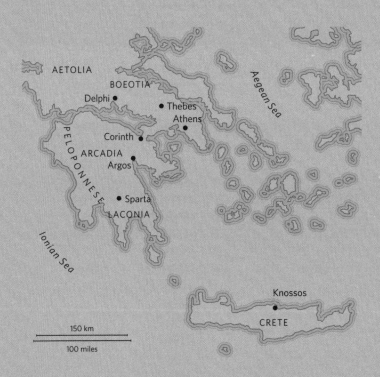

AETOLIA
BOEOTIA
Delphi
Thebes
Athens
Corinth
PELOPONNESE
ARCADIA
Argos
Sparta
LACONIA
Aegean Sea
Ionian Sea
Knossos
CRETE

150 km
100 miles

In 1300 BC Greece was a civilized land where kings ruled, traded and fought among themselves. Their people made substantial innovations in architecture, urban development and writing. These Greeks were the people who according to legend sailed to Troy in northwest Anatolia and destroyed that city, an event echoed in Homer's later story of the *Iliad*.

Two hundred years later their culture was gone. Archaeology shows that around 1250 BC the city of Thebes was destroyed by fire, and this was only the most prominent victim in a wave of destruction that swept across Greece. Other cities were damaged, and there are clear indications that following this the inhabitants made desperate attempts to strengthen their defences. All in vain. The next wave of destruction was even stronger. Barely a single city of note escaped devastation, the one exception being the fortress 'high city' – the Acropolis – in Athens.

After this, Greece fell into a dark age. Population levels plunged and trade routes that had once spanned the Mediterranean were now reduced to bartering between neighbouring villages. The sophisticated pottery of the previous era became crude lumps of poorly baked clay. Today, academics debate the cause of this epic collapse. Was it plague, climate change, internal warfare, foreign invasion or a combination of all of these? It is surely no coincidence that at the same time this collapse happened, the Hittite empire buckled in much the same way and the Egyptians struggled to fend off waves of invading Sea Peoples.

While modern scholars may be uncertain about what happened, the ancient Greeks reckoned they knew exactly who was responsible for their particular problems – the Dorians.

## The Heraclidae

Similarly, just as modern scholars are divided in their opinions about where the Dorians came from, the Greeks were very clear on this in their own minds. Dorus, the father of the race, was one of the sons of Hellen. The mythical Hellen was the man whom all Greeks considered their common ancestor, and is the reason why things Greek are called 'Hellenic'. The Dorians were a relatively minor Greek people, mostly based in Crete and possibly in the north of Greece. Then came Heracles (Hercules to the Romans).

While mostly known for his ability to kill things large and small, Heracles also managed to father a small army of children with numerous partners. By and large – though Heracles travelled widely – these children were of Dorian stock from the Peloponnese.

They were later driven from there and after numerous setbacks that delayed them for three generations, this group swept southwards again and conquered the south of Greece.

To nineteenth-century historians, this seemed rather convenient. Obviously the legend of the 'Return of the Heraclidae' was a confused recollection of a massive Dorian invasion from the north. This threw Greece into its dark age and displaced the original inhabitants of the Peloponnese, who fled, mostly eastwards, to found the East Greek cities of Ionia in Asia Minor and the Aegean islands. The warlike origin of the Dorians was even built into their name – 'dory' means spear in Greek.

The problem is that, despite a century of searching, no definitive evidence for a 'Dorian invasion' has been found. This has prompted

Hoplites in combat, with helmets, round shields and long spears. The Greek historian Thucydides saw many of the wars in Greece as a struggle between the native Ionians and Dorian usurpers.

a counter-argument which claims that far from being a migrant tribe of northern barbarians, the Dorians were always present in southern Greece (rather as the Greek legends had claimed all along). When the previous civilization was destroyed by a nameless disaster, the Dorians rather than invading simply took vacant possession of abandoned valleys and farmlands.

## Dorian Greece

By 800 BC Greece was again civilized, though it looked very different from the Greece of four hundred years previously. Where once kings had ruled from palace complexes, now the basic social unit of Greece was the *polis*, the city-state. The administrative script used to write an early form of Greek, today known as Linear B, had vanished completely, to be replaced by the Greek adaptation of Phoenician script that went on to become the modern alphabet.

However they had arrived, the Dorians were there. From Corinth to Sparta they occupied the Peloponnese. They were considered fully Greek, though they had their own distinctive dialect and some unique traditions. Like all Greeks they sang a battle-hymn known as the *paean* just before the battle-lines clashed, but the Dorian version was different from the others. On the other hand they did worship the same gods using the same rituals, and many of their traditions were similar to those of other Greek ethnic groups.

Like the Ionian Greeks, the Dorians sent their surplus population abroad as colonists. While the Ionians mostly settled in Asia Minor, the main centres of Dorian colonization were in the west. The city of Syracuse in Sicily was a Dorian settlement, as was Taranto (Tarentum) in southern Italy. There were some Dorian settlements in Asia Minor, notably Halicarnassus, home of the historian Herodotus and the warrior-queen Artemisia. The island of Rhodes was also Dorian.

And if they ever had been barbarian invaders, a demonstration that later Dorians were very civilized Greeks can be found in that most glorious representation of Classical Greek architecture, the Parthenon. Built on the Acropolis of Athens, the beating heart of Ionian culture, this iconic building uses the Doric order of architecture. Modern academics are uncertain exactly how much of Doric architecture can be traced back to the Dorians, but the ancient Greeks believed that the simple, strong lines of Doric architecture originated from the wooden temples originally built by the Dorians.

Much of what we know about the rivalry between Dorian and Ionian Greeks comes from the historian Thucydides (*c.* 472–400 BC).

His account of the Peloponnesian War (431–404 BC) had the Dorian Corinthians and Spartans pitted against the Ionian Athenians and their allies. While this seems to make the distinction clear, the question remains as to whether Thucydides exaggerated this division as a literary device to simplify a complex political situation. Certainly the Athenians had some allies who were Dorians, and their neighbours the Boeotians, with whom the Athenians feuded equally vigorously, were neither Ionian nor Dorian but Aeolian.

There is a tendency to identify the Dorians with their most famous offshoot, the Spartans. This has given the Dorian people a rather macho image, especially as the Cretan Dorians shared many of the cultural traits of the Spartans. However, the picture of the Dorians as a plain-spoken warrior race becomes more complex when we remember that Syracuse was a largely Dorian city, yet closer to Athens than Sparta in its institutions. And though Dorian, the pleasure-loving Corinthians frankly let the whole side down with their sybaritic ways. ('Not everyone can go to Corinth' was an ancient proverb with the meaning that some luxuries are not affordable to all.)

## The later Dorians

A famous marble bust often assumed to portray the Spartan king Leonidas (who died in 470 BC). The huge ridge on the helmet was probably originally painted to depict a horsehair crest.

Another reason for believing that Thucydides might have talked up the differences between Dorians and Ionians is that the distinction seems hardly to have mattered in the Hellenistic age. Following the conquests of Alexander in the late fourth century BC, there was massive emigration from Greece to Asia Minor. Greek colonists were eagerly sought by Hellenistic dynasts looking to consolidate their Asiatic kingdoms, and there are few indications that the settlers differentiated themselves by ethnic grouping.

By the time of the Roman empire the Doric dialect had largely been replaced by a form of Greek common to the entire Greek-speaking world (it was known as *koine*, meaning 'common'). The Roman province of Greece was called Achaea, after yet another different ethnic group of Greeks. In the end, most Dorians vanished through the same process of integration and absorption that befell many other peoples in antiquity, though the Spartans remained idiosyncratically distinct until the fifth century AD and the fall of the Roman empire.

## Future Echoes

Doric architecture is still used today to stress strength and simplicity – for example many of the columns of the Capitol building in Washington, D.C. are in the Doric style. When a display of wealth or culture is wanted, architects tend to choose the more ornate Corinthian style – popular with banks and museums. (The columns of the British Museum's distinctive frontage are based on the Ionic order.) Doric architecture is also often found in eighteenth-century university buildings – possibly because of all the orders of Greek architecture, Doric is the cheapest to construct.

The Doric order continued to be popular in architecture through the ages, as seen in this Italian drawing for a portico dating to the late eighteenth–early nineteenth century.

# *c.* 1000 BC – AD 600
# **The Phrygians**
# King Midas and the Gordian Knot

*Phrygia, clad in vineyards, where dwells [the mother-goddess] Rhea who tended Dionysus through childhood.*

Nonnus, *Dionysiaca* 34.214

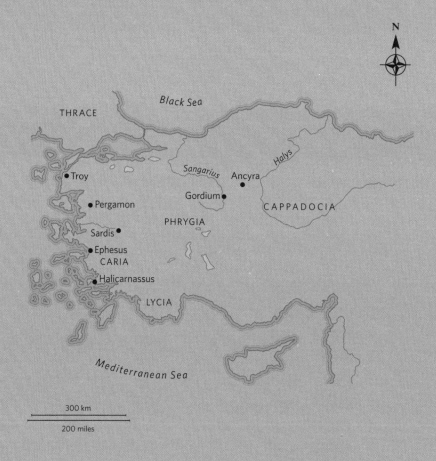

W hile most people may never have heard of the Anatolian Phrygians, they probably are familiar with the name of that nation's most famous ruler – King Midas. According to Greek mythology, Midas was granted a single wish by the wine god Dionysus (Bacchus) as a reward for helping one of his followers. After some thought the king asked that everything he touched should turn to gold. Regrettably, Midas had not thought through the implications of this talent. As a result his touch turned food and drink into distinctly un-nourishing gold.

Eventually Midas was forced to abandon his new ability. He did this by washing in the River Pactolus, near the site of the future city of Sardis. That river is today the Sart Çayi, and its sands became golden where Midas touched them. In fact so rich were the deposits of electrum (a naturally occurring gold and silver alloy) in this river that they made the king of the land downstream as rich as Croesus – mainly because he was, in fact, Croesus.

## Phrygians and Hittites

So who were the Phrygian people from whom Midas had sprung? The Phrygians themselves were a remarkably durable people, and they left enough of a mark on the ethnographic record for researchers to determine that they probably originated in the Balkans to the west of Greece. Their language was of the Indo-European group, while most native peoples of Anatolia spoke languages of Semitic origin. The Phrygians were evidently fond of their language, because its last speakers are recorded in the sixth century AD, around 1,600 years after its first appearance.

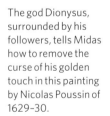

The god Dionysus, surrounded by his followers, tells Midas how to remove the curse of his golden touch in this painting by Nicolas Poussin of 1629–30.

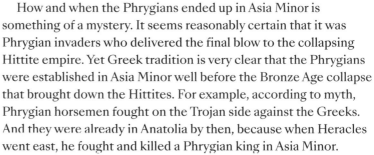

This statue from the second or third century AD of a Phrygian man is a rare example of a male 'caryatid', a supporting pillar carved in human form – usually the figure is female.

How and when the Phrygians ended up in Asia Minor is something of a mystery. It seems reasonably certain that it was Phrygian invaders who delivered the final blow to the collapsing Hittite empire. Yet Greek tradition is very clear that the Phrygians were established in Asia Minor well before the Bronze Age collapse that brought down the Hittites. For example, according to myth, Phrygian horsemen fought on the Trojan side against the Greeks. And they were already in Anatolia by then, because when Heracles went east, he fought and killed a Phrygian king in Asia Minor.

Their presence in the region seems supported by Assyrian records which refer to raiders called the 'Muski' – a name close to an ancient name for the Phrygians. The Assyrians later explicitly called the Phrygians 'Muski', but they had the confusing habit of sometimes calling different peoples by the same name.

One way of reconciling the evidence would be to assume a Phrygian presence in Anatolia as a subject people of the Hittites. Then in the turmoil at the end of the Bronze Age, the Phrygians were reinforced by other members of the tribe from neighbouring Thrace (a detail we learn from Herodotus). Once the Hittites collapsed, the Phrygians set up their own kingdom, which was a going concern by the time decent record-keeping began again around 850 BC.

### Gordium and the Gordian Knot

The Phrygians occupied the western area of the Anatolian plateau. Much of this land is bare, and the climate harsh. It is, however, excellent for growing grape vines and for horse-breeding, which explains the Phrygian reputation for horsemanship in antiquity. The capital, on the River Sangarius, was the city of Gordium, which appears to have developed around a natural citadel. Again, people who have never heard of Gordium will know of the extremely elaborate knot that tied an ox-cart to a post in the city centre.

The ox-cart was dedicated to the Phrygian god Sabazios, and an oracle had decreed that 'whoever can loosen the knot will become king of Asia'. Untying the Gordian Knot was no easy feat, as according to later reports it consisted of several intertwined knots, and since the rope was made from bark strips, it only became harder to untangle with age.

At first it seemed as though mastery of Asia might go to an invading barbarian tribe called the Cimmerians, regardless of the oracle, who captured and sacked Gordium in 696 BC. They had already tried their luck

against the Assyrians and been violently rebuffed, and they next attacked the kingdom of Lydia to the west. After initial successes, the Cimmerians were defeated in 619 BC by a Lydian-led coalition that included the Phrygians. The Cimmerians were scattered and eventually merged with the population of nearby Cappadocia. They too are now largely forgotten, apart from the most famous, albeit fictional, member of their tribe – Conan the Barbarian.

Despite being unsuccessful, the Cimmerian invasion appears to have brought about the end of Phrygia as a unified state, and thereafter it was briefly a geographical region occupied by a number of small principalities, each with its own minor monarch. Gradually the area came under the power of the neighbouring kingdom of Lydia. Gordium was rebuilt, but now as a Lydian stronghold.

Lydia in turn fell to the power of Persia as the empire of Cyrus the Great (r. 559–530 BC) expanded westwards. In 450 BC, the region was again unified, but this time as a satrapy – an administrative district of the Persian empire. The area enjoyed considerable prosperity, as the Royal Road linking the Persian heartlands with the Mediterranean ran through it – a line of communication which later became famous as the western end of the Silk Road.

Phrygia acquired a new ruler in 333 BC when the Greeks under Alexander the Great (r. 336–323 BC) conquered Anatolia. Alexander himself came to Gordium, and wrestled with the famous Knot. Eventually the frustrated conqueror pulled out his sword and 'untied' it by the simple expedient of slicing through it. Evidently this conduct fell within the acceptable terms of the prophecy, as

Alexander did indeed become the master of Asia (as the ancients called Anatolia), and of much else besides. 'Cutting the Gordian Knot' thereafter passed into language as a metaphor for finding a simple but drastic solution to a complex problem.

## After Alexander

Alexander's conquest of the region did not endure, because soon afterwards another rampaging tribe, the Galatians, came across from Thrace and they did to the Phrygians much the same as the Phrygians had done to the Hittites. The Galatians destroyed Gordium, and founded their own capital, Ancyra (modern Ankara). Eventually the city of Pergamon established a tenuous sovereignty in the region, which was in turn surrendered to the Romans in 133 BC.

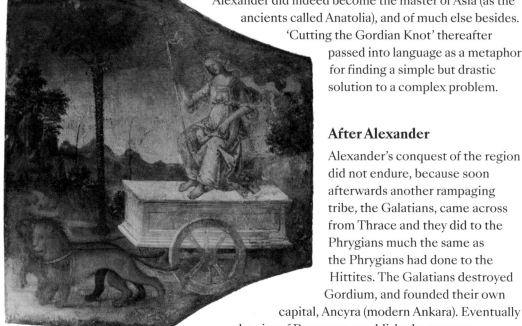

The great goddess Cybele on her chariot drawn by lions. While many Renaissance paintings are wildly inaccurate, this detail from a painted ceiling in Siena, Italy, seems to have been inspired by ancient sculpture.

Through all these changes in overlordship, the Phrygians seem to have quietly gone on as a people, with their own distinctive language, culture and religion. The language was now written using Greek letters, and their principal god Sabazios was identified with the Roman Jupiter. Nevertheless, the Phrygian god Attis also managed to find his way into the Roman pantheon, and even established a branch temple in Rome itself.

Attis mainly piggybacked on the even greater success of the Anatolian goddess Cybele, who had been worshipped in the region in one form or another for at least the preceding 5,000 years. The Greeks adopted the Phrygian rites of worship for this goddess, and she was enthusiastically welcomed in Rome under the name of the Magna Mater, the 'Great Mother' (or 'Great Goddess'). The Romans under the Republic later credited the goddess's aid as instrumental in the defeat of Hannibal and the Carthaginians.

The Roman Republic became an empire, and its Phrygian subjects were present in Judea to hear the apostles talking in tongues (Acts 2.10). With the end of the Roman empire, Phrygia peaceably became an administrative unit of the Byzantine empire. In the meantime, however, the Phrygians had become hosts to an unruly horde of Visigoths whom the Roman emperor Theodosius settled there in AD 399. These new arrivals joined several thousand Jews who had been deported to the region some 500 years previously. But if the survival of the language is any indication, Phrygian culture endured – and certainly even in the early Byzantine era some people identified as Phrygian: 'The bishop Selenas … was a Visigoth on his father's side, but his mother was a Phrygian, and so he could easily teach in church in both languages' (Socrates of Constantinople, *Ecclesiastical History* 5.23).

Only with the Ottoman conquest of Anatolia in the fifteenth century did Phrygia disappear as an administrative unit. Thereafter the Phrygians, who had seen the passing of their Lydian, Persian, Pergamene, Roman and Byzantine rulers, themselves step reluctantly from the stage of history.

## Future Echoes

The French Revolution of 1789 might seem a strange place to find Phrygians, but at least their hats were there. The soft felt brimless cap was adopted by the revolutionaries as a symbol of freedom thanks to confusion with the similarly shaped cap worn by manumitted Roman slaves. In fact the 'liberty cap' may have spread to France from the United States, where during the Revolutionary War it was held aloft on a Liberty Pole. Since then, the cap has often been used on state emblems, including on coins and the seal of the United States Senate, where the British, for instance, would use a crown.

The Tree of LIBERTY...with the Devil tempting John Bull.

John Bull, the archetypal Englishman, is tempted in this contemporary cartoon by the fruits of the Tree of Liberty. The Phrygian cap in the tree's centre is opposed to the British crown of the oak in the background.

# 10th century BC – 6th century AD
# The Illyrians
## Balkan Raiders

*The Illyrians were fond of plundering Messenia and Elis [in southern Greece], because they could attack anywhere on that extensive coastline ... and while help was slow in arriving they could over-run the countryside at will.*

Polybius, *History* 2.1.6

You would think that when meeting a strange people, it would be polite to ask them what they called themselves. Yet for most of recorded history this has not been the case. Rather, those doing the recording have tended to give arbitrary names to other peoples, which then become attached to them thereafter. Such is the case with the Illyrians. If there was an original Illyrian tribe, the Greeks probably encountered this relatively small group somewhere just north of Epirus, and promptly applied the name to the entire population west of Macedonia and south of the Danube.

Until that time, the peoples of the region did not know that they had very much in common apart from a taste for raiding the more settled lands of Greece and Macedonia. In fact, which peoples and what cultures made up the population of ancient Illyria has long been a topic of debate among modern ethnographers.

For example, the Illyrians spoke an Indo-European language (albeit in a variety of Indo-European dialects). This suggests that they came from the northeast, along with other prehistoric migrants who spoke the same language. However, the continuity of their pottery from earliest times to the early Iron Age suggests an autochthonous people (literally 'sprung from the soil' – a term meaning they were always there). It is also possible that waves of Indo-European migrants managed to bring about change in the language while most of the original population remained in place, rather as Norman invaders Frenchified the English language and before that Gallic was made French by Latin.

## Archaeology and myth

To add to the complicated ethnographic situation in Illyria, archaeology shows that there was a fresh influx of peoples in the early Iron Age which introduced into the region Celtic elements from what is today known as the Hallstatt culture. In short, what the civilized folks of the Classical era saw as a single, uncouth and extremely unruly people turns out on closer examination to have been a patchwork of different tribes with different dialects who shared elements of a common culture to a greater or lesser degree.

Greek mythology claimed the name of Illyria came from the son of a Greek hero called Cadmus, who founded Thebes. Illyrius was born while Cadmus was on a campaign against the peoples of the northwest and the child eventually went on to become ruler of that region. Other mythologers, with Illyrian misbehaviour in mind, reckoned it more probable that Illyrius was the son of the savage, man-eating cyclops Polyphemus, who features in Homer's *Odyssey*.

Indeed, when the Greeks and Macedonians used the word 'Illyrian' it was usually in combination with 'problem', 'raid' or 'pirates'. Generally speaking, the sole interest of Classical cultures when it came to Illyria lay in how to contain the predatory habits of its peoples. It is from such usages that we know, for example, of a tribe of Illyrians called the Liburni.

## Liburnian pirates and traders

The Liburni were a maritime people who lived in what is today Croatia. Their proclivity for piracy was powered by speedy and agile galleys of a type the Greeks called the *libyrnis*. Possessed of a sail and a single bank of oars, these ships ranged the Adriatic Sea and were a terror to merchantmen making the crossing between Italy and Greece. Because of their light build, these ships could easily hide in the many bays and rocky inlets of the Illyrian coastline, and could even raid upriver. In fact in later years the Romans adopted the Liburnian design and used such ships for their inland fleets on the Rhine and Danube rivers.

While the Liburni traded across much of the Mediterranean, the Greeks had a – probably justified – suspicion that should Liburnian traders come across an isolated ship, the 'merchants' would turn pirate in the blink of an eye.

It is debatable how much the seafaring Liburni had in common with other 'Illyrian' tribes. For example, an Illyrian people called the Dalmatae lived practically next door to the Liburni, yet had a strictly land-based pastoral culture. The Liburni were relatively sophisticated traders, but it appears from the archaeological remains that most of the Dalmatae lived in tents and caves and seldom ventured far from their native pastures. To some extent the Dalmatae were 'Illyrians' to the other Illyrians – that is, an uncultured and primitive people prone to savage bouts of tribal violence against their neighbours.

Though developed by the Greeks, this style of helmet is called 'Illyrian' because it was enthusiastically adopted by warriors there. The Illyrians favoured the greater visibility afforded by the helmet's open face.

### Raiding Greek lands

Insofar as the Illyrian tribes of the early Iron Age collaborated at all, it was in launching major assaults against the Greeks and Macedonians. In such joint enterprises against the Macedonians, the Illyrians sometimes co-operated with a related people called the Dardani. As time went on, Illyrians and Dardanians learned to keep a keen eye on the whereabouts of the

Centuries after they ceased to be used by Illyrian pirates, Liburnian boats were still employed by the Roman army. Here they are seen on Trajan's Column in action against the Dacians.

Macedonian army; the absence of that army in Greece or Thrace became the signal for an Illyrian plundering raid.

Even further north were another people loosely affiliated with the Illyrians. These were the Pannonians. Like the other Illyrian peoples they were largely illiterate, and left little record other than archaeological, which reveals that, like most Illyrians, the Pannonians had a simple culture which combined farming with raiding. People lived in tribal, family-based bands and were buried together in such groups (the warriors with their weapons). The Pannonians were more exposed to Celtic settlement and culture than the coastal Illyrians.

## Contending with Rome

Only in the Roman era did the Illyrians begin to act as a unified people. It seems that in the mid-third century BC a leader called Agron, who was based in what is today Montenegro, united several Illyrian tribes into a common kingdom. Agron broke with tradition by becoming an ally rather than an enemy of the Macedonians. The benefit was that when the Macedonians notified the Illyrians that they intended to launch an attack in southwestern Greece, the Illyrians enthusiastically joined in.

The disadvantage with becoming a somewhat more unified state was that those exasperated by Illyrian misbehaviour finally had a substantial target to attack. After Agron's death in 231 BC his widow Teuta expanded Illyrian maritime raids as far as Corcyra (modern Corfu), an island that was an essential way-point on the Adriatic crossing to Italy. Teuta may have had imperial ambitions here, for Corcyra was traditionally believed to have been Illyrian until Greek settlers kicked them off the island. Nevertheless, this threat to maritime trade was too much for the Roman Republic which now dominated Italy.

In 229 BC the Romans launched their first military expedition east of Italy against the Illyrians, the first in a series of campaigns that were to become known as the Illyrian Wars. As the decades turned to centuries, the Romans conquered Macedon, Greece and Asia Minor and continued fighting the Illyrians. The rough terrain and the decentralized Illyrian tribes made it hard for the Romans decisively to conquer them, especially as the Illyrians proved themselves adept at guerrilla warfare.

Tiberius fought a series of tough campaigns against the Dalmatians in the years before he became emperor of Rome.

By the time of the emperor Augustus (r. 27 BC–AD 14) the Romans controlled most of the coast, but were finding it hard going against the Pannonians. The Roman effort completed the process the Illyrians had begun themselves – it united them as a people. In AD 6 all of them, in perfect harmony, rose up in rebellion against Rome. The Dalmatae, the Liburni, the Pannonians and other tribes such as the Iapodes, the Breuci and the Pirustae had finally found common cause. It took the future emperor Tiberius (r. AD 14–37) four years and five legions to bring the revolt under control. Fortunately, his adoptive father Augustus had also campaigned in the region when he was younger and was sympathetic to the difficulties involved.

The region became the Roman province of Illyricum, which was later divided into the provinces of Pannonia and Dalmatia. Over the centuries the Illyrians became gradually so Romanized that they saved the empire. During the third century AD, when Rome was in danger of falling apart under the strains of barbarian raids, it was a series of 'Illyrian emperors' – men of Pannonian or Illyrian stock – who stabilized the empire. Emperors such as Decius (r. AD 249–51), Claudius Gothicus (r. AD 268–70), Aurelian (r. AD 270–75) and Diocletian (r. AD 284–305) had mostly short and always violent reigns, but by the time of Diocletian their efforts had largely brought the crisis to an end.

When Rome did finally fall, it was another Illyrian, Justinian I (r. AD 527–65), who took control of what was to become the

Byzantine empire. By now the Illyrians were fully Romanized, and it is doubtful that they appreciated the irony of the fact that they were finally destroyed by Slavonic barbarian raiders. They vanish as a people around the seventh century AD.

## Future Echoes

The pastoral Dalmatae tribe doubtless had dogs to protect and control their herds. These dogs were probably the distant ancestors of the breed which today ultimately derives its name from the tribe – the Dalmatian. Dalmatian dogs were around in the seventeenth century and are known for their energy and loyalty to those they love but are standoffish or even hostile to strangers. These are certainly qualities with which the ancient Dalmatae could identify.

Modern Albanians have a rather romanticized view of the Illyrians as part of their ancestral identity. They consider as possible ancestors a tribe called the Albona, who are described as being in Illyria during the Roman invasion. The Italians call the dawn 'Alba' possibly because Albania is the land from which they see the sun rise.

The familiar spotted Dalmatian dog originally came from Dalmatia. It was introduced into England in the eighteenth century and was favoured as a 'coach' or 'carriage' dog, running alongside to protect the occupants from highwaymen.

DALMATIAN OR COACH DOG

# 7th century BC – 546 BC
# **The Lydians**
# As Rich as Croesus

*As far as we know, the Lydians were the first people to make and use gold and silver coins. They were also the first people to become retail traders.*

Herodotus, *The Histories* 1.94

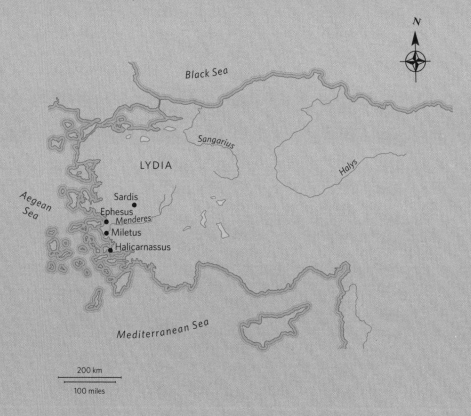

Lydia was beautiful and prosperous, which might in itself be reason enough for the name of an ancient kingdom to become a modern girl's name. There is also the respectability of biblical antecedents (St Paul converted a dye-seller named Lydia to Christianity). Thus the name survives, even though the ancient Lydians themselves are almost forgotten.

Apart from the name itself, two kings of Lydia and a river there have made their way from Asia Minor into the contemporary world. The river is a winding waterway that ran along the border of the kingdom. So gently does it twist and turn on its route to the sea near the ancient Greek city of Miletus that anything following a similar route 'meanders', just as did the River Meander. (It is now the Menderes river in modern Turkey.)

That the land around the river is flat enough to allow so convoluted a course suggests that the main reason for Lydia's wealth was agricultural, and the Lydians were indeed famous for the horses raised on those lush pastures. Another source of the nation's wealth was the River Pactolus, which was rich in gold washed down from the Anatolian highlands. Legend had it that the literally golden sands of the river came about because King Midas of Phrygia had washed in its waters to cure himself of his legendary golden touch.

## Lydian kings

The envious Greeks compared their mountainous and generally unproductive homeland with the rich farmlands of Lydia and made one of that country's kings a simile for wealth. Even today many dream of becoming 'as rich as Croesus'.

A further tantalizing trace of the ancient Lydians comes from a mythological king of that nation. King Tantalus was invited to host a feast for the Olympian gods, and in a desperate search for something suitable for the main course, he decided to serve up his own son. Far from being flattered by the king's sacrifice, the gods were sickened and horrified. Tantalus was punished for his bad taste by being chained for eternity waist deep in a pool of water with succulent fruit dangling from branches above him. Tormented by hunger and thirst, Tantalus is unable to drink the water, which recedes as he bends down towards it, nor can he eat the fruit, for the branches lift it out of his reach as he tries to grasp it.

Another mythological Lydian monarch exposed to temptation was Queen Omphale, who had Heracles as her servant for a time. Heracles was in servitude as punishment by the gods for a particularly gratuitous killing. Omphale

The earliest Lydian coins, such as this example from around 550 BC, were a standardized weight but not a standardized shape.

took advantage of her relationship as the hero's employer to the extent that Heracles left behind a son who eventually became the kingdom's ruler. According to Herodotus, such behaviour was acceptable among Lydian females. In fact it was customary for Lydian girls to charge for sex until they had accumulated a satisfactory dowry, after which they became respectable married women.

## Emergence of the kingdom

Through mythology and diplomatic contacts, Lydia was already well known to the Greeks by the time the kingdom emerged from the wreckage of the Bronze Age collapse as one of several Anatolian states which replaced the former Hittite empire. Herodotus also tells how a man called Gyges overthrew the dynasty established by Heracles sometime in the seventh century BC. More probably, Lydia was a Phrygian possession until the invasion of Cimmerian barbarians from the east, when the tables were turned. At that time Gyges took advantage of the chaos to set up his own kingdom.

Gyges was also probably responsible for establishing the Lydian capital at Sardis. There is some dispute as to where the main city of the Lydian people had previously been. Homer suggests an otherwise unknown place called Hyde. Modern scholars note that in the Hittite era the people of the region were called Maiones, and the later Roman writer Pliny the Elder (AD 23–79) notes that there was a Lydian city called Maeonia even in his day.

The Lydians flourished as an independent people – their state was well situated to take advantage of trade between Europe and the Middle East, and Lydian leatherwork and textiles were renowned for their quality. Famously, the Lydian contribution to trade was the invention of coinage. Lydian coins were basically nuggets of electrum stamped with a lion's head to show that they were an 'official' standard weight. These proto-coins were of relatively high value, and the current theory is that the idea evolved as a simple way to pay the army. Nevertheless, coinage was a concept whose time had come, and soon every nation with claims to statehood had its own mint.

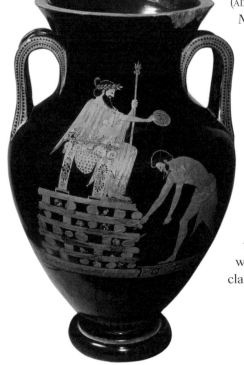

Croesus is about to be burned alive by his Persian captors on a Greek red-figure vase. He was allegedly reprieved at the last moment by the Persian king Cyrus.

The ruins of Sardis, the Lydian capital, in a picturesque location at the foot of Mount Tmolus.

## King Croesus

The last king of Lydia was the fabulously wealthy Croesus (560–546 BC). By this time Lydia was closely connected, through trade and warfare with the Greek cities of Asia Minor, to the wider Greek world. Indeed, the steady expansion of Lydian territory had forcibly incorporated several formerly independent Greek cities into the kingdom, which now occupied most of western Anatolia as far east as the River Halys (Kızılırmak).

Croesus gave generously to the rebuilding of the temple of the goddess Artemis at Ephesus, and it is largely thanks to his substantial contribution that this edifice became so splendid that it was recognized as one of the seven wonders of the ancient world. Croesus was also convinced of the efficacy of the Oracle of Apollo at Delphi in Greece. So it was to this oracle that he turned for advice in around 548 BC.

In previous years Lydia had clashed with the new dominant power in the Middle East – an expansionist people called the Medes. Generally, the Lydians had held their own thanks to their superior cavalry and archers. Then, abruptly, the Medes were gone, replaced by a usurping people called the Persians. Like the Medes, the Persians were camped right next door to Lydia on the eastern

Lydians bringing tribute to their Persian overlords in a relief at Persepolis, the great city and palace built by Darius (522–486 BC).

bank of the Halys. It was only a matter of time before the Lydian kingdom and Persian empire would come to blows. Should he take the initiative, Croesus asked the Oracle, and try to crush the threat before the Persians had firmly established their rule over the lands they now held?

'Do that,' advised the Oracle, 'and you will destroy a great empire.' It was only in 546 BC, as a prisoner in the smoking ruins of his capital, that Croesus realized that Lydia might have been considered a 'great empire' also – and by taking the war to the Persians, Croesus had certainly destroyed it.

The Greeks had a theory that some Lydians, unable to accept Persian rule, loaded their families and possessions on to ships and emigrated to Italy, where they became the Etruscans. It is certainly true that both Etruscans and Lydians possessed a language largely incomprehensible to outsiders (and which scholars struggle to understand today). Nevertheless, this romantic theory has been discredited on the grounds that Lydian and Etruscan inscriptions are as wildly different from each other as they are from anything else, and genetic sampling of the Tuscan population suggests native Italic ancestry.

Lydia survived as a Persian, Hellenistic, Roman and Byzantine province. But rather like modern girls called Lydia, it was only in name. The distinctive Lydian culture and language had largely disappeared well before the Roman era.

## Future Echoes

Many people who have never heard of King Gyges of Lydia are familiar with one of the stories about him. When exploring a cave in the mountains, Gyges – who at the time was a humble shepherd – came across a golden ring. When he twisted the ring on his finger, he immediately became invisible, and Gyges used this power to take control of the kingdom. The Greek stories do not tell what later became of this ring, but it has a remarkable parallel in Middle-earth, where a wandering Hobbit came upon a ring with a similar power. (J. R. R. Tolkien, author of *The Hobbit,* was a scholar of language and myth.)

After Tantalus had been punished for serving the gods a cannibalistic dinner, it is worth noting what became of the main course. This young man was restored to life again, albeit with an ivory shoulder to replace the one the goddess Demeter had absent-mindedly eaten. The youth moved to mainland Greece, married a king's daughter and became ruler of southern Greece. His name was Pelops, which is the reason why the Peloponnese is so called. To win his bride he was the victor in a chariot race at Olympia, thus launching a minor athletic festival that came to be known as the 'Olympic Games'.

# *c.* 1000 BC – 450 BC
# The Sicels
## Settlers of Sicily

*The Sicels crossed over from Italy to the island ...*
*which thus came to be called Sicily. After they*
*crossed over they continued to enjoy the richest*
*parts of the country for nearly three hundred*
*years before the coming of the first Greeks.*

Thucydides, *History of the Peloponnesian War* 6.28

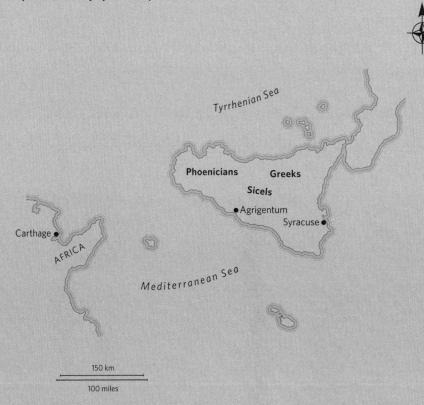

W e are accustomed to colonization being a violent, brutal affair which ends with the colonists exploiting and often massacring the people whose lands they have forcibly seized. Yet what if the colonists were cautiously welcomed, and were not too oppressive, and they and the original inhabitants eventually become one and the same? While there were inevitably a number of violent episodes, when it came to colonization it seems the Sicels were remarkably accommodating, both as an occupying and occupied people.

Whatever their origins, the people who have given their name to the island of Sicily did not begin there. It seems reasonably certain that ancient writers are correct in their claim that the first peoples who occupied Sicily were a tribe called the Sicani. Then came the chaos of the Bronze Age collapse.

The Egyptians report that one of the seafaring confederations they repulsed included a tribe called the Shekelesh. According to later tradition, the Shekelesh rebounded from Egypt to the western Mediterranean and settled in southern Italy. Here they gradually adopted Italic ways and the local language before crossing into Sicily at some time around 1000 BC. Indeed, the ancient historian Diodorus Siculus says exactly that (5.6): 'And many generations later, the people of the Sicels crossed over *en masse* from Italy into Sicily and made their home there.' As the 'Siculus' part of his name informs us, Diodorus was a local from the formerly Sicel town of Agyrium in the centre of the island, and his report probably draws on the same tradition.

As ever with such migrations, the people into whose lands the Sicels migrated were not particularly happy to see them. But there was not a lot the original Sicani could do about it, since as one of the Sea Peoples (if this was indeed the case) the Sicels will have been proficient with Iron Age weaponry.

A lion attacks a bull in a Sicel relief on a votive altar found at Centuripe, Sicily, dating from the Hellenic era.

Nevertheless, modern archaeological studies suggest that the Sicel invasion was far from an apocalyptic event. Throughout antiquity, Sicily was relatively thinly inhabited, especially in the interior where the Sicels chose to settle. While it was not quite the case that land was available for all, archaeological evidence indicates that by and large, once the Sicani had been bumped from prime sites they settled in the second-best locations, mostly in the west of the island.

## Sicels and Greeks

By the time civilization got back on its feet in the Archaic era of around 800 BC, the Sicels were recognized as the dominant people of the island. The poet Homer gives wandering Odysseus a Sicel servant woman who already lived at his home farm before the Greek hero set off for the Trojan War, which suggests there was interconnection between early Iron Age Greece and Sicily.

The Greeks of the Classical era imagined that Sicily in former times had been a wild, distant and romantic place – but definitely part of the Greek world. It was in Sicily, for example, that Hades, the grim god of the Underworld, was believed to have abducted Persephone to be his bride. Other nations have also claimed the location, but Lake Pergusa near the formerly Sicel town of Enna has a good claim, not least because its shores are abundant in flowers, which Persephone was said to be gathering when she was kidnapped.

Persephone gathers flowers in this delicate Roman wall painting from Villa Varano, Stabiae, Italy.

Another people with whom the Sicels came into contact – often violently – were the Phoenicians, thanks to Carthaginian settlement in the west of the island. Sadly, today we know few precise details about Carthaginian-Sicel interactions, because the Sicels did not leave a written record at this period, and modern historians are grateful for any scraps of information from the Carthaginians about themselves, let alone about other peoples.

Much of what we know of the Sicels comes from the Greeks, since while it seems clear that the Sicels originally

The intricate mouldings and painted decoration of this covered dish (*lekanis*) from Sicily demonstrates the level of technical skill of the people of Centuripe, Sicily, in the third century BC.

spoke an Italic language, by the time they came to set things down in writing they mostly used Greek. The Greeks settled by and large on the eastern side of the island, and rather like the Sicels before them, they had the military technology to ensure that no one could seriously object to their arrival. Then again, as with the Sicel settlement, it seems that no one particularly minded them being there in any case. The Sicels, as already noted, were largely settled in the island's interior, and as Cicero later observed, the Sicel city of Enna was about as far from the Mediterranean in every direction as it is possible to be on the island. Therefore the arrival of strangers on a coast the Sicels generally had little use for occasioned them as much curiosity as distress. And the Greeks came bearing gifts.

The colonization of Syracuse may be considered something of a template for Greek settlement in Sicily. First the Greeks occupied the (probably uninhabited) island of Ortygia just off the coast. Then through trade, bribery and diplomacy they developed friendly relations with the locals (probably Sicani in this case, but the same pattern applied to colonies with a native Sicel population). Eventually the Greeks acquired land on the mainland and the colony of Ortygia became Syracuse.

The Sicels were a tribal-based people who practised rudimentary agriculture but were mainly pastoral. The Sicilian interior met their needs well, and it turned out to be rather useful to have Greeks to trade with on the coast. Where the Greeks and Sicels did have a common interest in the same fields, ownership changed hands as much through sale and marriage arrangements as through more violent forms of acquisition.

Indeed, stories of how sophisticated Greeks managed to trick the rustic Sicels out of land actually show that the Greeks preferred not to simply take those lands by brute force. One might suspect that for every Sicel tricked out of his landholding, there was an undocumented Greek who came out worse in a trade deal. (Modern anthropology has shown that native peoples were in reality shrewd bargainers when dealing with more sophisticated cultures – it was simply that they often assigned higher values to certain goods.)

As the Classical era went on, Sicel society rapidly developed. What had once been small towns expanded as the Sicels discovered the joys of urbanism, and at least three settlements grew to sufficient size for the Greeks to refer to them as 'cities'. At the same time there was a marked decline in relationships between the Sicels and Dorian Greek cities led by Syracuse.

## Conflict and assimilation

According to Diodorus Siculus, a man called Ducetius took advantage of anti-Syracusan sentiment and united the Sicels under his leadership. (They had formerly been led by individual chiefs of different tribes.) For a while the Sicel confederation dominated the island's interior. Ducetius was able to retake lands the Greeks had seized from the Sicels, but the rapid growth of his power alarmed the Syracusans. They allied with the nearby Greek city of Agrigentum and in 450 BC their combined power destroyed the Sicel army in battle. Ducetius demonstrated the remarkable lack of hatred between Greeks and Sicels by riding into Syracuse and offering his surrender. The Syracusans reciprocated in kind by exiling him to Corinth with sufficient funds to maintain himself comfortably. It is also worth noting that Ducetius founded at least one city and repopulated others with a mixed Greek-Sicel population.

Sadly, the good relations did not last. Ducetius broke his parole and returned to Sicily. He died soon after his reappearance, but that was itself enough to provoke a Syracusan assault and the conquest of much former Sicel territory. Nevertheless, the real conquest was not physical but cultural. Increasingly the Sicels were indistinguishable

from their Greek neighbours in language, culture and (thanks to intermarriage) ethnicity.

By the time the historian Diodorus Siculus was writing in the first century BC, he was able to deliver this pronouncement on the disappearance of his ancestors (5.6.5):

> Once sufficiently large numbers of Greeks came to Sicily, those already living there adopted that language. Eventually they grew into the Greek way of life. Finally they lost not only their barbarian tongue but also themselves.

## Future Echoes

There appears to be a clear etymological link between the Shekelesh Sea People, the Sikeloi of Italy and the Sicels who emigrated to Sicily. The Sicels certainly gave the island the name it has today. It is interesting that it has endured, even though Sicily has seen so many peoples come and go in subsequent ages that geneticists attempting to untangle the island's complex ethnic heritage have had difficulty isolating 'original' Sicel genes.

That the Sicels originated in Italy seems to be generally agreed. According to Thucydides, one of their kings was named Italus, and it was he who gave his name to Italy. The people who drove the Sicels from Italy were a tribe called the Aborigines. They were in central Italy before the Romans, so 'aboriginal' has come to mean any people who first occupied a land.

Fifth-century BC coins from Greek Sicilian cities, including one from Syracuse in the centre. The Sicels were eventually completely absorbed into the Greek culture embodied by these coins.

## c. 1500 BC – 550 BC
# The Medes
## Destroyers of Nineveh

*Behold, there stood before the river a ram which had two horns: and the two horns were high; but one was higher than the other, and the higher came up last. I saw the ram pushing westward, and northward, and southward; so that no beasts might stand before him, neither was there any that could deliver out of his hand; but he did according to his will, and became great.*

Daniel 8:3–4

N

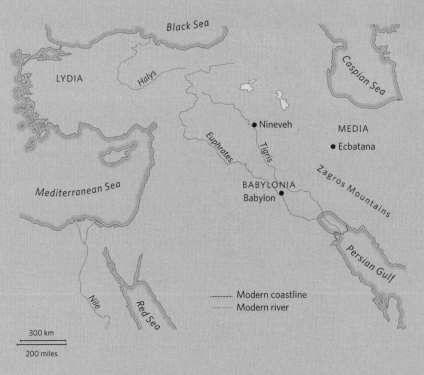

Black Sea

LYDIA

Halys

Caspian Sea

Nineveh

MEDIA

Ecbatana

Euphrates

Tigris

Mediterranean Sea

BABYLONIA
Babylon

Zagros Mountains

Persian Gulf

Nile

Red Sea

......... Modern coastline
------- Modern river

300 km

200 miles

This strange prophecy in the Bible describes the empire (the 'ram') of the Medes and the Persians. The otherworldly description seems an appropriate way to begin a history of the Medes. Even people who have never heard of them know of their priestly caste, the Magi – from whom we get the modern word 'magician'. To the peoples of ancient Judea and Europe, the Medes were a faraway exotic people with strange rites and beliefs.

The ram's 'higher horn' was the Persians, who occupied the higher reaches of the river Tigris. The lower 'horn' was the homeland of the Median people, much of which is today Iran. The Medes were of Aryan stock (the word 'Iran' actually comes from 'Aryan', though it is much disputed what 'Aryan' actually means). Beyond that basic fact, the origins of the Medes are a mystery. It may be that they were the descendants of the Elamites who had occupied the land before them, or they may have been invading pastoralists who arrived around 1500 BC. Perhaps they were a mixture of both, for the Greek historian Herodotus tells us that there were originally six different tribes who united to become the Medes.

Relief from Persepolis of a Median soldier in typical dress carrying a lamb, probably as a sacrificial offering.

It should also be noted that the Greeks had a mystical theory about where the Medes came from. According to Greek mythology, the Medes were descended from the premier witch of antiquity, the fearsome Medea. There are different versions of the legend, but they all involve Medea fleeing east after a career of murder and magic in the Greek world. Medea's son Medus was a great warrior and an even better ruler, so the people of what had previously been the land of Ayria changed their name to Medes in his honour.

According to the Roman-Jewish historian Josephus, the Medes were descended from one of Noah's grandchildren. 'Now as to Javan and Madai, the sons of Japhet; from Madai came the Madeans, who are called Medes' (*Antiquities of the Jews*, 1.6.1). It appears that the only people not eager to tell us where the Medes came from are the Medes themselves. Their language has not been preserved and we have no texts giving the Median version of their origins, magical or otherwise.

## From rebels to rulers

The earliest and more factual accounts of the Medes come from those conscientious record-keepers of antiquity, the Assyrians. In the ninth century BC the Assyrians campaigned against the 'Madai'. Assyrian reports state that the original homeland of the Medes was 'along the Great Khurasan Road just east of Harhar to Alwand'. The Khurasan Road later became part of the fabled Silk Road, and ran from near Babylon to Central Asia. Harhar and Alwand are assumed to be in the Zagros Mountains, where in later times the Median people bred cattle and horses famed for their quality.

The Medes that the Assyrians knew were scattered in different small kingdoms. It may have been Assyrian oppression after they had conquered the Medes that made the subject people think of themselves as a single nation. The Assyrians record several Median rebellions which they bloodily suppressed.

Though the Assyrians helped to protect the Medes from barbarian raiders such as the Cimmerians, the depth of Median feeling against Assyria was demonstrated when the Medes allied with a Babylonian-led confederacy of former Assyrian subjects determined to wipe their oppressors off the face of the earth. Median troops were among the rebels who razed the Assyrian capital of Nineveh in 612 BC.

The fall of Assyria created a power vacuum in the Middle East, and the Medes seem to have been among the people who stepped up to fill it. They made their capital at the former Elamite

An archaeologist's drawing of an ancient relief showing Assyrians attacking a Median city. It is probable that the cities were independent and failed to support one another, making them easy prey for their predatory Assyrian neighbours.

Medes and Persians in a relief from Persepolis. The Medes have round hats and carry their bows in cases, while the Persians have their bows slung on their shoulders.

city of Ecbatana and, as the prophet Daniel had foretold, pushed northward and westward and (slightly) southward. It is uncertain how much actual warfare was involved in this process, and how much was simply the Medes taking over wholesale administrative structures left vacant by the now vanished empire of the Assyrians.

If we are to believe Herodotus – and many modern historians don't – between 625 and 549 BC the Medes ruled a substantial empire, which included the former Assyrian domains in what is today Iran, much of northern Mesopotamia and Armenia. Under King Cyaxares (r. 624–585 BC) the Medes pushed into Anatolia, reaching as far as the kingdom of Lydia before they met determined resistance and stopped at the River Halys. By now, along with Babylonia and Egypt, the Medes were considered one of the great powers of the known world.

## The mystic Medes

Despite this, we know little of Median society and culture. One reason is that in some ways the Medes were very similar to their close relatives the Persians. As far as later Western historians were concerned, Persians and Medes were one and the same, and often Greek historians who should have known better refer to the Persians as 'The Mede'. Consequently it is difficult to isolate specifically Median traditions and behaviours.

We can assume a feudal-type society in which lords of the five Median tribes held lands and owed fealty to their king, whom they supplied with soldiers upon demand. The sixth tribe was the Magi – a priestly caste who interpreted dreams and promoted the fire-worship of the god Ahura-Mazda. In the later history of the empire of the Medes, this religion was strongly affected by the teachings of Zarathustra.

As a result of the skill of the Magi at interpreting signs, portents and dreams their name gradually came to mean any accomplished user of the arcane arts, and it is probably in this sense that the Gospel of Matthew (2.1) has three Magi from the east (in other traditions they are given very un-Median names) who followed a star to Bethlehem.

## The conquering Persians

Things came unstuck for the Medes when King Astyages (r. 585–550 BC) married his daughter to the Persian king Cambyses (r. c. 580–559 BC). At the time the Persians were subordinate to

Astyages ordering the death of the infant Cyrus, in a 1709 painting by Jean-Charles-Nicaise Perrin. Cyrus was the grandson of Astyages, king of the Medes, but later overthrew him, as had been foretold, and the Medes became part of the Persian empire.

the Medes, but the child of Cambyses and his wife had his own ideas. When that young man, Cyrus II – today called Cyrus the Great – came to power in Persia he immediately rebelled against his grandfather. Astyages sent an army to reclaim the rebellious province, but its general defected and joined the rebels. Eventually Cyrus stormed Ecbatana and captured Astyages, whose daughter he married (if so, she might also have been his aunt). This marriage made the rebellion more of a palace coup in much of Astyages' former domains, and these peacefully transitioned from being part of the Median empire to part of the Persian empire. Cyrus went on to conquer the rest.

Once their lands became Persian, apparently so did the Medes. Inscriptions suggest that the Medes quickly adopted the Persian language, and the few distinctions between the two cultures vanished as the Medes and Persians merged into a single people – as the Greeks had considered them all along.

## Future Echoes

One of the benefits of being a subject of the Median/Persian empire was that the system was based less on the whims of local bureaucrats and more on the rule of law. Even today 'The law of the Medes and Persians' refers to something which cannot be changed by circumstances.

The Median word *magush* (root – 'to wield power') as with Magi and 'magician' has mutated through the ancient Greeks *magike* to become the modern word 'magic'.

A controversial question is whether the Medes remain in the Middle East as a separate people – namely the Kurds. Genetic testing has proved inconclusive because we do not know what the genome of the Medes looked like, or indeed, whether the Medes all belonged to the same ethnic group. With definitive evidence lacking, the entire question has become deeply entangled in modern regional politics.

## c. 1000 BC – 539 BC
# The Chaldeans
## Masters of Magic

*O daughter of the Chaldeans ... Stand now with thine enchantments, and with the multitude of thy sorceries wherein thou hast laboured from thy youth.... Let now the astrologers, the stargazers, the monthly prognosticators, stand up, and save thee.*

Isaiah 47:1, 12–13

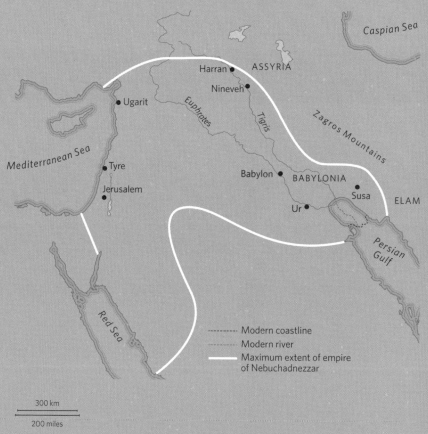

N

Caspian Sea

Harran

ASSYRIA

Nineveh

Ugarit

Euphrates

Tigris

Zagros Mountains

Mediterranean Sea

Tyre

Babylon  BABYLONIA

Susa

ELAM

Jerusalem

Ur

Persian Gulf

Red Sea

- - - - - - -  Modern coastline
- - - - - - -  Modern river
————  Maximum extent of empire of Nebuchadnezzar

300 km

200 miles

It is not just the Hebrews who regarded the magical and prophetic abilities of the Chaldean people with both suspicion and awe. The Chaldeans were so renowned across the ancient world that by the time of the Roman empire anyone claiming to foretell the future tended to go by the name 'Chaldean'.

## Unruly arrivals from the north

When the Chaldeans first met the peoples of ancient Mesopotamia, they were far from welcome arrivals. The original Chaldeans were what historical anthropologists call 'proto-Akkadian peoples', which made them relatives of the Assyrians – but that did not stop them violently invading Assyria at some point in the tenth century BC.

At the time, the Assyrian empire was in the first flush of its youthful strength, and its armies easily deflected the invaders to lands along the southern banks of the River Euphrates. The Arameans who lived there lacked the Assyrian talent for warfare and grudgingly had to make room for the newcomers, who repaid their hospitality by speedily dispossessing them altogether.

According to the Bible, a man called Abram left from the city of Ur 'in the land of the Chaldeans' to seek his fortune in Canaan to the west. This is our first connection between the Chaldeans and unearthly powers, for Abraham (as he is known today) is revered as the father of the Hebrew, Christian and Muslim faiths.

The Chaldeans ruling in Ur were being roughly treated by their Assyrian cousins. From references written on cuneiform clay tablets by the scribes of Assyrian kings Ashurnasirpal II (r. 884–859 BC) and Shalmaneser III (r. 859–824 BC), it is clear that by this time the Chaldeans were subjects of the Assyrian empire. That the Chaldeans were unhappy with this development goes without saying, for the Assyrians were brutal rulers.

Assyrian repression did not stop the Chaldeans from rebelling with some regularity, and they were usually joined in their uprisings by the Babylonians and Elamites, people who liked their Assyrian rulers no better than did the Chaldeans. Each time, the

A striding lion on a wall made of glazed bricks, from Nebuchadnezzar's Babylon. Even after thousands of years it is possible to appreciate the brilliant colours and striking appearance.

An imaginative image of Chaldean astronomers observing the heavens atop a ziggurat. At this time there was little distinction between astronomers and astrologers.

Assyrians were able to bloodily suppress the rebellion, but an explosive resentment was building among the people of the empire.

## The imperial Chaldeans

In 626 BC the Assyrians proved to be their own worst enemy. A massive convulsion of civil wars so weakened their empire that a minor Chaldean king called Nabopolassar was able to wrest Babylon from Assyrian control. The subject peoples of Assyria's empire had tired of civil war and their brutal rulers' ever-rising demands for manpower and money. The Chaldeans, Medes, Parthians and Persians allied with the barbarian Scythians and Cimmerians to form a coalition bent on the total extermination of Assyria.

The coalition was highly successful. By the time Nabopolassar died in 605 BC the Assyrian capital of Nineveh was a smoking ruin and the Assyrians were extinct. Meanwhile Nabopolassar and his Chaldeans had leveraged their control of Babylon into an empire of their own. It was at this time that the Chaldean rulers of Babylon immersed themselves in that ancient city's detailed studies of astronomy and astrology. (It is from the Babylonians that we get both the twelve signs of the zodiac and the 60-minute hour, the latter because Babylonians used a sexagesimal system – base 60 – for astronomical calculations.)

Modern archaeology has unearthed large number of texts which demonstrate the Chaldean preoccupation with magic. Like numerous other ancient peoples, the Chaldeans believed the world was swarming with spirits. Many of these were malign and responsible for bad luck and disease, while others could be persuaded into the service of humanity.

A fragment of text from a tablet now in the British Museum gives a flavour of the Chaldean approach to demonology:

May the wicked demon depart!
May they seize another!
The propitious demon, the propitious giant,
may they penetrate into his body!

Many who have never heard of the Chaldeans know something of them, even apart from Abraham. There are, for example, the famous Hanging Gardens of Babylon. By some accounts these were built for the Persian wife of the Chaldean king Nebuchadnezzar II (*c.* 604–562 BC) to ease her homesickness for the mountains of her homeland. Nebuchadnezzar is best known for his starring role in the Bible's Book of Daniel. It was not priests poring over the liver of a sacrificial victim, or stargazers looking up from a Babylonian ziggurat who eventually predicted the doom of the Chaldeans' Neo-Babylonian empire, but the God of the Hebrews. The Hebrews had little love for the Chaldeans, as told in the Book of Habakkuk (1:6–10):

> The Chaldeans, that bitter and hasty nation.... Their horses also are swifter than the leopards, and are more fierce than the evening wolves: and their horsemen shall spread themselves, and their horsemen shall come from far; they shall fly as the eagle that hasteth to eat. They shall come all for violence ... and they shall gather the captivity as the sand. And they shall scoff at kings ... they shall deride every strong hold; for they shall heap dust, and take it.

## Enemies of God

The Hebrew God held a grudge because in an attempt to undermine Chaldean rule in the Levant, the Egyptians had encouraged the Hebrews to rebel. This proved disastrous for the house of Judah when Nebuchadnezzar captured Jerusalem in 586 BC, razed the temple of Solomon and deported thousands of Jews to exile by the rivers of Babylon.

Despite his kingdom's overlordship of many lands and peoples, it was clear that Nebuchadnezzar was uneasy that his people might share the fate of the Assyrians. The Bible reports that he dreamed of a statue which represented his empire. That statue was made of brass, and iron and gold, but had feet of clay. While that fundamental flaw might have indicated a lack of respect for Yahweh, the Hebrew God, the demise of the Chaldeans can be partly attributed to the fact that they became assimilated with the people of Babylon. Long ago they had abandoned their native Semitic tongue and adopted the Aramaic spoken by most peoples in Mesopotamia. Now, in their customs, religion and dress, the Chaldeans gradually merged with and became indistinguishable from the Assyriac-Babylonian mix in the kingdom's heartlands. Despite this, Chaldeans continued to dominate the priestly caste of the empire. Gradually a 'Chaldean' ceased to represent a member of a fast-vanishing people and came instead to mean an expert in magic and prognostication.

By the year 540 BC, in the time of Nebuchadnezzar's later successor Belshazzar, the writing was on the wall. According to the Book of Daniel (5:5), the ruler was holding a lavish banquet when a hand appeared and wrote upon the wall a prophecy of the destruction of the kingdom. The words were interpreted by the Hebrew prophet Daniel, who informed the king that he had been 'weighed in the balance and found wanting'.

The mortal instrument of divine judgment was the Persian king Cyrus the Great. The Persians were a rising power in the east that had already subjugated the earlier empire of the neighbouring Medes. When Cyrus turned his attention to the Neo-Babylonian empire it fell into his hands like a ripe fruit in 539 BC – partly because the governor of the province of Assyria adroitly defected to the Persians at the critical moment.

Another reason for the rapid fall of Babylon was that the Chaldeans had imported not only Jews in vast numbers but also other disaffected peoples whom they had exiled from their homelands. Naturally all these peoples supported Cyrus, who reciprocated by releasing them from their captivity and allowed them to return to their homes. With the end of their empire, the Chaldeans as a people vanish from history.

## An enduring name

Still, the name lived on. Four hundred years after the defeat of the last Chaldean king, sceptics in the Roman Republic are found disputing whether latter-day Chaldeans could indeed see the future, as recorded by Cicero (*On Divination* 47; in reality all those he names met violent and premature ends).

> I recall the many prophecies which the Chaldeans made to Pompey, to Crassus and even to the recently assassinated Caesar, saying that all of them would die in old age, at home and in great glory.

The collapse of the Roman empire and the rise of Christianity between them erased the Chaldeans from history for the next thousand years. But so evocative a name is hard to forget. The Chaldeans popped up again after administrative rearrangements of the Catholic church in 1500–1600 which recognized a group of

Christians in the region of Assyria who sought communion with Rome. Established as the Chaldean Catholic Church, this congregation has existed ever since. It still maintains a tenuous existence in its now largely Muslim homeland and there is also a growing community of expatriates. Many of these identify with the ancient Chaldeans – though establishing the veracity of this claim would indeed require sorcerous skills.

## Future Echoes

Rembrandt's painting *Belshazzar's Feast*, 1635, captures the evocative moment when a divine hand begins to write on the wall, ruining the Chaldean king's dinner. Though the Hebrew characters in the painting are not in the conventional right-to-left arrangement, any reasonably proficient priest should have been able to decipher it.

The phrase 'feet of clay' has been worked into the title of numerous books and songs. In the 1940s Frank Sinatra sang 'Too late, too late, I realized my idol had feet of clay'. More recently, in 1996, the phrase was used by the late Terry Pratchett as the title for one of his books in the bestselling Discworld series.

The writing on the wall in Rembrandt's 1635 painting *Belshazzar's Feast*, now in the National Gallery, London.

# *c.* 1000 BC – AD 350
# **The Kushites**
# Egypt's Southern Conquerors

*They are the tallest and most handsome men in all the world. Their customs are completely different from the rest of humanity – and particularly in how they choose kings. They find the tallest of all their people, and should his strength be equal to his height, they make him their ruler.*

Herodotus, *The Histories* 3.20

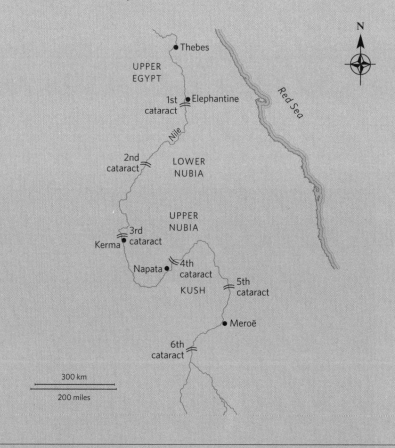

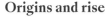

Historians have long known that the Greeks acquired many of their ideas from the Egyptians, and others (such as writing), indirectly, via the Phoenicians. Yet did the Egyptians receive some of their ideas from a people even further south, from an African civilization that reached from the headwaters of the Nile to the shores of Lake Victoria?

The people at the heart of this intriguing theory are an African nation called the Kushites. These southern neighbours of the Egyptians have long been regarded as a sort of appendix to Egyptology, and it is only in recent decades that the study of the Kushites has developed as a discipline in its own right. Certainly, the Kushites and Egyptians have a long and storied history of interaction, with each state dominating the other in turn. As a result, it is sometimes hard to disentangle which aspects of Egyptian civilization came from Kush and which aspects the Kushites obtained from the Egyptians.

The round head and delicate features of this bronze statue identify this person as Kushite, while the leopard's head on the kilt reveals he was a priest.

## Origins and rise

The Kushite kingdom evolved in the area of northern Africa which the Egyptians called Nubia, probably from 'nub', the Egyptian word for gold. Another Egyptian name for the region was the 'land of bowmen' (Ta-Seti), since invading Egyptians found out the hard way that the local people were expert archers. This was a very old culture, with the first unified kingdoms beginning to form around 3000 BC. Indeed, it may have been the need to meet the growing threat from the south that forced the Egyptians themselves to unify into a single state.

When the Egyptians in the mid-second millennium BC finally threw out the Hyksos people who had dominated their land for over a century, Egypt became an expansionist power. Egyptian armies not only marched far north into Canaan, but also moved southward into Nubia, destroying in the process the Nubian kingdom of Kerma. For several centuries thereafter, northern Nubia was a province of Egypt. The two cultures interacted to a very substantial degree, though the Egyptians record a number of rebellions, which suggests that the Nubians were not entirely satisfied with their status as part of southern Egypt.

By the tenth century BC, Egypt was in trouble. Successive assaults by waves of migratory Sea Peoples had been repulsed, but at the cost of leaving the kingdom bankrupt and exhausted. Egyptian power in the south declined to the point where the local aristocrats were able to seize power for themselves and set up an independent Kushite kingdom based on the city-state of Napata on the Nile in what is today Sudan.

The Egyptians found that they also faced a new enemy in the resurgent power of Assyria, which had expanded in the Levant and appeared to be seriously intent on conquering Egypt too. While the Egyptians focused on the northern threat, the kingdom of Kush took the chance to make serious inroads into Egypt's southern domains. A series of warrior Kushite kings then pushed their kingdom's borders past Elephantine towards the ancient Egyptian city of Thebes.

By 728 BC Egyptian rule had fractured under the strain of military, social and economic pressures. At least three pharaohs each claimed to rule a part of the divided kingdom. While these squabbled among themselves, a Kushite king called Piye decisively resolved the argument by taking control of the entire state. Once again Egypt and Nubia were united, but this time under the Kushites. Piye and his successors became the Twenty-fifth

dynasty of Egyptian pharaohs, ruling a land that stretched almost 2,500 kilometres (1,550 miles) from Gaza to the fabled city of Meroë, around 200 km (125 miles) north of modern Khartoum in Sudan.

### 'Great Meroë'

Meroë was the second city of Kush, and the nexus through which gold, ivory and slaves were funnelled northwards. The Greek historian Herodotus, writing in the fifth century BC, describes a utopian city (*Histories* 3.17–25) where people lived to be a hundred years old and dined on 'meat and milk'. Excavations in 1910 found evidence that supported the identification of the city described by Herodotus as Meroë, and his 'Temple of the Sun' where food spontaneously appeared for the people has been tentatively located. Herodotus says he heard of the 'great city' of Meroë, while he was at Elephantine, an island in the Nile near the First Cataract, fifty days travel to the north.

Meroë was certainly well urbanized. According to the first-century AD geographer Strabo, the houses were made from palm wood interwoven with brick. The city is today so comprehensively ruined that it is impossible to hazard a guess at even an approximate

Kushite pyramids at Meroë (now in Sudan), the second city of the Kushite kingdom. So closely were the Kushite and Egyptian cultures intertwined, it is now impossible to tell which civilization learned what from the other.

maximum population, but those ruins still contain more than 200 substantial steep-sided 'Nubian-style' pyramids.

So much of Kushite culture has been lost that we now struggle to identify aspects of it. It would certainly help if we could read the few texts to survive in the Merotic language, which was used at least by the later Kushites. However, as yet no Rosetta Stone has been discovered which can unlock the enigmatic clay tablets unearthed by archaeologists, and until then much of the administrative and social lives of the Kushites must remain a mystery.

Kushite domination of Egypt lasted less than a century, from around 750 BC to 656 BC. The Kushite pharaohs got off to an energetic start, striving for control of the Levant and assisting the Hebrews in the defence of Jerusalem against the Assyrians. (It is a salutary reminder that while students of Classical history are concentrating on the Greeks and the local squabbles of the tiny town that was to become Rome, on the eastern shores of the Mediterranean at the same time people from Sudan were fighting people from Iran for control of Syria.)

## Retreat from Egypt

This imperial overreach stretched their resources too far, and the Kushites were not only unable to take the Levant, they even lost northern Egypt, where the Assyrians set up a puppet government. The last Kushite pharaoh, Tantamani, made a spirited attempt to regain Egypt, but failed, and by 650 BC the Kushite kingdom was once again based at Napata. The pyramid tomb of Tantamani can still be seen at the royal burial site of El-Kurru (in modern Sudan), near Napata, alongside those of King Piye and his successors.

The Egyptians followed the retreating Kushites and attacked Napata, pillaging and burning the city. After 590 BC, the Kushites decided that their northern neighbours had become too powerful and retreated further south to make their new capital at Meroë.

After Assyria vanished amid a welter of civil wars and vengeful former subjects, Egypt became subject to the Achaemenid Persian empire established by Cyrus the Great. The Persians had heard of the fabulous wealth of Meroë, and made a determined attempt to seize it for themselves, but an expedition under their king Cambyses II (r. 530–522 BC) failed. Thereafter the Kushites were left to their own devices.

Napata was not completely abandoned, and when the Romans had conquered Egypt, they ventured southwards in the first century BC. They found Napata at that time ruled by a warrior queen called Candace, who also gets a mention in Acts of the Apostles 8:26. ('Candace' may actually have been the Kushite word for 'queen' and not a personal name.) The Roman general Petronius sacked Napata, but was taken aback by the vehemence of the response as waves of warriors attacked his garrisons. ('Their women carry weapons!' remarked a mildly shocked Strabo.) Eventually Candace asked to negotiate. When Petronius told her that her ambassadors must speak with Caesar (Augustus), the baffled reply was, in effect 'Caesar who?'.

Meroë to the south remained largely peaceful, but had problems of its own. The area was rich in minerals and forests, but mines require large amounts of timber for tunnel supports and smelting. Eventually Meroë used up all the local wood, causing massive environmental degradation. When the neighbouring Axumites of Ethiopia sacked Meroë in AD 350 they finished off a city that had for the most part already destroyed itself.

A kneeling Kushite pharaoh of the late eighth to early seventh century BC, with his distinctive regalia including a 'cap' crown and ram's head amulets.

## Future Echoes

When the Greeks went east under Alexander they came across a massive mountain range, similar to the mountains of the Ethiopian highlands east of Kush. This is one theory (of many) as to how the Hindu Kush got its name. (Today the name Kush is applied to a strain of cannabis from that region, which is being investigated for use in medicine.)

One of the most controversial theories about the origins of Greek civilization is the hypothesis put forward by author Martin Bernal in his book *Black Athena* (1987–2006). Subtitled 'The Afroasiatic Roots of Classical Civilization', this argues that Greek culture was heavily influenced by ideas and even settlers from Africa. This brief summary cannot do full justice to Bernal's theory, and not everyone agrees with it, but it is intriguing to think that the lost Kushites may have helped to shape Western civilization.

# 329 BC – AD 10
# **The Bactrians**
## Powerful Traders on the Silk Road

*Though more civilized than nomads, one of the worst traits [of the Bactrians] … was that those made incapable by old age or sickness were thrown alive to dogs which treated them as prey. The dogs were raised for that specific purpose and the locals called them 'undertakers'.*

Strabo, *Geography* 11.11.3

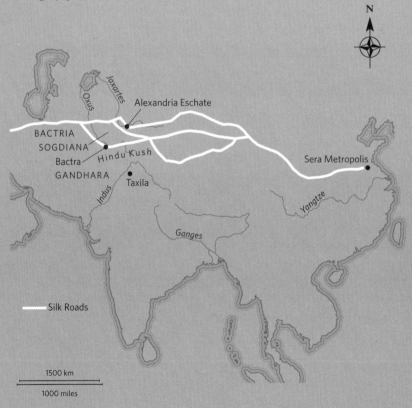

N

Joxartes
Oxus
Alexandria Eschate
BACTRIA
SOGDIANA
Bactra — Hindu Kush
GANDHARA
Indus
Taxila
Sera Metropolis
Yangtze
Ganges

— Silk Roads

1500 km
1000 miles

The city of Balkh in northern Afghanistan lies some 75 kilometres (46 miles) south of the border with Uzbekistan. It is over 5,000 kilometres (3,100 miles) from Greece, and even today a flight between Athens and Balkh takes over nine hours. Why this is interesting and what makes it remarkable is that in the Classical era, Balkh was called Bactra, and was the capital of a substantial Greek kingdom which, in one form or another, lasted for around 300 years.

## Alexander in the east

The history of the Greeks in what is today Afghanistan began in 329 BC with Alexander the Great's pursuit of the last claimant to the throne of the Achaemenid Persian empire, Bessus, who was satrap (provincial administrator) of Bactria. Alexander's conquest of Bactria made him the master of all the former domains of the Persian king.

The Bactrians, who had been part of the Persian empire since the sixth century BC, did not become Greek subjects without a struggle. Most of the population of Bactria and the neighbouring state of Sogdiana followed the teachings of their native prophet Zarathustra, whose doctrine of Zoroastrianism still has many followers today. Fire and earth were sacred to the native peoples, who were therefore appalled by the Greek practice of either burning or burying corpses. Their dead were left in the open to decompose and be devoured by scavengers – a practice which shocked the Greeks as much as the Bactrians were shocked by them.

A lively rebellion followed, and the pragmatic Alexander realized he would either have to compromise or live with a state of permanent insurrection. Exactly what was worked out is unknown, but it involved Alexander marrying a native Sogdianan princess called Roxana (or Roxanne).

Cities were certainly not new in the region (at already over a thousand years old, Balkh/Bactra was of so venerable an age that it was known as the 'Mother of Cities'). However, Alexander and his subordinates took urbanism to a new level, founding a multiplicity of new cities and also remaking others – including Bactra – in a Hellenistic form. By the time Alexander left in search of new worlds to conquer, the kingdom of Bactria-Sogdiana had several hundred 'cities' and a population of some 35,000 Greek settlers.

Many of these settlers were opportunists who hoped to start a new life in the frontiers opening up in the east. Others were veteran soldiers forcibly retired by Alexander and not at all happy about finishing their lives thousands of miles away from home. In fact when news spread that Alexander was dead, most of the settlers

The fifteenth-century tomb of Ali at Mazar-i-Sharif near Balkh, as Bactra is now called. There are few Classical-era monuments in the city, which was razed to the ground by Genghis Khan in the late twelfth century.

attempted to pack their bags and return to Greece, but the caravan of returnees was blocked by Alexander's successors, who well knew that a Greek settler presence was essential if they were to hold on to this, their most easterly conquest.

Greek settlers and Bactrian locals were forced into uneasy co-habitation for the next century – a period when this kingdom was largely ignored in the dynastic struggles between Hellenistic monarchs based much further west. The virtual isolation of Bactria became a reality in 245 BC when the Parni people rose in rebellion and established the independent kingdom based on Mesopotamia that was soon to become the Parthian empire.

## An independent kingdom

By this time the Bactrian people had formalized what was already the *de facto* situation: they declared themselves an independent kingdom, with the former satrap becoming Diodotus I of Bactria-Sogdiana. This new kingdom was no isolated appendix of Greek culture but a powerful and dynamic state in its own right. Known to later geographers as the 'kingdom of a thousand cities', Bactria had all the ingredients necessary for success.

Geographically the land was protected from invaders by the Hindu Kush mountain range to the south and an inhospitable desert beyond Sogdiana to the north. Between the two was a fertile land watered by run-off from the mountains, and, further north, by the River Oxus (Amu Darya). Though cut off from the Hellenistic Seleucid empire to which it had formerly belonged, the kingdom now traded with Ptolemaic Egypt by way of India and – also via India – developed an extensive indirect trade with China. In fact, it was through the Bactrians that the Chinese first became aware of Mediterranean culture and began to establish stations along that trading route that was later to become famous as the Silk Road.

Trade was greatly helped by a species of the native livestock – the Bactrian camel, which still runs wild in this region. Immediately identifiable by its distinctive twin humps, the Bactrian camel was the ideal animal for regional long-distance trade. A Bactrian camel is capable of taking in over 100 litres (22 gallons) of water at a time and then going without while carrying loads up to 50 kilometres (30 miles) per day. While hospitable in other ways, the region's temperatures range from minus 30°C (minus 22°F) in winter to 40°C (104°F) in summer – conditions the Bactrian camel seems to tolerate without undue discomfort.

## A Greco-Indian fusion

It was not long before the Bactrian kings started to develop a predatory interest in their neighbours. Most of Alexander's conquests in India barely survived his death, but in the early second century BC a Bactrian king called Demetrius I launched a series of campaigns which resulted in the establishment of what is usually called the Indo-Greek kingdom, reaching into the northwest of the Indian subcontinent. There followed a period of cultural exchange that led to the partial fusion of Greek and Indian cultures into something that contained much of each but was uniquely different. This fusion is well represented in artefacts of the period, which also demonstrate other aspects of the mingling of Greek and Indian. For example, there are coins minted in the Hellenistic style with Greek inscriptions, but square in shape, as were contemporary Indian coins, and depicting – for example – avatars of the Indian god Vishnu instead of the traditional Hellenic deities.

In fact it seems clear that as well as following Zoroastrian and Hindu religion, much of the population had converted to Buddhism, added to which there was a large degree of syncretism as well – the process by which one religion adopts elements of another.

Demetrius I, king of the Greek kingdom of Bactria, wearing distinctive headgear. He and his successors often used an elephant motif in their propaganda.

## Bactrian demise

Two factors combined to bring the rule of the eastern Greeks to an end. These are poorly documented in our sources, since ancient historians, rather like the Hellenistic kings of the west before them, were completely focused on events around the Mediterranean. It is clear, though, that the Bactrian monarchy suffered the same unfortunate vulnerability to usurpation and civil war as their western relatives. Civil war in a state surrounded by alien and predatory peoples is never a good idea, and things were made worse when one of the region's periodic waves of nomadic migration struck the northern frontier.

Entire towns were destroyed, and contact was lost with others, such as Alexandria Eschate (literally 'Alexandria the furthest') on the River Jaxartes. This city was several hundred kilometres northeast of the capital Bactra, and over 9,650 kilometres (6,000 miles) from Greece. The last mention of the city reveals it was still a going concern in 30 BC.

Weakened by constant warfare, the Bactrians were unable to resist opportunistic attacks by the Parthians, Yuezhi nomads from northwestern China and aggressive Indian kings, and over the course of the first century BC their kingdom slowly crumbled away. First Bactria itself was overwhelmed, and finally, in AD 10, the last remnants of the Greek kingdom in India vanished. Exactly how this happened we have no idea, and the 'when' is only made possible by the discovery of coins of the otherwise unknown king Strato III Philopator.

Bactrian camels have long been important in their homeland – this little statuette from the region is at least four thousand years old.

## Future Echoes

Today the Bactrian Greeks are almost completely forgotten by westerners, many of whom are surprised to find Greek ruins even in Turkey, a great distance to the west of Bactria. Art historians are less surprised, because Gandharan art – the fusion of Greek and Indian styles – survived in the region for another thousand years until the Islamic conquest. Perhaps the most famous examples of this Indo-Greek style were giant monumental carvings of the Buddha at Bamiyan along the route of the Silk Road in Afghanistan, the tallest of which was over 50 metres (165 feet) in height. The statues survived Genghis Khan and European occupation, but in 2001 the then Taliban government of Afghanistan decided that they were 'against Islam'. Despite worldwide protests, including from many Muslim nations, the statues were dynamited. This barbaric act erased one of the last remaining traces of the Greek presence in the region.

One of the monumental sixth-century Buddhas of Bamiyan, Afghanistan, carved in Gandharan style and destroyed in 2001.

# Part Three
## The Coming of Rome
### Civilization Spreads Beyond the Mediterranean

Ancient Rome – the words evoke powerful images in the modern mind. 'To the glory that was Greece, and the grandeur that was Rome' exclaimed Edgar Allan Poe in one of his poems ('To Helen', written in 1845). That 'grandeur' has been emphasized in dozens of sword-and-sandal epics on television and in film, and generations have become accustomed to the idea of Roman soldiers striding around in long red cloaks, unconvincing leather cuirasses and huge copper arm guards.

In reality, Romans seldom wore any of these articles of clothing, and the grandeur of Roman architecture was somewhat spoiled by a more mud-splattered reality, in which those noble marble temples were surrounded by teeming market stalls. There is also the idea that Rome carried the torch of culture into a howling, uncivilized wilderness, weaning barbarians from their middens and mud huts with aqueducts, roads and decent sewers.

This, to a certain extent, was true of ancient Britain – though even this northern island was somewhat more civilized than most people imagine. And because British historians have long exercised a powerful influence on Anglo-Saxon views of ancient Rome, there is a tendency to think that the British experience was shared by conquered peoples across Rome's growing empire.

Again, not so. In fact the opposite was often true – those peoples conquered by Rome tended (often with considerable justification) to consider that it was the Romans who were the barbarians, to whom it was their unwanted task to teach the arts of civilization. The Augustan poet Horace (65–8 BC), looking at the dominance of Hellenism in Roman art, literature and architecture in his day remarked that 'Greece has conquered her rough conqueror'.

Certainly the Greeks had little to learn from the Romans in terms of aqueducts, roads, sewers or the other accoutrements of municipal civilization. They had learned these hundreds of years earlier from Mesopotamia and Egypt, and were unimpressed by Rome's achievements to date. Indeed, when Pyrrhus, king of the **Epirots** in western Greece, fought an unsuccessful series of wars between 280 and 275 BC against the Roman Republic, he admired the order of Roman army camps, remarking that in this at least, 'These barbarians don't look so barbaric.'

Before Greece, the Romans had conquered their fellow Italians. Again, there are few signs that the peoples of Italy felt overwhelmed by the superiority of Roman civilization. Overwhelmed by the power of the Roman legions, certainly, and by the ferocity and discipline of the average Roman soldier, very definitely, but by Roman art, architecture and poetry, not in the least. These aspects of civilization were common to all of Italy with the exception of the Gallic north. The great names of Latin literature, from Plautus (north-central Italy) through Horace (Samnite Italy) and Virgil (Cisalpine Gaul), to Martial (Spain) and Juvenal (Aquino, on the border with Tuscany), include very few actual Romans from Rome. Even that quintessential Roman, Marcus Tullius Cicero, was from Arpinum, a Samnite town captured by Rome two hundred years before his birth.

The example of these writers tells us wherein lay the true power of Rome. It was its ability to take enemies defeated on the battlefield and make them into Romans. Recognizing, however, that there might be lingering hard feelings among the peoples whose lands they had invaded and whose cities they had pillaged, the Romans of the Republic withheld the vote from their newest citizens for several decades until they had become at least partly romanized.

And romanized they did become. Usually the first among a conquered people to become Roman citizens were the aristocracy. These aristocrats had to get used to the idea of no longer being the largest fish in a very small pond and instead denizens of a larger world with limitless potential. The experience of one Publius Ventidius Bassus encapsulates in the experiences of one man the manner in which Rome absorbed other peoples.

Ventidius was from Picenum in the Po valley of northern Italy. In the Social War of 90 BC, when he was still a boy, the Roman legions attacked the region, pillaged Picenum and took thousands of prisoners. Among these was Ventidius. He thus first saw Rome when he was marched through the city with his captive mother as exhibits in a Roman triumph. Yet Rome was open to men of talent, and one of the city's great strengths was that it did not care from which peoples they originated, as long as they were prepared to become Romans. Conscripted into the army, Ventidius became Roman, and being talented, he rose rapidly through the ranks. By 40 BC Ventidius was a Roman general whose task was to fight back against a Parthian invasion of Rome's eastern provinces. A few years later, Ventidius was back in Rome, where he appeared for the second time in a Roman triumph – now not as a miserable prisoner prodded along at spear-point, but as the conquering general for whom the entire event was staged.

In short, Ventidius became as Roman as the Romans, as did the remaining people of his native Picenum. The fate of the Picentines was far from unique. Many of the tribes and cultures in this section did indeed vanish – not through extirpation, but by absorption. Rome was barbaric as a conqueror, but welcoming to the conquered. Cultures which survived initial pillage and massacre by the legions were defenceless against a process which assimilated them into the Roman mainstream.

The **Sabines** were absorbed so early that one of their number became the second king of Rome after Romulus, and the Etruscans soon followed. Some Italian peoples held out for centuries, and parts of northern Italy still resisted Rome even as the **Galatians** and **Thracians** were being folded into the empire. The Gallic tribe of the **Arverni**, conquered by Julius Caesar in the 50s BC, became an integral part of Roman Gaul, while the **Batavi**, a Germanic tribe from the Rhine delta, likewise became assimilated. The Romans so appreciated their military prowess that Batavi formed the bulk of the emperor's personal bodyguard from the reigns of Augustus (27 BC–AD 14) to Galba (AD 68–69).

The British proved particularly obdurate, which is why Caratacus of the **Catuvellauni** and Boudicca of the **Iceni** are still national heroes of the British today. (Though successive waves of later invaders of Britain mean that Frenchmen in Brittany are more probable descendants of Caratacus than the average modern Briton.) Yet even in Britain the pattern was the same. First the Roman legions marched in against vehement resistance. Then decades or centuries later, the legions marched out again with their ranks swelled by the descendants of the very people who had fought them so bitterly.

Modern archaeology has shown that the Roman empire was no homogeneous cultural monolith. There was no deliberate drive to make peoples identically 'Roman', even though they were assimilated. **Nabataean** and **Celtiberian** Romans, at the eastern and western ends of the empire respectively, were very different people, for all that they shared a common Roman culture alongside their own. The **Samaritans** in the Levant maintained an identity that survives to a limited extent to this day.

Only on the empire's outer edges – the **Garamantes** and **Numidians** in the deserts of North Africa and the **Dacians** beyond the Danube in their Transylvanian stronghold in the Balkans, with the nomadic **Sarmatians** even further out on the central Eurasian steppe – was the magnetic power and dominance of Rome fragile at best, as well as temporary. And it was from the Eurasian steppe, as we shall see in the final section, that the ultimate challenge to Roman power would come.

# c. 1500 BC – AD 550
## The Thracians
## Masters of Metalworking

*Each man among the Thracians has several wives and no sooner has a man died than a dispute breaks out among them as to which of them their husband loved the most.*

**Herodotus,** *The Histories* 5.5.1

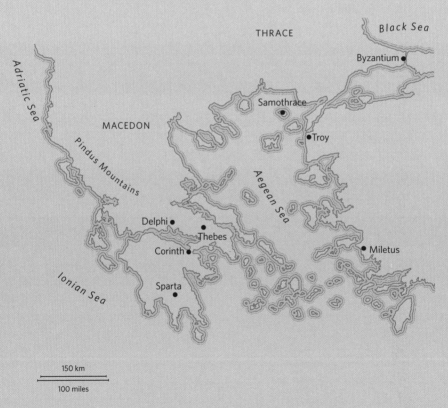

In the early Classical world, the equivalent of the Wild West was Thrace. And like the settlers in the American West, the Thracians outnumbered their neighbours and had the advantage of superior weaponry.

Thrace covered a wide area, consisting today of European Turkey and most of Bulgaria apart from the northwest. Much of the land is flat and fertile, although Thracian warriors were unenthusiastic farmers – they preferred banditry and plundering their enemies. Horse-rearing too was socially acceptable, and the Thracians were keen horsemen. We know little about Thracian religion, since the Thracians were as contemptuous of writing as they were of most of the arts of civilization. However, it is clear that their main deity was a horse god. He is so often depicted on horseback that modern researchers simply call him 'the Thracian horseman'.

Apart from rich fields, Thrace also had abundant reserves of timber, gold and precious stones. (It is indeed mainly through gold artefacts and jewellery that we know of the early inhabitants of Thrace.) Gold ornaments and copper tools from 3000 BC show that even as civilization was taking hold in Mesopotamia, the proto-Thracians were producing sophisticated metalwork, and they kept their reputation as metalworkers through the remainder of antiquity.

Some time around 1500 BC, the Thracians known to the Classical world came thundering into the Greek orbit on their horses – tall, red-haired warriors, with pale skin and blue eyes. They swept aside local overlords and made themselves the dominant caste, mixing with the local population. Perhaps for this reason, genetic research has shown considerably more diversity among the Thracians than the red hair and blue eyes of the ancient stereotype.

This gold mask of a Thracian king testifies to the metalworking skills for which the Thracian people were renowned.

## A warrior people

The Thracians were given their name by the Greeks, who called them after Thrax, a son of the war god Ares. Unable to resist a good fight, the Thracians joined the war between Greeks and the Trojans, taking the Trojan side. In the *Iliad*, Homer talks of the Thracians 'who wear their hair in a tuft on their heads' and gives this description of one of their kings (*Iliad* 10.430ff.):

His horses are the finest and strongest that I have ever seen, whiter than snow and faster than any wind that blows. His chariot glows with silver and gold, and he has brought his marvellous golden armour, of the rarest workmanship – too splendid for any mortal man to carry, and suitable only for the gods.

The next writer to take a serious interest in the Thracians was the historian Herodotus, in the mid-fifth century BC. It has often been pointed out that Herodotus was as much an anthropologist as he was a historian, and some of his first-hand observations have been borne out by archaeologists. For example, Herodotus claims that when a Thracian warrior died, his wives would literally fight to decide who had been his favourite (as quoted at the beginning). The prize for the winner was to be sacrificed and buried alongside her husband. One tomb of a Thracian aristocrat has been discovered which contained, along with spectacular gold grave goods, the body of a dead woman, with another female body in the antechamber. By one interpretation this latter woman had come second in the contest for her husband's affections in the afterlife. Herodotus also remarks (*The Histories* 5.1):

Other than the Indians, the Thracians are the most numerous people on Earth. It is my opinion that if they could ever unite under a single ruler, nothing could stop them from taking over the world. However, there is absolutely no way that this could happen.

To the Greeks, Thracian males appeared as wild, macho characters with a huge appetite for life untrammelled by 'civilized' considerations. For example, one late second-century AD Greek author reported that a Thracian drinking game consisted of a warrior standing on a stone with a sword in his hand and a hangman's noose around his neck. The stone was kicked away and the dangling warrior attempted to cut himself free, to much hilarity if he failed.

If anything, Thracian women were even more alarming to the Greeks, since they tended to be extremely forward in expressing their sentiments to any males they were attracted to, and they saw no reason why they should remain virgins until marriage. Thracians were polygamous, and the Athenian playwright Menander has a Thracian woman remark scornfully that a man with only five wives would be considered a 'miserable creature who could barely count himself as married'.

The Thracians must have had some feeling for the finer arts, as the most famous musician of mythology was the Thracian harpist Orpheus, whose playing and singing was said to charm the birds from the trees. Heartbroken after the death of his wife Eurydice, and an ultimately unsuccessful attempt to bring her back from the Underworld, Orpheus, according to Ovid, turned from women and was the first Thracian to embrace homosexuality. His failure to succumb to their charms so enraged the local women that they literally tore Orpheus to pieces.

## Greeks and Thracians

By the fifth century BC the Greeks had considerable experience of the Thracians because the wealth of that land to their north enticed them there in droves. Fortified Greek colonies dotted the Thracian coastline from the borders of Macedonia to the shores of the Black Sea. These colonies had to be fortified, because the Thracians did not take kindly to the new arrivals, and there was some bitter fighting before the two groups learned to live alongside one another.

Greek and Thracian tactics and weaponry were so different it was actually quite hard for them to fight each other. When not on horseback, the typical Thracian warrior was a peltast – a man armed with a javelin, a long spear, and rudimentary armour, often carrying a distinctive curved shield. These warriors were disorganized, opportunistic and agile – the very opposite of the close formations of heavily armoured, disciplined Greek hoplites who faced them. The Thracians would stand no chance taking on a Greek phalanx

The site of the ancient Thracian city of Perperikon was settled and devastated many times over the millennia. Now in ruins, it was a thriving city in Roman times.

head-on, and there was no possibility of a phalanx closing with their more agile opponents. The result was something of a stand-off until the Greeks began recruiting Thracians into their armies and the Thracians started hiring Greek mercenaries.

This led to a degree of cultural interchange, though initially with a few misunderstandings on both sides. In his play *Lysistrata* of 411 BC the comic playwright Aristophanes describes a Thracian mercenary simply chasing a market vendor away from her stall before helping himself to her produce. The writer and historian Xenophon (*c.* 431–354 BC) once entered the service of the Thracian king Seuthes II. A rather appalled Xenophon later wrote of a banquet in which the king did an impromptu dance and served his guests by literally hurling chunks of bread and meat down the table at them.

## Foreign rule

The Persians were the first to attempt to unite the Thracians under one ruler. In 516 BC they tried to bring at least the southeastern part of Thrace under their control, though it is uncertain exactly how comprehensively Persian rule extended over their conquests. In pursuit of a long-running grudge against the Greeks, the Persians brought a massive army into Thrace. This persuaded many overawed Thracians to throw in their lot with the Persians, who maintained a longstanding presence in Thrace, thanks to the attraction of its mineral wealth.

Thrace became an integral part of the Roman empire, as shown by this Thracian-style gladiator depicted on a fragment of a Roman bowl discovered in London.

In the fourth century BC, King Philip II of Macedon and his son Alexander were also tempted to seize Thrace because of the land's mineral wealth, which they then used as the financial springboard for their conquest of the Persian empire. However, the full subjugation of the region had to wait until the arrival of the Romans, and the steady, methodical expansion of roads, mines and settlements under Roman law.

Oddly enough, Herodotus now proved prophetic, because, united under one ruler, the Thracians – or at least one Thracian – did indeed rule the world. This was Maximinus Thrax, a gigantic Thracian (his party trick was knocking out a horse with a single blow) who rose from the ranks to become Roman emperor in AD 235. By some accounts he was the only Roman emperor to have been born outside the empire. While Thrax was largely Romanized by the time he became emperor (though his Thracian was always better than his Latin), it was not long before his outraged subjects conspired together to replace their 'barbarian' emperor with someone more suitable and he was assassinated in AD 238. A later Roman emperor, Licinius – who was defeated and killed by Constantine the Great – was also a Thracian.

As with many warrior peoples, the Thracians settled down under Roman rule, though 'Thracian'-style gladiators were always a draw at the Roman arena. As a nation, the Thracians passed into Byzantine control with the fall of the western Roman empire and largely vanished when overwhelmed by Slavic tribes which arrived in the sixth century.

## Future Echoes

Almost everyone has heard of Thrace's most famous son, though no one knows his real name. He was a deserter from the Roman army who became a bandit. Captured by the Romans he was forced to become a gladiator, and – as did many gladiators – this man adopted a stage name, choosing to call himself after the town where he was born – Spartacus.

While every bit as brutal as the Romans against whom he led his army of escaped slaves, Spartacus is today renowned as the ultimate rebel – the man who took on a powerful, corrupt empire and for years defeated everything that empire could throw at him. And when he went down, in 71 BC, he went down fighting.

Spartacus was an inspiration for later revolutionaries, and books, music as well as a famous Stanley Kubrick film have been based on his story. One of Russia's most successful football clubs, FC Spartak Moscow, is named after him, as are numerous other sports teams.

# *c.* 1200 BC – 171 BC
# **The Epirots**
# The Original Pyrrhic Victory

*While Antiochus [ruler of the Seleucid empire] was at Chalcis ... Charops came to him as envoy on the part of the whole nation of Epirus.... The Epirots begged Antiochus not to drag them into a war with Rome, since their geographical position meant they would bear the brunt of any war.*

Livy, *The History of Rome* 36.5

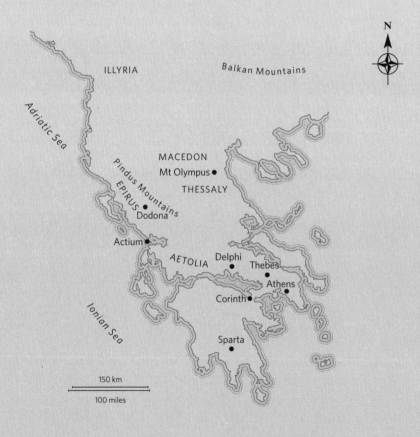

Few today have heard of the Epirots, but their victories are famous. That is because under King Pyrrhus, the men of the Epirot army fought a number of battles against the Romans. Each time they won, but at so high a cost that they might as well have been defeated. Even today a victory that costs more than it achieves is known as a 'Pyrrhic victory'.

So who were these people who challenged the Romans for the mastery of Italy? They came from the mainland of western Greece across the Adriatic Sea. In fact, the name of their land – Epirus – is derived from the local word meaning 'mainland', to differentiate it from the many islands off the coast.

The land of ancient Epirus is today divided between northwestern Greece and southern Albania. Due to prevailing winds, it receives substantial rainfall each year and would be one of the most fertile parts of Greece were it not for the fact that the rain falls almost entirely upon mountains. Apart from an agriculturally viable strip of coast, Epirus consists basically of a series of mountains, the Pindus range, running from north to south, which become increasingly precipitous further inland. (The Vikos Gorge in the Pindus mountains is perhaps the world's deepest, being only metres wide in some places and with a drop of almost a kilometre on each side.)

Consequently, the only result of the abundant rainfall for the Epirots was that their sheep were wetter than most, for the land was mostly suitable only for grazing animals with a good head for heights. Another effect of the landscape was that it could not support major cities, so rather than adopting the city-state system of their southern neighbours, the Epirots lived in scattered mountain communities.

## Warriors and oracles

Since for most Greeks the city-state (*polis*) was the only suitable habitation for civilized folk, they tended to look down upon the Epirots as barbarians. It is also true that the Epirots did not produce much in the way of great literature or epic poetry, and that fighting the mountains for every meal produced a nation of hardy warriors. Indeed, there is an opinion – held by some ethnologists both ancient and modern – that the Dorians who invaded southern Greece during the Bronze Age collapse originated in Epirus. If correct, this would make the most famed warriors in ancient Greece – the Spartans – descendants of the Epirots.

What is known for certain is that when record-keeping resumed after the dark age following the Bronze Age collapse, Epirus was inhabited by Greek-speaking tribes, the three main ones being Thesprotians, Chaonians and Molossians. Of these, the Molossians were the most important. Their royal family, the Aeacidae, claimed descent from the Greek hero Achilles. There is tenuous support for this in that Mycenaean-era ruins are relatively abundant in Epirus, so the Greeks of the Heroic Age were certainly familiar with the place.

The haunted canyons of the Pindus Mountains also held considerable religious significance for the Greeks. The Epirots regularly hosted visitors to the oracle of Zeus at Dodona, a site ancient enough to be mentioned by Homer in around 800 BC, and where one of the largest theatres in the ancient world was built in the Hellenistic era. It may be significant that during the Trojan War, Achilles – alleged father of the Epirot kings – prayed to 'Zeus at Dodona' to protect his companion Patroclus. Substantially rebuilt in the modern era, Dodona remains open to visitors, as it has been for thousands of years.

The theatre at Dodona was built to entertain the huge crowds who came to seek the wisdom of the oracle of Zeus.

Another important feature of the landscape of Epirus was the sinister River Acheron, the 'River of Woe'. The Acheron runs through 50 kilometres (30 miles) of southern Epirus, and, according to the ancient Greeks, one branch takes a downward turn and flows on through the kingdom of Hades, the land of the dead. Perhaps unsurprisingly, the Necromanteion, 'the Oracle of the Dead', was situated on the banks of the Acheron. Flocks of visitors came here hoping for answers from the Beyond – ordinary folk with questions about the family inheritance, or Greek tyrants seeking guidance on matters of state.

The Epirots were largely insulated from Greek affairs by sea and mountains, though because the mountain ranges ran from north to south, the Epirots also had the thankless job of insulating southern Greece from barbarian invaders from Illyria who used the mountain valleys as avenues of attack. In this the Epirots were like their eastern neighbours, the Macedonians, who also were involuntary defenders of Greece's northern borders, and who, like the Epirots, were casually dismissed by the southern Greeks as 'barbarians' for their efforts.

## The two Alexanders

Epirots and Macedonians both enjoyed their moment of supremacy at the same time, in the fourth century BC, when a Macedonian king, Philip II, married an Epirot princess called Olympias. The son of that marriage was Alexander the Great, the man who consolidated his father's subjugation of the southern Greeks and then led them on his wild eastern adventure that ended with the conquest of the Persian empire.

Meanwhile, the Epirots had united their fractured political entities into a single federation under the command of the Molossian kings, and while Alexander went east, the Epirots went west – with far less success. Alexander the Molossian, uncle of Alexander the Great, took his army to southern Italy, ostensibly to defend the Tarentines there against Roman aggression. (As the Epirots considered themselves ancestors of the Spartans, and Tarentum (Taranto) was a Spartan colony, there was a family connection.) Eventually the Epirot Alexander was killed in battle in 331 BC, but the Romans had not seen the last of the Epirots. They returned under the greatest of the Epirot kings, Pyrrhus (319–272 BC).

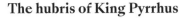

## The hubris of King Pyrrhus

Pyrrhus was a warrior king who pushed the Epirot boundaries to their largest extent, and in the process greatly enriched his nation. Many of the most impressive buildings at Dodona and elsewhere in Epirus were constructed in this period. However, glory was quickly followed by ruin. Pyrrhus attempted to convert his early military success into world domination. Starting with the conquest of Italy, his aim was then to defeat prosperous Sicily and later Carthage. With the west under Epirot rule, Pyrrhus would subsequently turn east and conquer the Hellenistic kingdoms of the Macedonians, Ptolemies and Seleucids.

This master plan hit a snag at the outset – the nascent republic of Rome already had a grip on most of Italy and was not going to let go without a fight. Since the Romans were numerically superior to the Epirots, they could weather defeat after defeat to fight Pyrrhus to a standstill. Eventually Pyrrhus was forced to return home to Greece. He died in a minor war while trying to take the city of Argos, his plans for world domination considerably diminished.

The Epirots after Pyrrhus fell on hard times – his military ambitions had financially exhausted the state just as they had once enriched it. The new power of the Aetolian League to the south in central Greece meant that Epirus was threatened by Greeks from that direction as well as by invaders from the north. Unable to stave off two threats at once, the Epirots saw their oracle at Dodona plundered by the Aetolians in 219 BC.

Worse was to come. By the turn of the century, the Romans had seen off the threat of the Carthagnian Hannibal's invasion of Italy and turned their malevolent attention eastwards. Rome's primary target was Macedon, because the Macedonians had allied with Hannibal in the recent war. The Epirots tried hard to steer a neutral course between the great powers, but the political stress tore their fragile federation apart. In the third Macedonian war which began in 171 BC, the Molossians sided with Macedon, while the other Epirot tribes took the Roman side.

Rome won the war, and Aemilius Paullus, the Roman general, proceeded to rip the heart out of Epirus by plundering the state and exporting almost the entire Molossian tribe – 150,000 men, women and children – back to Italy as slaves. Thereafter, Epirus was a subdued, peaceful and eventually prosperous province of the Roman

This bust of the Epirot king Pyrrhus was found at Herculaneum in a Roman villa. Pyrrhus' Roman foes came much closer to conquering the known world than he did.

empire. But the Epirots had largely lost their identity as a people, and while the land remains (and is one of the last undiscovered tourist treasures of modern Greece), the Epirots as a nation have vanished from history.

## Future Echoes

Epirus exported gold, silver and slaves, but for the Romans the most prized inhabitants of Epirus were not human but canine. Molossian hounds – an early version of the Rottweiler – were used by hunters, householders and shepherds. While relatively bad at herding sheep, Molossian hounds were very good at protecting shepherds. 'With them at your back, you never have to worry about midnight thieves, attacks by wolves, or ambushes by Spanish bandits', remarked the poet Virgil (*Georgics*, Book 3).

Although it was not the way Pyrrhus had planned it, Epirus – or rather the waters off its coast – was the stage for a pivotal battle for world domination in 31 BC. The venue was the promontory of Actium. The event was the showdown between the heir of Julius Caesar, a young man called Octavian, and the combined forces of Mark Antony and Cleopatra of Egypt. At stake was control of the Roman empire. After an uncertain start, Octavian's admiral Agrippa routed the enemy, Octavian became the emperor Augustus, and the rest, as they say, is history.

A Roman copy of a Hellenistic original of a ferocious Molossian hound, now in the British Museum, London.

# *c.* 900 BC – 290 BC
# **The Sabines**
# Co-founders of Rome?

*Some thought it intolerable that the Sabines,
after getting a share in the city and its territory,
should insist on ruling those who had granted them
such privileges. Yet the Sabines ... felt they could
reasonably demand the ruler [of Rome] should be
one of them. They ... argued that their contribution
had added to the number of the people so that
[Rome] could properly be called a city.*

Plutarch, *Life of Numa* 2

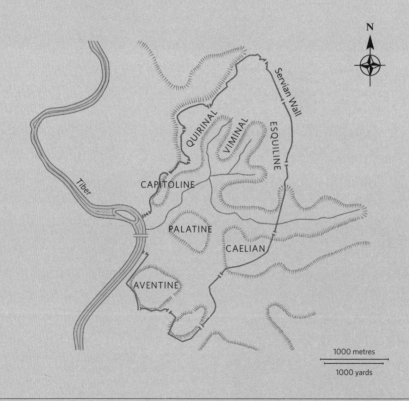

Without a doubt, the Romans were the most influential people and culture in the history of Europe. Yet Rome might not even have registered in the history books without the contribution of another, almost forgotten tribe – the Sabines.

## Foundation or evolution?

What happened in the early years of the city of Rome is one of the most fiercely debated topics in Classical history. Essentially there are two schools of thought. The first believes that Rome grew organically as a hilltop fortification on the Palatine Hill. As 'Rome' expanded, the hamlet's inhabitants became ever closer to the villagers on the adjacent Viminal Hill, who were members of the Sabine tribe. Despite the fact that the proto-Romans were a different people, the two groups got along well. (The Romans were of Latin stock, whereas the Sabines spoke another Italic dialect called Oscan.) Trading between the two hamlets took place in the valley between the two hills, in what became the Roman forum.

In time Rome was ever more successful, as the settlement lay at the nexus of not one but two trade routes. Rome was at the 'head of navigation' on the River Tiber – the furthest point that a seafaring ship could reach upriver. And the second nexus, the Via Salaria, was an ancient (even then) road which transported salt from the salt flats at Ostia to the mountains of the Italian interior. Since Rome sat at the first point that the Tiber could be bridged, this gave the city control of this vital trading route.

With success came expansion, and with expansion the Sabine settlers on the Viminal were gradually folded into the new city. By the time the historical record becomes trustworthy, Latins and Sabines were a single people – the Romans.

This is pure poppycock, says the second traditional school of thought. The idea that cities in the ancient world grew organically is a myth, perpetuated by western historians who base their theory on the manner in which towns grew in Britain and the United States. The archaic world around the Mediterranean was a different and more violent place. Cities there were founded by groups of well-armed

An eighteenth-century engraving schematically showing the ancient city of Rome. The Romans were on the Palatine (A) and the Capitoline (B), and the Sabines on the Viminal (H) and Esquiline (L).

The Rape of the Sabine Women was frequently depicted in art, here by Baldassare Peruzzi in 1496 on a wooden panel now in the Prado Museum, Madrid.

settlers who imposed themselves on the landscape, whether the locals liked it or not. Any hamlet growing organically would have lasted precisely up to the point at which its size made it profitable to be raided. The Etruscan inhabitants of the city of Veii nearby, for example, would have cheerfully sacked Rome for pleasure and profit.

In this view, Rome survived because it had strong walls from the beginning, which is exactly why, in legend, when Romulus founded the city his very first act was to build a wall. This is what the founders of Tarentum did, too, as did the founders of Syracuse, Naples and every other contemporary Italian city worth mentioning. It is how ancient cities were established. Rome was no different.

## The Rape of the Sabines

If the second school of thought is correct, then the Sabines as the local people would have been both startled and somewhat offended when a large number of Latin settlers arrived and soon converted the Palatine Hill into a substantial fortified town. And Roman tradition rather agrees with this version of events. The story adds the extra information that the Latin settlers were not prime citizen material, but whatever human odds and ends the city founders had been able to muster in their effort to create a population of colonists. They included criminals on the run, escaped slaves and retired mercenaries.

Unsurprisingly, most of these had been unable to find wives to accompany them, so the city of Rome faced the prospect of perishing within a generation – a prospect its unhappy Sabine neighbours faced with equanimity and were disinclined to remedy by providing their daughters in marriage. The Roman solution was to hold a celebration allegedly aimed at reconciling the Sabines to their presence. In the space between the Sabine and Roman settlements, games, feasting and dances took place – until the moment when, at a prearranged signal, the Romans seized every nubile woman present and dragged their victims back to Rome.

This was the infamous 'Rape of the Sabine Women'. It should be noted that in the ancient world 'rape' meant capture and carrying off rather than sexual assault (from the Latin *raptus* from which we also get 'rapture' and the 'raptor' birds of prey). The women thus became the unwilling brides of their Roman abductors, and horrific as this is, abducting brides had a long tradition in the ancient world. (Indeed, one of the reasons a bride traditionally stands on the left of the groom in a modern wedding ceremony is so that the husband has his sword arm free to fight off outraged relatives opposed to the marriage.)

The parents of the Sabine women certainly were outraged, and hostilities promptly commenced. According to legend, it was the Sabine women themselves who brought an end to the fighting. They pointed out that their marriages were an accomplished fact and they now had children as a result. All their parents could reasonably do was to sort out the matter of outstanding dowry payments. Reluctantly, the Sabines agreed. Since Rome now consisted mostly of their sons-in-law and grandchildren, a closer relationship was impossible to avoid.

## A union of peoples

At this point gradualists and traditionalists are in agreement. The local Sabines and the Romans merged into a single people. This was not the end of the Sabines, however, because while the Romans populated a single town, the Sabines as a tribe occupied a considerable tract of land east of the Anio and Tiber rivers. Most of what we know of the non-Roman Sabines comes from later tradition, though this is not completely trustworthy.

For example, some Romans floated the romantic idea that the Sabines were descended from early Spartans who had defected from Greece following a civic disagreement. This is flagrant invention, as the Sabines seem to have shared the same language and culture as other Italic hill peoples. More probably the Sabines were related to another Italic people called the Samnites, with whom the Romans were to feud bitterly for centuries. Like many other hill peoples, the Sabines from necessity embraced a lifestyle of frugality and simplicity, which may have been what evoked the Spartan connection.

The Romano-Sabines quickly became the equals of the Latin settlers, a fact reflected by the tradition that the second king of Rome, Numa Pompilius (traditionally 715–653 BC), was a Sabine. While Romulus was a warrior-king, it was the Sabine Numa who is credited with setting up many of the laws and traditions which endured through the later centuries.

Another early Sabine of note is an aristocrat called Attus Clausus. Originally belonging to one of the many Sabine groups living outside Rome, after a falling out with the local townspeople Clausus packed up his entire household and possessions and moved to Rome. In this way Attus Clausus founded the first of the great Roman families – their name was Latinized to become Appius Claudius.

## Sabine ancestors

For the next half a millennium the Claudii exasperated the Romans with their aristocratic arrogance, and at the same time drew reluctant admiration for their leadership in Rome's many wars. The Claudian family provided Rome with the emperors Tiberius,

Claudius and Nero before internecine family politics killed off the clan. (Nero alone stands accused of murdering his mother, adoptive father, wife, unborn child and step-brother.)

Another proud Sabine of the late Republic was Quintus Sertorius (*c.* 123–72 BC), a rebel general who held Spain almost as a private fiefdom for nearly a decade while fighting off a succession of Roman armies. In doing so, Sertorius probably felt some kinship with his ancestors from the Sabine mountain town of Nursia (in modern Umbria). These Sabines were among the many who did not get along with their Roman relatives. Between 504 BC and 468 BC Romans and Sabines clashed repeatedly, with the Sabines generally coming second to the more numerous and better-equipped Romans. The last recorded clash between Romans and independent Sabines was as late as 290 BC, when the Sabines and their Samnite relatives made a last attempt to withstand the Roman juggernaut.

Later Romans regarded Sabine ancestry as a point of pride. (Certainly it would seem preferable to descent from robbers or escaped slaves.) Several Roman clans went so far as to regularly use the suffix (cognomen) 'Sabinus' as part of the family name. An example is the first-century AD customs officer called Titus Flavius Sabinus, who is better known as the father of the Roman emperor Vespasian.

## Future Echoes

The Rape of the Sabine Women and the aftermath of that atrocity have been depicted numerous times in sculpture and painting, including by Giambologna, Nicolas Poussin and Jacques-Louis David, with a more recent rendering by Picasso. The incident was also memorably adapted into the 1954 musical film *Seven Brides for Seven Brothers*.

Many modern married couples have also unknowingly re-enacted part of it. The tradition of carrying the bride across the threshold of the marital home derives from the Romans, who according to Plutarch (*Life of Romulus* 15) did this in acknowledgment of the fact that the first brides in their city did not come willingly.

A dramatic rendering of the abduction of a Sabine woman by the Flemish artist Giambologna, 1582, which can be seen in Florence.

# *c.* 1100 BC – today
# **The Samaritans**
## Survivors of Antiquity

*A man was going from Jerusalem to Jericho,
when he was attacked by robbers. They stripped
him of his clothes, beat him ... leaving him half
dead. A priest happened to be going down the
same road, and when he saw the man, he passed
by on the other side. So too, a Levite....*

*But a Samaritan traveller came upon the
man and when he saw him, he took
pity on him. He went to him and
bandaged his wounds, pouring
on oil and wine. Then he put
the man on his own donkey,
brought him to an inn and
took care of him.*

Luke, 10:30

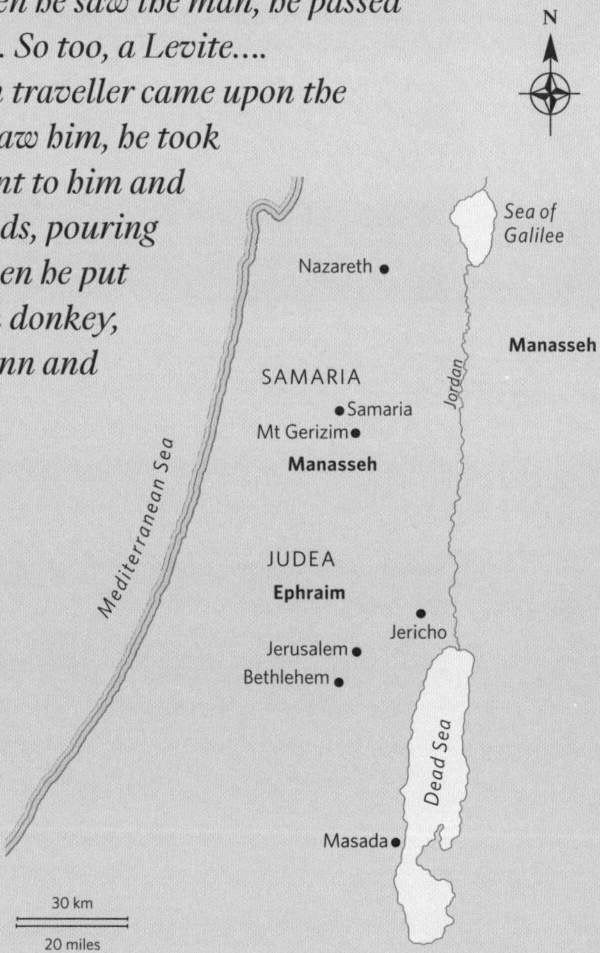

N

Sea of
Galilee

Nazareth •

Manasseh

SAMARIA
• Samaria
Mt Gerizim•

**Manasseh**

Jordan

Mediterranean Sea

JUDEA
**Ephraim**

Jericho
•

Jerusalem•
Bethlehem •

Dead Sea

Masada•

30 km

20 miles

In the parable told by Jesus, a priest and a Levite passed by the injured man. The Levites were a tribe descended from the High Priest Aaron, so this man's avoidance of the injured man is as shocking as the conduct of the priest. (In their defence, there were religious strictures about these individuals approaching a naked man.)

The Samaritan, on the other hand, could easily have passed by the wounded man and no one would have condemned him. In fact, Jews and Samaritans got along so badly that Jews travelling north would often take a very extensive detour to avoid passing through the lands of the Samaritans. So what the parable tells us is that the deeply felt differences between Jews and Samaritans should be overridden by their shared humanity.

From the Jewish perspective, the problem with the Samaritans was that they were not Jews, but neither were they Gentiles. They were somewhere in between – sharing many Jewish beliefs, but in a different way, and celebrating similar religious festivals, but at different times.

Both peoples were monotheists and worshipped the same god. Yet the Jews of the time felt that the best – perhaps the only – place to do this was the temple in Jerusalem. For the Samaritans, their most sacred place was Mount Gerizim, in the Samarian heartland (where Samaritans still go to pray today). Likewise, while the Samaritans scrupulously followed the first five books of the Torah, the Hebrew Bible, the rest they rejected as not being authentic scripture. In short, the disagreements between Samaritans and Jews was something of a family feud – and no feuds can become quite so bitter.

The root of the problem began around 1000 BC after the separation of the land of Israel into the northern kingdom (with its capital at Samaria) and the kingdom of Judah in the south. The Samaritans claim that they are descended from the tribes of Israel in the north, namely those of Ephraim and Manasseh, and that their lineage can be traced back through the High Priest Aaron all the way to Adam, the first of men.

The one Samaritan that most people have heard of has his good deed commemorated in this stained glass window in a church in Northamptonshire, England.

## Surviving the Assyrians

The Israelites of the time disagreed. According to them, their ancestors in the northern kingdom had been scooped up by the Assyrian conquest and forced into exile in the eighth century BC, and the Samaritans were basically descended from miscellaneous vagrant peoples who had drifted, or had been moved, in thereafter. Support for this argument came from the Assyrians, with one of their texts (the so-called Nimrud Slab of 797 BC) claiming that the former people of the northern kingdom were 'settled among the Assyrians', while people from other conquered lands were moved into the now unoccupied territories.

The Samaritans (then and today) refute this and uphold their claim that they have been in the land all along. Some scholars argue that there is a middle way. It is very hard for even the most conscientious officials to extract every last person from a country that a people know well and do not want to leave. It is possible that large numbers of Samaritans remained after the forced Assyrian deportations, and others may have found their way back. Newcomers moving into a land where a substantial Samaritan population remained found it easiest to adopt Samaritan ways. This hypothesis would also explain the Jewish tradition that the Assyrians sent priests to teach the people living in Samaritan lands the proper way to behave.

## Surviving the Persians

Over the following centuries the Jews and Samaritans adopted an attitude of mutual disdain, with neither wanting to have anything to do with the other. This is despite the fact that in belief and culture they were much closer to one another than to any of the other peoples living nearby.

In 539 BC the area came under the domination of the Persians. The Persians had been helped in their rise to power by displaced peoples whom they had promised to restore to their homelands, and this was certainly honoured in the case of the Jews who had been exiled to the rivers of Babylon. (Though by this time the Lost Tribes of Israel had been gone too long to be recovered.) Some Samaritans certainly returned. The Talmud (rabbinic commentary) gives these returnees the name of 'Kuthim' after the land of 'Kuth' to which the Samaritans had been exiled and where they had doubtless picked up a number of foreign traits. The Persians were generally tolerant rulers, and during the era of their domination the Samaritans were free to feud with the Jews, and the two peoples grew ever further apart.

The sacred site of Mount Gerizim in Samaritan tradition is the oldest mountain, located at the centre of the world. Samaritans believe that it was here that Abraham was on the verge of sacrificing his son Isaac.

## Surviving the Greeks

After the conquest by Alexander the Great and his death in the late fourth century BC, Samaria became part of the Seleucid empire under its Hellenistic rulers. Rather like their Jewish relatives, the major problem for the Samaritans with their new situation was that Greek culture was very attractive to some. There was a strong temptation to abandon the puritanical strictures of a deeply religious society in favour of gymnasia, theatres and a varied choice of possible religions and cults.

Among the Jews the enticements of Hellenism caused a religious backlash. And Jewish reactions to those members of their society whom they saw as dissolute in turn angered the Seleucid rulers. As the Seleucid kings tried to punish Jewish religious obduracy, the Jews responded with armed rebellion under the Maccabees. It appears that the Samaritans tried hard not to make this a three-cornered fight, and as usual with those who attempt to stay out of a fight, both parties in the argument accused them of siding with their opponents. In his *Antiquities of the Jews* (12.5) the historian Josephus has the Samaritans writing to the Seleucid authorities, saying 'We beg you ... to leave us in peace and not to hold us responsible for what you claim the Jews have done. We are a different nation with different customs.'

## Surviving the Romans

Under the Roman empire, the main challenge for the Samaritans lay initially in persuading the Romans that they were not related to the Jews, who displayed their usual recalcitrant attitude to foreign conquerors. Nevertheless, Samaria became part of the province of Judea, and the people suffered through the two major Jewish uprisings of AD 66–70 and AD 131–35.

Christianity was an issue for both Jews and Samaritans. The early church considered the conversion of the Samaritans as a halfway house between the mission to the Jews and the mission to the Gentiles. The apostles Peter and John paid a special visit to the region, according to Acts 8:14–17. Yet somehow Samaria and its idiosyncratic religion managed to flourish under Roman rule, and well into the Byzantine era.

## Surviving still

Unlike the Romans, the Byzantine empire which continued after the fall of Rome was both Christian and intolerant. The usually peaceable Samaritans objected so strongly to Christian interference with their religious practices that in AD 484 the emperor Zeno had personally to quell unrest in the area.

Then in AD 529 the Samaritans made the fatal error of rebelling in an attempt to set up their own independent state. Until this point they had enjoyed some of the same sort of protection as the Jews as worshippers of a religion which was a precursor to Christianity. Rebellion gave the authorities reason to strip away those protections and the Samaritan population was more than decimated in the subsequent purges. It is always hard to put a number on ancient populations, but it is probable that fewer than 100,000 Samaritans were left at the end of the Byzantine era.

The Samaritans lived on beyond antiquity, though very few in number, and are still extant as a people even now. They are rightly described as 'forgotten', however, since very few today know that the Samaritans stubbornly continue to exist. This is despite time under Islamic rule, which fluctuated between tolerance and savage persecution, and the stresses of the modern era, when politics have certainly not become simpler. Around 700 Samaritans remain – an improvement from the 1920s when there were just 100 Samaritans.

## Future Echoes

Today when most people think of the Samaritans, it is not of a small community living in the Middle East, but an organization founded in Britain in 1953 with the intention of helping in confidentiality those in distress or contemplating suicide. The name of the organization was derived from the good Samaritan of the Bible.

This parable from the New Testament is another that has attracted many artists over the centuries, including Rembrandt and Eugène Delacroix. Delacroix painted two versions of the subject, one of which was copied and modified, including reversing the motif, by Vincent van Gogh in 1890 when he was in the asylum in Saint-Rémy in Provence, France.

Samaritans still worship at Mount Gerizim, though there are now only around 700 Samaritans remaining.

# 1100 BC–AD 700 and 202 BC – 40 BC
# The Garamantes and Numidians
## Forgotten Peoples of North Africa

*The swarthy Garamantes leave their tropic home;*
*They, whose horses are free of bit or saddle,*
*Yet obey the guiding whip in the rider's hand.*
*The hunter, his home a fragile hut*
*Goes roaming far, and should his spear not hit the mark*
*With his flowing robe, he binds the angry lion.*

Lucan, *Pharsalia* 4.770ff.

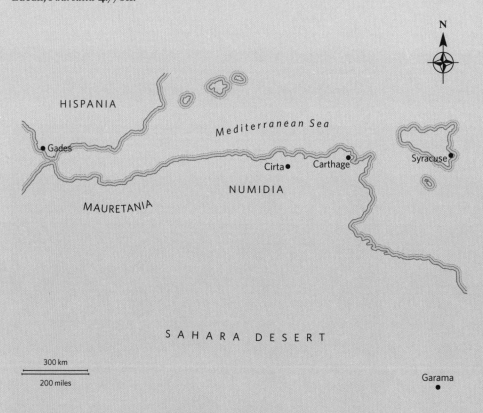

The Sahara was not always a desert. Many thousands of years ago, part of it was a savannah through which substantial rivers rolled to the Atlantic Ocean. Then, for reasons which science does not fully understand, the Sahara began to dry out, turning slowly into the parched land that it has become today. Yet even three thousand years ago the desert had advanced nowhere near as far as it has now. On its northern edge lived Berber peoples, farmers, nomads and hunters, unaware that climate change was already slowly destroying their lands and their culture even before the Romans came from the north. The Romans extinguished Berber Numidia as an organized state, but the Berber Garamantes to the south and east endured. They outlasted the Roman empire, though in the end the desert was the victor.

## The Garamantes

When the first Greek and Phoenician explorers reached the coast of North Africa, the Garamantes were already there. By 1000 BC they were the dominant population in the Fezzan. Today this is a rocky and sparsely inhabited land in southern Libya, yet when the Garamantes moved there it was fertile enough for agriculture and the herding of cattle. Greek and Roman sources tell us that the native diet consisted of figs, grapes, wheat and barley. To the north of the land of the Garamantes lay a long, narrow tract of dry land which was the only place on earth where silphium grew, a plant eagerly sought by the Greeks and later the Romans for its medicinal and culinary properties (it was extinct by the end of the first century AD).

Protected by mountains to the north and the expanding desert to the south, the early Garamantes enjoyed a peaceful agrarian existence. According to Herodotus, their main enemies were a cave-dwelling people called the Troglodytes, whom they hunted with spears from chariots. The colonization of northern Libya by Greeks certainly caused the Garamantes little distress. Instead they broadened their activities to include mining (mostly of a green semi-precious stone called amazonite, found in the southern mountains of their territory) and trade.

The Garamantes quickly established themselves as the middlemen in goods passing between the trans-Sahara region and the Mediterranean world, and traded with peoples to the south for gold, ivory and slaves. (Ivory was also available from the North African elephant, a smaller and more tractable beast than the sub-Saharan elephant. As with the Garamantes, climate change has made the species extinct.)

The ruins of Garama in Libya are today set in an arid wasteland, yet in its prime the city was surrounded by lush farmland.

Few literary traces have been left by the Garamantes of their society, and most of what archaeologists have found is in an as yet indecipherable proto-Berber script. We also know little of their religion, though according to the first-century AD Roman writer Silius Italicus, the Garamantes consulted their gods in 'prophetic groves' (*Punica* 1.393). The same author names the main deity of the Garamantes as Ammon, perhaps conflating him with Ra-amon (or Amun), the principal god of Egypt.

While not especially warlike, the Garamantes were ready enough to join in the quarrels of their neighbours, and later to fight off the encroachments of the Roman empire. Even in the first century AD the Roman Pliny (the Elder) remarked with some disgust that it was impossible to travel to the land of the Garamantes, as that people had blocked access by systematically filling in the wells which once provided water for travellers.

By this point the Garamantes had begun to urbanize, and we know of at least six substantial Garamantine settlements. The largest of these was Garama, which now lies abandoned deep in the Sahara desert of southern Libya. An estimated 10,000 people lived in or around this city. The locals supplemented their income by raiding into the more settled Roman provinces to the north, until in AD 203 the exasperated Roman emperor Septimius Severus came south with a punitive force. It is believed that he captured Garama, but the length of supply lines would have made it impossible to hold the city, and eventually the Romans withdrew.

By the end of the Roman era the Garamantes had developed a sophisticated irrigation system which helped to cope with ever-decreasing rainfall. This eventually became a network of tunnels extending thousands of kilometres. Nevertheless, year by year the water level in the wells and aquifers dropped until finally life in their homeland became unsustainable and the Garamantes dispersed as a people. By AD 700 they have vanished from the historical record.

## The Numidians

> The younger generation (of Persians in Africa) under the name of Numidians ... took possession of the region next to Carthage, which is called Numidia.... Finally, the greater part of northern Africa fell into the hands of the Numidians, and all the vanquished were merged in the race and name of their rule.
>
> Sallust, *Jugurtha* 17.11

The first-century AD Roman writer Sallust is certainly wrong in his wild guess about the origins of the Numidians, who once occupied an area of North Africa somewhat larger than Italy. He thought that they were descended from the Persian remnants of an army raised by Heracles in the Middle East which ended up in Africa. Modern ethnologists also query a once accepted origin of the name of Numidia. It was believed to have been derived from the Greek for nomads, which was then corrupted by the Romans in their description of this North African people. In fact the name may have had its roots in one of the languages of the people who came together to become the Numidian nation.

The catalyst that formed this nation was the city of Carthage. The people themselves had always been around, but as a medley of semi-nomadic desert tribes living in autonomous bands which felt little loyalty or kinship towards one another. However, the Carthaginians preferred to deal with their neighbours as a single group (it is hard to negotiate with dozens of tribes individually) and their patient diplomacy as much as anything else helped to create two rough tribal confederations by around 200 BC. These were the eastern Massylii and the western Masaesyli. Between them, these two formed a nation that occupied most of modern Algeria, and spilled over into Mauritania in the west and Tunisia in the east.

Political 'unification' meant little more than the fact that disputes over grazing rights and the harvest at various oases were now resolved by a chieftain/king rather than through feuding as previously. Such quarrels had been the stimulus which trained

Numidian horsemen were considered by the Romans to be the finest light cavalry in the known world.

Numidian men to become superb horse riders. In fact the Romans, whose cavalry the Hellenistic Greek historian Polybius generally despised, were quick to adopt what they could of Numidian tactics, though they found it difficult to imitate the Numidians' skills, which made them arguably the finest light cavalry in the known world.

The Numidians as a nation were caught in the crossfire of Rome's wars with Carthage (264–241 BC and 218–201 BC). Towards the end of the third century BC the clash between these two powers had moved to the African mainland, and both Romans and Carthaginians lobbied hard for Numidian support. Originally the Numidians supported Carthage, with whom they had traded and served as mercenaries. Then the young king of the Massylii, a man called Masinissa, switched his allegiance to the Romans.

This proved a shrewd move. Because the Masaesyli adhered to their Carthaginian alliance too long, the victorious Romans made Masinissa supreme king of Numidia. He ruled for almost half a century as a loyal ally of Rome. Under his leadership the Numidians settled down in towns, the state developed a limited coinage, and trade – especially exports of olive oil – flourished through the Romano-Numidian port of Cirta (in modern Algeria), which became the kingdom's *de facto* capital.

'His greatest and most divine achievement was this: Numidia had been before his time universally unproductive, and was looked upon as incapable of producing any cultivated fruits. He was the first and only man who showed that it could produce cultivated fruits just as well as any other country.' So wrote Polybius (*The Histories* 38), who may have met Masinissa personally.

Even after the death of Masinissa all was going swimmingly until Jugurtha came to the Numidian throne in 118 BC. He achieved this by bribing and flattering the most corrupt members of what was then a very corrupt senate in Rome, and by murdering rivals wherever he could find them. Indeed, after one particularly egregious case of bribery, Jugurtha was summoned to Rome to testify about his activities. He took advantage of the immunity he was offered to kill another rival who was sheltering with the Romans. When ejected from Rome afterwards, Jugurtha remarked contemptuously 'The whole city is doomed, if it can only find a buyer.'

However, Jugurtha had overreached himself on this occasion, and the Romans attacked his kingdom. The Jugurthine War (112-105 BC) was initially marked by the incompetence and corruption of the

Roman generals, but eventually Rome prevailed. Jugurtha was captured and executed, and Numidia lost much of its western territory to Rome's client state of Mauretania.

After the civil war that brought Caesar to power, the Numidian state was partitioned between Mauretania and the Roman province of Africa. A king called Arabio tried to revive the Numidian kingdom in 44 BC after Caesar's assassination. He managed to rule for four years, but was eventually killed during the struggle between Caesar's would-be successors. Thereafter, Numidia ceased to exist as a nation, though as members of the Roman empire, the Numidians achieved considerable prosperity.

## Future Echoes

Sophonisba was a Carthaginian princess who was married to a Numidian king in a diplomatic alliance. When Carthage was defeated by Rome, Sophonisba faced the prospect of being displayed in a Roman triumph. Preferring death to indignity, the princess poisoned herself. This heroism caught the attention of later eras, and Sophonisba has been the topic of numerous tragedies, plays, paintings and operas. Those who have taken Sophonisba as a theme include the composer Henry Purcell, the artists Rembrandt, Guercino and Mattia Preti, while Voltaire wrote a play on the subject.

Sophonisba takes a cup of poison, preferring death to capture by the Romans, as depicted in a painting by Mattia Preti of 1670.

# *c.* 500 BC – AD 529
# **The Sarmatians**
## Horse Riders of the Steppe

*In Europe there is a Scythian race, called the Sarmatians*
*... different from all other peoples. Their women ride*
*on horseback, use the bow and throw the javelin.*
*They can fight in war as long as they are virgins, and*
*they stay virgins until they kill three of their enemies....*
*Whoever takes to herself a husband gives up riding on*
*horseback unless she has to join a general expedition.*

Hippocrates, *About Airs, Waters and Places* 17

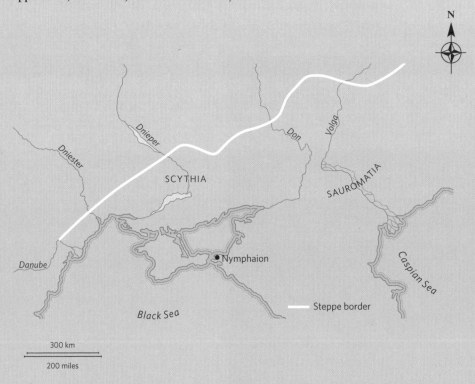

Few ancient peoples had female warriors – not because of sexism but because childbirth was already dangerous enough. A handful of male survivors from a catastrophic battle might be able to repopulate their tribe, but a people that lost too many women was itself lost. In the ancient world it was a struggle for most populations to grow, even without losing females in battle.

Hence the astonishment at the female Sarmatian warriors. Not a few scholars have noted that the Sarmatians occupied steppe land to the north of the Black Sea, in what is now Ukraine and southern Russia, which was the legendary home of the Amazons, and so have wondered if it was Sarmatian women who gave rise to the myth.

## Horsemen and fire-worshippers

The Sarmatians arrived in this region at some time between 500 and 200 BC. The difference of three centuries in estimates is the result of an academic debate as to whether the 'Sauromatians' of 500 BC are the same as the Sarmatians of later eras. In both cases the Sauro-sarmatians were of Iranian stock, tall (in the ancient world anything near 2 m or 6 ft counted as tall) and red-haired – though one source describes members of one Sarmatian tribe, the Alans, as more blond than the others. Apart from the Alans, the other major Sarmatian tribes were the Iazyges and the Roxolani. The men of all tribes favoured long, flowing beards.

Amazons, one on horseback, battle against Greeks in a frieze from the Mausoleum of Halicarnassus. Even the proudly chauvinistic Greek males respected the Amazonian warrior ethos.

The Sarmatians were superb horsemen. They needed to be to displace the Scythians, to whom they were related, who already lived in this area and were very good on horseback themselves. The usual Scythian technique for dealing with invaders was to take advantage of the open steppe country. In battle they would stay on their horses and fall back before attackers while peppering them with arrows. Eventually the enemy would tire of chasing round in circles after an enemy who kept inflicting casualties without ever closing into 'proper' combat. The Sarmatians solved the problem by also fighting on horseback and charging into close contact, where they could inflict casualties with the 4-m (13-ft) long lances which became their signature weapon.

Like many Iranian peoples the Sarmatians seem to have been fire-worshippers. 'Seem' because the Sarmatians did not leave any written record, and the nature of their religion is obscure. Stone bowls may have served as portable altars, for another distinguishing mark of the Sarmatians is that they had no fixed temples or altars. At the most simple, a Sarmatian place of worship was created by a sword thrust point-first into the ground, as described by the late fourth-century AD soldier and historian Ammianus Marcellinus (31.2).

The Sarmatians buried their dead, probably regarding cremation as defiling the purity of flame, in accordance with their beliefs as fire-worshippers. Chalk laid under the corpses suggests an attempt also to insulate the body from the earth itself. Horses, cattle and even humans (probably slaves or servants) were sacrificed and buried alongside a deceased aristocrat. The graves have been found in clusters, each generation of burial mound lying slightly further from the most ancient ones in the centre.

These burial mounds have yielded a rich treasure for archaeologists and grave robbers alike. Sarmatian weaponry was both simpler and more elegant than that of their Scythian cousins, and the Sarmatians had a fondness for semi-precious stones

As a people who lived on horseback, it is not surprising that Sarmatians produced elaborate horse trappings such as this pommel and roundel.

Sarmatians in their distinctive scale armour on Trajan's Column. Their steel lances were later stripped from the sculpture for the metal.

which they often worked into their weapons, for example in sword pommels. Gold jewellery, cups and plaques found in tombs reveal the Sarmatian appreciation of fine metalwork.

Ornate armour has also been discovered, for the Sarmatians were among the first armoured knights in history. Legend has it that their warriors kept the hooves of every horse they ever owned. Eventually these hooves were split and used to fabricate armour, 'each piece smoothly overlapping on the body like the scales of a python'.

## Greek and Roman foes

The Greeks were well aware of Sarmatian military prowess, and generally kept well clear. (A hoplite on foot can do little against a cavalryman who does not want to be caught, while the Sarmatians would demolish Greek cavalrymen without breaking their stride.) In situations where the Sarmatians and Greeks did come into violent contact it was the Greeks who gave ground, and this led to the development of some permanent Sarmatian settlements in former Greek territory in what is today the northern Crimea.

The full extent of Sarmatian territory at its greatest is still uncertain, for their lands ultimately reached far beyond the ken of Mediterranean-based civilizations, from the plains of what is now

Ukraine to the borders of modern Poland. To the south, especially along the eastern Danube, the Sarmatians were a troubling presence even for peoples protected by the formidable power of the Roman legions.

One of those legions, Legio XXI Rapax, found out about the Sarmatians the hard way. Sent to the province of Pannonia (on the lower Danube) in AD 92 to forestall a barbarian attack, the legion was instead wiped out by the Sarmatians. This led to the emperor Domitian himself taking the field (and to the poet Martial offering up prayers that the emperor's breastplate would be up to the challenges it was about to face).

Domitian's campaign proved inconclusive. The Sarmatians remained a steadily escalating threat that culminated almost a century later in AD 174 in a series of clashes intense enough to count as a war during the reign of the emperor Marcus Aurelius. In this conflict both the Romans and Sarmatians could claim victories, but both also realized that they were mainly weakening each other to the benefit of their many enemies elsewhere. A peace treaty was therefore arranged, with several novel features, including an agreement that neither side would approach within a day's march of the other. The Sarmatians also released their Roman captives – an estimated 100,000 of them – which shows that their war had not been without success.

Apart from occasional clashes, the treaty by and large held until the fourth century AD, when the Sarmatians fell out with the emperor Constantine. A large raid westwards across the Danube was thrown back, and the Sarmatian king was killed. This is the first indication we have that the Sarmatian confederacy had become a single kingdom. Contact with the Romans had also led to the Sarmatians becoming somewhat more patriarchal. Female warriors no longer joined their brothers in battle, but the Romans continued to sneer at the Sarmatians for being 'dominated by their women', which suggests that Sarmatian women still enjoyed more rights than their equivalents in the Roman world.

In late antiquity Romans and Sarmatians were forced to collaborate in a vain attempt to defend themselves against the waves of migratory tribes from the east, which were eventually to overwhelm them. Both peoples helped to build and garrison the *Limes Sarmatiae* – a line of fortifications which was moderately successful in holding back the Goths, but which crumpled when it was hit by Attila and his Huns. This forced yet another realignment, and the year AD 378 saw an alliance of Goths and Sarmatians meet with temporary success against these new invaders.

The continual pressure of fighting back waves of invaders eventually broke the Sarmatians as a people. They went down under yet another wave of migrating humanity, the Ostrogoths, and the survivors were then forced westwards. The last remnants of the Sarmatians are reported in what is now Lombardy in Italy, and after 529 they vanish from the record entirely.

## Future Echoes

In the peace treaty between Marcus Aurelius and the Sarmatians it was agreed that both sides would keep a distance of a day's march from each other. The land that lay between the Roman and Sarmatian domains formed the world's first demilitarized zone.

The Sarmatians also provided the Romans with some 8,000 cavalrymen. Most of these were stationed in Britain as the *ala prima Sarmatarum*. When these Sarmatians retired, they did not return to their homelands and have left gravestones and descendants around northern Britain. The Sarmatians were still in Britain when the island fell to Germanic invaders in the later fifth century. Many have noted the connection between armoured Sarmatians and the knights of King Arthur, and legends from the former Sarmatian heartlands have many points in common with Arthurian myth.

This ceremonial helmet from Ribchester, Britain, probably belonged to the *ala prima Sarmartarum* (First Sarmatian Cavalry) unit which was stationed there.

# *c.* 550 BC – AD 600
# **The Nabataeans**
# The People of Petra

*But from the rock as if by magic grown, eternal,*
*  silent, beautiful, alone!*
*Not virgin-white like that old Doric shrine,*
*  where erst Athena held her rites divine ...*
*The hues of youth upon a brow of woe, which*
*  Man deemed old two thousand years ago,*
*Match me such marvel save in Eastern clime,*
*  a rose-red city, half as old as time.*

John William Burgon, 'Petra' (1845)

The last line quoted opposite sums up all that most people have heard about the Nabataeans. Petra, the beautiful, now abandoned, rock-carved city was but one of that people's settlements in the bitterly hostile desert in the lands between the Arabian Peninsula and the fields of Syria and Judea.

However, 'half as old as time' certainly qualifies as poetic hyperbole, as it seems the first Nabataeans moved into the area only around 550 BC. Their arrival might be connected with the fact that shortly before, the Assyrians report having put down a rebellion by an Arabic tribe called the 'Nabatu'. Given that the Assyrian response to rebellion usually included flaying the leaders alive and impaling most of the remaining population on stakes, the deep desert may well have appeared an attractive alternative.

Even once the Nabataeans had taken up residence in the territory which is now in the southern part of the kingdom of Jordan, they did not immediately start building. For several centuries the Nabataeans were simply another minor tribe of desert nomads, shifting their herds between the few patches of vegetation that could be found in the wilderness.

A sculpture found in the Nabataean Temple of the Winged Lions, bearing the inscription 'Goddess of Hayyan son of Nybat'. Hayyan is believed to be the Nabataean equivalent of Aphrodite/Venus.

## Building a kingdom

Yet eventually the skill and ingenuity which were later to become a Nabataean trademark began to make themselves apparent. The Nabataeans developed techniques that enabled them to grow crops, usually of fruit, in a country where the rainy season might consist of three thunderstorms and a shower. Elaborate irrigation systems channelled water falling over a wide area to one stand of trees, or even a single fruit tree. With the greater population that resulted from more available food, the Nabataeans were able to displace other tribes from the local oases.

At this time these oases were vital links across the desert through which ran the only southern land route from Syria to India and beyond. Therefore, once they had control of the oases, the Nabataeans had control of a significant and highly lucrative trade route. By 400 BC the Nabataeans were as renowned as traders as they were as farmers, and as farmers their reputation was considerable. The few tracts of arable land in Nabataean territory were some of the most intensively cultivated in the known world, and a network of dams and canals extended that land beyond the limits of what might have seemed possible.

By this time the Nabataeans also lived in permanent settlements. The largest of these was known to the Greeks as Petra, a name which simply means 'rock'. Before the third century BC, this probably was a fortress of last resort to which the local Nabataeans would flee. One of the region's few perennial streams ran nearby, and with their customary skill the Nabataeans built a series of conduits and dams to create a substantial artificial oasis.

The Nabataean kingdom was now a ncxus between the Greek, Persian, Indian and Egyptian civilizations. Along the developing trade route – later to become the famed Silk Road – passed camel trains carrying exotic goods from the Orient, some from locations so distant that their original location was unknown. Alongside spices, perfumes and fabrics from the east came incense from Arabia, ivory and copper from Egypt, sugar from India and the specialized products of a dozen other lands.

## Greeks and Nabataeans

Naturally, the Nabataeans kept a share of all the wealth flowing through their land, and, being shrewd traders, their kingdom rapidly became wealthy. Such wealth attracted the attention of larger predators. One of Alexander's former generals, Antigonus I (Monophthalmus), attacked the kingdom in 312 BC. The Greek historian Diodorus Siculus records how a force of men under a commander called Athenaeus attacked Petra by night, when merchants were busy trading as it was too hot for such activity during daytime.

Athenaeus' men spent the rest of the night loading up tons of silver and spices and gathering as much of the population as they could to be sold as slaves. They then set out confidently for home, at which point they discovered that as well as developing their trade routes, the Nabataeans had become highly experienced at protecting them from bandits – even ones sent by a foreign king. Their large and well-trained cavalry force, mostly mounted on camels, quickly caught up with the heavily laden attackers. Diodorus reports that all of the 4,000 infantrymen on the raid were slain, and only a handful of the 600 cavalrymen made it home, 'though most were wounded'.

The Nabataeans then sent a strongly worded complaint to Antigonus, doubtless pointing out that if the king wanted to cut his lands off from trade with the east, he was going the right way about it. Antigonus got the message, and disowned his commander. Yet instead of keeping his word to leave the Nabataeans in peace,

The 'Treasury' at Petra: what it was originally built for is uncertain but it may have served a funerary purpose.

he sent his son Demetrius to launch a further attack. Presumably the hope was that Demetrius, a skilled commander, could do better than his hapless predecessor. But the Nabataeans it seems were natural cynics and had been expecting another attempt. Thanks to Demetrius' excellent generalship much of his force survived the vigorous Nabataean defence, but thereafter Antigonus carefully kept his distance from the Nabataeans.

One interesting detail we learn from reports of Demetrius' expeditions is that the Nabataean kingdom now extended as far north as the Dead Sea. The Nabataeans were in the habit of using boats to skim off the blobs of bitumen which rose naturally to the surface from cracks in the lake bed. Bitumen was a prized product in the ancient world for its many qualities and was used for waterproofing, as an adhesive and even in embalming, so gaining access to the precious material was probably the reason the Nabataeans extended their reach so far north.

While the Seleucids then warred with the Ptolemies of Egypt, the Nabataeans remained safe from military conquest. Nevertheless they were not immune to the charms of Hellenistic civilization, and a degree of cultural conquest took place. Later Nabataean architecture and artefacts show clear signs of this influence. Nabataean gods (of whom we know very little apart from the fact that their principal deity was called Dushara) were originally represented by plain blocks of sacred stone, but after centuries of contact, they began to be carved with human features, as were the Greek gods.

The samples of Nabataean language we have suggest that they were largely bilingual in their own dialect – an Arabic-based tongue – and Aramaic, which was the lingua franca of the region.

## Romans and Nabataeans

With the arrival of the Romans, the Nabataeans became reluctant participants in the struggles which shaped the Middle East in this era, at different times fighting with the Parthians against the Romans and being helped by Cleopatra in a war against the Jews. While largely unfortunate in their foreign adventures, the Nabataeans were more successful in defending their homeland. This was partly because they controlled the water supplies, and had become experts at maintaining large reservoirs of water in deep underground storage tanks, the location of which was a carefully guarded secret.

Despite the turmoil, under King Aretas IV (r. 9 BC–AD 40) the Nabataeans reached their peak as an independent nation, and it was during his rule that many of the famous structures at Petra, including 'The Treasury', were carved from the cliffs. However, it was clear that some accommodation would have to be reached with the growing power of Rome. King Rabbel II came to an agreement that so long as Rome kept peace with him, on his death his kingdom would then pass into Roman hands, and around AD 105 or 106 this is what happened.

As citizens of the Roman province of Arabia Petraea the Nabataeans did very well, and archaeological examination of the ruins of Petra suggests that at this time the population peaked at around 30,000 inhabitants. That made it a substantial city anywhere in the ancient world, let alone one in an artificial oasis in the middle of a forbidding desert.

A Nabataean mosaic portraying a camel with giraffe-type markings, or a giraffe with a camel's hump.

## Demise

Yet even in the Roman era, trade was slowly shifting north to the city of Palmyra, and Petra was losing some of its glory. Desertification, caused by the gradual drying out of the region, combined with over-farming to feed the large population meant that the Nabataeans went into a slow decline through the early Byzantine era. They had switched from speaking Aramaic to Greek and adopted Christianity by AD 600, but by then Petra was abandoned and the Nabataeans were well on the way to reverting to the same nomadic tribal existence as when they had first arrived.

At that point the Arab invasion that was to sweep the Byzantines from the Middle East reached the Nabataeans. The last remnants of the Nabataean people vanish from history as vassals whose lands were divided among half a dozen minor Arabic states.

## Future Echoes

Petra was abandoned without fuss, and as a result the city sat almost undamaged in the desert until it was rediscovered for the West by explorers in the early nineteenth century, in particular Johann Ludwig Burckhardt. Thereafter it was almost immediately recognized as one of the wonders of the world (a title now formally bestowed upon it by UNESCO). Today the city is visited by up to three times its original population as tourists every year, and its streets are as packed as they were in Petra's prime.

The 'rose-red city' featured in the film *Indiana Jones and the Last Crusade*, in which Indiana Jones's distinctive brand of archaeology led to the wrecking of the Temple of the Holy Grail. Fortunately this building, which is actually the iconic Nabataean Al-Khazneh, 'The Treasury' (though it may have been associated with the cult of the dead), survived the filming and remains a major attraction today.

# c. 650 BC – 133 BC
# **The Celtiberians**
# The Celts of Spain

*In Celtiberia when a man urinates in the morning,*
*He habitually rubs this on his teeth and red gums.*
*So [Egnatius] the shinier those teeth of yours,*
*The more they testify to the urine you've swallowed.*

Catullus, *Carmina* 39

The majority of the Roman Republic's most significant conquests were of peoples at least as civilized as themselves. Where the Romans did have to face 'barbarians' they struggled, and nowhere did they struggle as mightily as against the Celtiberians of the Iberian peninsula.

## Disputed origins

A Celtiberian sword – such swords were the prototype for the fearsome stabbing sword of the Roman legions, the *gladius hispaniensis*.

Where the Celtiberians originally came from is today a matter of much scholarly debate, but for the Romans it was straightforward. They noted elements of Celtic culture in this particular group of Iberian peoples (the Celtiberians were never a nation as such) and concluded that they were a Celtic tribe that had somehow fought its way into the heart of the Iberian peninsula and remained there. This is not such an unreasonable theory since Gaul was next to Iberia, and a Gallic tribe (the Galatians) had – much more improbably – done something similar and ended up in the middle of Asia Minor.

Modern research considers the matter much more nuanced. For example, study of Celtiberian inscriptions cannot even claim with certainty that the Celtiberian language was Celtic in origin. Come to that, ethnographers today are in considerable confusion about what it even meant to be Celtic, let alone to be an Iberian offshoot. Furthermore, some distinctively 'Celtiberian' features seem to have been in place even before 650 BC, which is the earliest that elements of the Celtic western European Hallstatt culture could have arrived in Celtiberia. Overall, it seems best to step back from the controversy and accept that by the time written records began, the mountains of north-central Spain were occupied by a hardy warrior people who had no desire to submit to would-be conquerors.

## Society

The Celtiberians were a largely agricultural people whose trade was limited to interactions with Iberian tribes living nearby. As a result, it is unsurprising that many of their material possessions were of the same type as those of their neighbours. For instance, the Celtiberians, like other Iberian tribes, favoured a short-bladed stabbing sword which they used to deadly effect when at close quarters with the enemy. This form of attack so impressed the Romans on the receiving end of these swords that they promptly developed their own version. Thereafter, the *gladius hispaniensis* became the standard sword of the Roman legions.

A funerary marker of the first century BC–first century AD showing a Celtiberian warrior on horseback carrying a shield and spear, from Clunia, Spain.

Warfare in what the Romans called Hispania was endemic until the (eventual) Roman conquest at the end of the first century BC, and consequently the Celtiberians tended to live in well-defended hillforts called *castros* by modern researchers and *oppida* by the Romans. It seems possible, through archaeological excavations and a close study of the hints in the Roman written records, to trace a slow evolution of Celtiberian society from one in which aristocrats dominated their own particular clans and feuded with the others, to a later, more civic society based around a sort of city council.

The main Celtiberian tribes were the Titti, the Lusones, the Belli and the Arevaci, who were the most dominant. These tribes only united against a major existential threat (such as the Romans), but sometimes not even then. They seem to have been just as happy to join together to fight their Iberian neighbours as they were to ally with one of those neighbours to attack a tribe of fellow Celtiberians with whom they were feuding.

Celtiberian lands began well south of the Pyrenees, with the lowlands between their own mountainous territory and that mountain range occupied by a variety of other Iberian tribes such as the Vascones. Yet other tribes prevented the Celtiberians from reaching the Mediterranean coast, but in any case they seem to have preferred their mountainous homeland, despite this being one of the more inaccessible parts of the country.

## Meeting 'civilization'

Inaccessibility proved an advantage in 241 BC when the Carthaginians, smarting from their defeat in the first Punic War with Rome, made a determined effort to regain an empire by conquering Iberia. The Carthaginians were somewhat nonplussed by the savage opposition put up by the Celtiberians and other Iberian hill-peoples, and mostly got around this by leaving the Celtiberians aside as a problem to be dealt with later. Meanwhile the Celtiberians were more than happy to fight for the Carthaginians as mercenaries and assist with conquering other Iberian tribes.

All this came to an end around 201 BC when Carthage fell to the Roman legions. The Romans felt that Iberia now belonged to them by right of conquest, and it became Hispania, with the country duly divided into provinces. There then came the problem of persuading the Celtiberians that they were now Roman subjects. This proved difficult. As mentioned previously, Celtiberian settlements were hard to reach, and the hostile reception on arrival seldom made the trip worthwhile. Furthermore, the broken landscape which the Celtiberians knew intimately lent itself to sudden ambushes and quick escapes.

It was partly because of the difficulty of fighting against such an enemy in the rough ground of Spain that the Romans abandoned their previous military tactics and formations and began to fight in smaller squads of handfuls of men (literally *maniples*).

This elaborate golden helmet was probably part of the regalia of a Celtiberian chieftain. In general the Celtiberians possessed little treasure for their disappointed Roman conquerors to loot.

## The Celtiberian wars

By 185 BC the Romans recognized that they had a serious problem, and set about conquering the Celtiberians. This was the start of fifty years of near continuous warfare. The Romans enjoyed considerable success, but also suffered some stinging defeats. In the early stages of the war, the Romans were fortunate in having a commander, Tiberius Gracchus, who was able to conduct the Roman side of the war with enough

An engraving depicting the siege of Numantia. Many Celtiberian families chose suicide rather than surrender to the Romans, who eventually took the city in 133 BC.

sensitivity and understanding that he gained the trust of many of the tribes he fought against.

A second round of conflict erupted in 150 BC. The Celtiberians routed a Roman army and killed almost 6,000 men before Roman superiority in numbers began to tell. Eventually the Celtiberians were forced to send envoys to Rome to sue for peace. This state of affairs lasted less than seven years, partly because broken Roman treaties and massacres elsewhere in Spain eroded Celtiberian trust. A succession of inept Roman commanders then suffered a series of defeats. One such commander negotiated a peace which the Roman senate promptly repudiated, reinforcing Celtiberian belief in Roman duplicity.

Nevertheless, the Celtiberians tried once more to make peace in 136 BC. They had defeated a Roman army and had it at their mercy when a son of Tiberius Gracchus (also called Tiberius Gracchus, as was the Roman way) offered to negotiate. Remembering the fair dealing of the elder Gracchus, the Celtiberians agreed terms and the Roman army escaped unharmed. The Roman senate then reneged on the agreement and war resumed.

## Ultimate defeat

By now few Romans wanted to fight the Celtiberians. Such campaigns offered little booty, much discomfort and the very real possibility of sudden death. It took a final effort under Scipio Aemilianus to bring the war to a conclusion. He forced the final remnants of the Celtiberian army into their fortress town of Numantia and besieged it. The Numantines held out even after their food was gone, and in the end most of those who did not die from starvation committed suicide. This defeat in 133 BC saw the end of the Celtiberians as an independent people.

But the Celtiberians were not yet extinct. There is a record of a Celtiberian cohort serving later in Britannia as part of the Roman army. Also, a man 'born of the Celts and Iberians, a man of the Tagus' made a career out of insulting the Romans in numerous ingenious ways, for all that he was a naturalized Roman himself. This was the first-century AD poet Martial, whose 'Epigrams' still make hilarious – and often startlingly obscene – reading today. Yet even by Martial's time the Celtiberians were blending with the other peoples of Hispania, and today they survive only as oddly Celtic place names in the Spanish countryside, especially in modern Galicia, which means 'Land of the Gaelic People'.

## Future Echoes

While the Romans had long counted ten months in their year from January to December (*decem* = ten, as in decimal system), their year formally started in March with the inauguration of the consuls. This changed in 153 BC because of the threat of war with the Celtiberians. Realizing that by the time a consul could raise an army and take it to fight in Spain the campaigning season would be half over, the Romans moved the date of consular inaugurations to January, thus starting the official year and the calendar year on the same day.

This has continued to be the case in Europe and much of the world ever since, though two new months, July and August (named after two leaders of Rome), were later added to bring the months in line with the number of days of the year.

# 279 BC – c. AD 500
# The Galatians
## Gauls in Asia Minor

*O foolish Galatians, who has bewitched you?*

St Paul to the Galatians 3:1

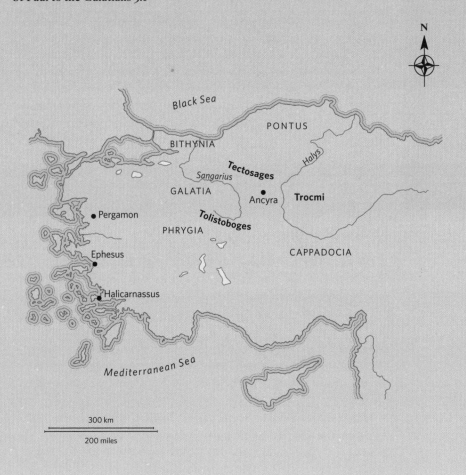

Those unfamiliar with the expansionist tendencies of the ancient Gauls are rather surprised to discover that Milan in Italy was once a Gallic city (captured by the Romans in 222 BC). Even more surprising is that the city of Ankara, the capital of modern Turkey, was once also Gallic. In fact the highlands of central Anatolia formed the heartlands of the Galatian state – an outpost of Celtic warriors far from their native Gaul.

## An unexpected journey

How the Galatians (whose name simply means 'Gauls' in the local dialect) ended up in central Anatolia is a convoluted tale which began when a Gallic ruler called Brennus decided that it had been a while since any barbarian raids had penetrated deep into Greece. By now a rich stock of treasure should have been deposited as offerings in places like Delphi, which enterprising warriors might help themselves to.

A marble head of a Galatian warrior. The Greeks of Asia Minor were proud of their victories over these ferocious warriors and often commemorated them in stone.

Accordingly in 281 BC Brennus led a sizeable army eastwards. Many warriors took along their wives and livestock, in case they came across anywhere decent to settle while travelling. 'Settlers' and 'raiders' were unable to reconcile their different motives, and in 279 BC the army split, with the 'settlers' heading east through Thrace. Brennus continued on to Delphi, where his raid failed disastrously, since the Greeks proved unexpectedly determined to keep their treasure for themselves.

Those travelling east initially had slightly better fortune, since the startled Macedonians were not expecting the mass incursion of a people from half a continent away. However, if there was one thing the Macedonians were accustomed to, it was repelling barbarian invasions. With Illyrians to the west, Scythians to the east and Germanic tribes on the Danube to the north, the Macedonians were extremely well practised at defending their homeland. The Gauls were summarily ejected from Macedonia and found themselves rather at a loss about what to do next.

### Finding a new home

Salvation came in the form of Nicomedes of Bithynia, ruler of a newly founded breakaway kingdom in northwest Asia Minor. Nicomedes was having a violent argument with his brother about who should be king, and he invited the Gauls to Asia Minor to help him in his struggle. Even among the 'settlers' the Gauls could muster some 10,000 ferocious warriors – easily enough to secure Nicomedes on the throne in 278 BC. So the problem then became what to do with the Gauls now that they were no longer needed.

For a while the Gauls bounced around Anatolia like a tribal wrecking ball, plundering territories and extorting ransoms from large towns. They eventually became enough of a nuisance for the Seleucid king Antiochus I, who was at least nominally suzerain of Asia Minor at the time, to feel that he had to deal with them (even though the Seleucid empire was in trouble elsewhere at the time). And this he managed to do, partly because his army included elephants. The Gauls had never seen these gigantic beasts before and had absolutely no idea how to contain them. After the elephants had trampled once or twice through packed ranks of terrified warriors, the Gauls fled in total rout.

They escaped to the Anatolian highlands, from where it was too much trouble for Antiochus to flush them out. Therefore the chastened Gallic tribespeople were left to quietly subdue the native Phrygians and settle down in what turned out to be their long-term home of Galatia. By and large the Galatians left the ordinary Phrygians in peace while displacing their landlords, and allowed the larger cities to continue as before, but under new management. The Galatians established themselves in farms and villages in rural areas, and proved surprisingly adept at cultivating the lands of the arid and inhospitable Anatolian interior.

The Galatians had never encountered elephants in battle before 275 BC, and when they did it was a complete shock that led to a massive defeat.

## Life in Asia Minor

The Galatians consisted of three tribes, the Tolistobogii, the Trocmi and the Tectosages, the last being the largest and most powerful. Each tribe was governed by its own ruler, whom the Greeks called tetrarchs (usually meaning one of four rulers). The Galatians soon resumed their traditional habits of raiding and warfare. It quickly became clear to them that inter-tribal skirmishes were far less rewarding than fighting their neighbours. Asia Minor was in the process of withdrawing from the Seleucid sphere of influence, and local politics were messy and violent.

As mercenaries, the Galatians happily sided with the highest bidder, and if the losing offer was good enough they were quite prepared to fight on both sides of a battle. Also, because local armies were too busy fighting one another to properly defend their own territory, the Galatians made repeated and profitable raids into Phrygia and Cappadocia.

Matters in Asia Minor reached a showdown between an alliance headed by the breakaway king of Pergamon, Attalus I (r. 241–197 BC), and the Seleucids, who still felt Anatolia should belong to them. The Galatians fought alongside the Seleucids, which turned out to be the wrong choice. Attalus won a decisive victory in 241 BC, and with it the independence of his kingdom, while the Seleucids and their Galatian allies were soundly beaten. (It is at this time that the statue famously known as the 'Dying Gaul' was created. It became one of the classics of antiquity, and many copies were made.)

## Galatians and Romans

In 189 BC the Galatians were again drawn into regional politics when a new player entered the game. This was the growing power of Rome, which allied with Pergamon against the Seleucids. Again the Galatians picked the Seleucid side and again this proved to be the wrong choice. The Galatians marked the centenary of their arrival in Asia Minor by being defeated by the Roman

This famous statue known as the 'Dying Gaul' in fact depicts a Galatian and was carved to celebrate the victories of the Pergamene leader Attalus I over the Galatians in the 220s BC.

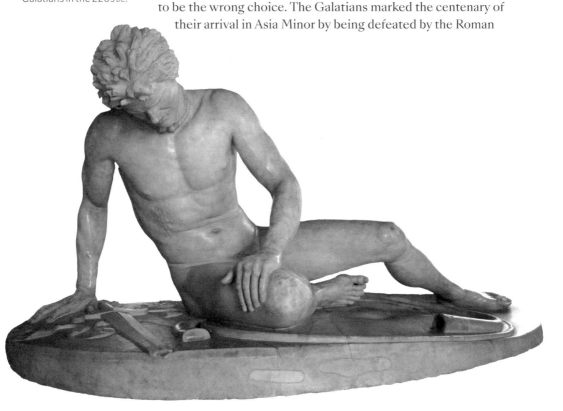

legions in two battles, the second of which was outside Ancyra (Ankara). The number of Galatian warriors before the battle is given as 50,000 (a figure which declined sharply that afternoon), which shows that the Galatian force had increased five-fold since the tribe first arrived in Asia Minor.

Defeat at Roman hands forced the Galatians to sue for peace, and thereafter they were largely subordinate to Rome. In the following century, with the rise to power of Mithridates VI of Pontus (r. 120–63 BC), this turned out to be no bad thing. Mithridates was one of the most capable and ambitious characters ever to stride the stage in Asia Minor, and he quickly set about gaining political control of Bithynia and Cappadocia. The Romans naturally objected, and for once their Galatian allies were on the right side in the wars that followed. After the defeat and conquest of Pontus in 64 BC, Galatia was still at least nominally an independent state.

At this point the leader of the Tolistobogii, Deiotarus, made a successful bid for power and displaced his fellow rulers to become overall king of the Galatians. Under Deiotarus the Galatians reverted to form and were on the wrong side in the Roman civil war between Pompey and Julius Caesar. In 47 BC Deiotarus had to explain his actions to the victorious Caesar. Cicero wrote a speech in Deiotarus' defence, which seems to have helped, because he survived and kept his kingdom. After Caesar's assassination in 44 BC, Deiotarus promptly threw Galatian support behind the assassins. Fortunately, the king realized at the last moment that he was yet again on the wrong side, and adroitly switched his allegiance. He died a few years later, around 40 BC, having achieved a ripe old age and having kept his kingdom intact.

The last king of Galatia was a man called Amyntas who took over in 36 BC. Amyntas was intent on enlarging his kingdom, and in the process killed the prince of a neighbouring statelet. The prince's vindictive widow arranged a successful ambush, and on that day in 25 BC the Galatian kingdom came to an end, along with the life of Amyntas. Augustus, now emperor in Rome, made Galatia a Roman province soon thereafter.

The Galatians settled down contentedly as Roman subjects. They turned their fondness for warfare to useful ends as soldiers in the legions – Legio XXII was mostly composed of Galatians and named 'Deiotariana' after the former king. The Galatians as a whole were gradually Hellenized and absorbed into the native population. As late as AD 420 the Galatians reportedly still spoke a version of Gallic that was understandable in Gaul, but they vanish from the historical record soon afterwards.

## Future Echoes

When spreading the gospel of Christ to the Gentiles, one of the early missions of St Paul was to first-century Galatia. Paul founded a number of churches, and wrote to the Galatians sternly warning them not to stray from the doctrines he had taught.

This Epistle to the Galatians is one of the most significant documents in Christianity, as it laid down the principles by which Gentiles could become Christian. Converts were excused from adopting large parts of the laws of Moses which would effectively make them Jews. This established a template for conversion which was adopted in the rest of the Roman empire, and subsequently by a considerable portion of the world's population.

St Paul writing his epistles in a painting attributed to Valentin de Boulogne, c. 1618–20.

# c. 300 BC – AD 475
# The Arverni
## For Vercingetorix and Victory

*There were two factions in all of Gaul.*
*The Aedui led one of these, the Arverni*
*the other.*

Julius Caesar, *Gallic Wars* 31

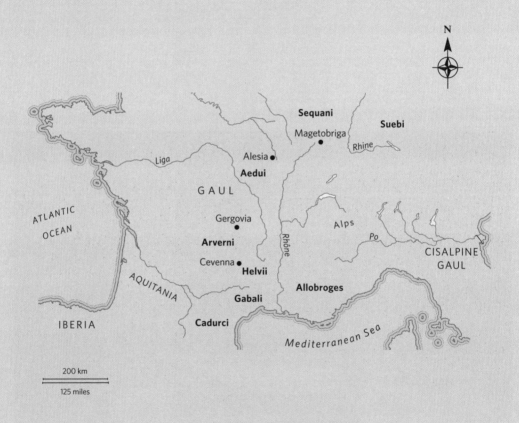

Resisting the vicious juggernaut of the Roman legions was a perilous task. Yet for a few brief years, the Arverni made a spirited attempt to challenge Roman supremacy in Gaul. Until the coming of the Romans, 'Gaul' was a geographical description of the land between the western Alps and the North Sea. The various Celtic peoples who occupied the region did not think of themselves as a nation, and in fact generally regarded each other as enemies. Of the many tribes in Gaul, one more than any other felt it had a divinely ordained right to dominion. This tribe was the Arverni.

## Blessed by nature

The Arverni had a lot in their favour. For a start, they occupied a strategic location in south-central Gaul. Their territory of mountains and rolling hills had abundant fresh water and rich volcanic soil. Large herds of cattle and sheep grazed in the highlands, which were dotted with mines producing gold, silver and copper. The tribe also controlled the fertile farmlands along the region's major river, the Liga, which in Gallic means 'silt' – a reference to the alluvial deposits that produced abundant crops. The Romans called this river the Liger. Today the name has mutated to the Loire.

The mineral and agricultural wealth of the region was sufficient to support several large towns, including the fortress town of Gergovia, and Cevenna, on the border with the Helvii. A powerful nation, well-fed and wealthy, and with a population estimated at between 175,000 and 200,000, the Arverni of the third century BC were well on their way to dominating Gaul. A number of minor tribes, such as the Gabali and Cadurci, were so cowed by the Arverni that they were somewhere between subjects and allies, paying taxes and supplying warriors at their overlords' request. Such affiliations meant that the Arverni's power extended deep into Aquitania (modern-day Aquitaine). The Arverni also had connections with northern Italy, since members of their tribe had joined a Gallic confederation that had swarmed over the Alps in the mid-sixth century BC and founded, among other cities, what is today Milan.

## The enemy from the south

The second century BC was an exciting time in Gaul. New ideas percolated northwards from the Gallic settlements in Italy and from lands further east with which the Gauls had trading relations. No one had much to teach the Gauls about metalworking or sword-crafting – they were acknowledged masters in that field.

But coinage, contracts and the other accoutrements of civilization were rapidly changing the Arverni way of life.

Fatally for the Arverni, it was not just new ideas that came north from Italy. The Romans came too. Until then, the Arverni's main rivals had been the Aedui, who now saw potential allies in the newcomers. Their diplomats came to terms with the Romans, who were mainly intent on keeping open their land route to Iberia, which ran along the Mediterranean coast of Gaul.

The Arverni had their own allies in the region, a people called the Allobroges. Matters came to a head in 121 BC with a four-cornered fight featuring the Aedui and Romans on one side and the Allobroges and Arverni on the other. War with Rome turned out to be unlike anything the Arverni had experienced before. At first confident in their previously unmatched numbers, bravery and superb weaponry, they soon discovered that courage alone was no match for the grim discipline of the legions. And even Gallic resolution faltered at the hitherto unknown sight of war elephants, which the Romans had brought over from North Africa.

The Arverni were crushed and retreated to make a last stand. This climactic battle was fought near the River Rhône in southern Gaul. Over 75,000 of the Arverni perished, and their king Bituitus and his son were taken captive. Fortunately for the Arverni, the Romans were not interested in conquering their lands. What they wanted – and acquired – were the lands of the Allobroges, through which ran the road to Spain.

The loss of tens of thousands of warriors was a blow from which even a great tribe like the Arverni needed generations to recover. But the Arverni never regained their royals. Their king Bituitus was paraded in a Roman triumph and was then exiled to Alba Fucens, an Italian town often used as a detention centre for high-profile prisoners, while his son was sent elsewhere. Kingless and decimated, the Arverni spent the next sixty years subordinate to the resurgent Aedui.

### Dangerous friends

Inviting outsiders to participate in Gallic tribal feuds was a dangerous game that not only the Aedui could play. So when a neighbouring tribe, the Sequani, later fell out with the Aedui in 63 BC, they turned to the Arverni, sure that the tribe would help against their old enemies. The Arverni in turn called on the Germanic king Ariovistus of the Suebi to bring his army across the Rhine to join the war.

Ariovistus and his men were the deciding factor in the battle of Magetobriga, which once and for all put an end to the dominance of the Aedui. Regrettably, Ariovistus proved to be in no hurry to return to his Germanic territory. He and his people instead settled in Sequani lands, despite bitter protests from his former allies.

This crisis presented an opportunity for the ambitious Roman governor of the lands confiscated from the Allobroges, a man named Julius Caesar. The Aedui, along with the Sequani, petitioned for his help in evicting the Germans. The campaign against the Suebi proved a lot tougher than Caesar would have liked, but Ariovistus was finally defeated and fled. So narrow was his escape from the Romans that the Germanic king had to swim the Rhine, abandoning his wives to be taken captive.

With the Aedui crushed, leadership of the Gallic people reverted to the Arverni. But the Arverni were not really in charge – Caesar was. The Gauls now discovered that ejecting Ariovistus from the lands of the Sequani had simply installed the Romans in the rest of Gaul. And, like Ariovistus, the Romans showed no signs of leaving.

## Vercingetorix and Caesar

A young Arverni nobleman called Vercingetorix (*c*. 82–46 BC) decided to forcibly eject the unwelcome Romans. Caesar had run into political difficulties in Rome, and was at that time on a mission

In this evocative painting of 1886, the artist Henri-Paul Motte shows Vercingetorix surrendering to Roman legionaries who wear anachronistic armour from a century later.

The siege of Alesia: as with the earlier siege of Numantia in Iberia, this represented the last holdout of a desperate people before their absorption into Rome's expanding empire.

to raise troops in Cisalpine Gaul (the Gallic part of Italy). The elders of the Arverni had been governing the tribe since the end of the royal line of Bituitus, and they strongly disagreed with Vercingetorix's fiery rhetoric. In the end, Vercingetorix was forced to stage a coup to gain leadership of the tribe in 52 BC.

Once in power, Vercingetorix used a mixture of smooth diplomacy and savage terror to subdue his rivals and acquire allies. In the process he created for the first time a sense among the Gauls that they were a single nation. Therefore it can be fairly said that Vercingetorix led a nationalist uprising against the Romans.

At first things went well. Caesar returned to Gaul at speed, but was rebuffed, sustaining heavy casualties in his attempt to take the Arverni fortress town of Gergovia. Vercingetorix knew that the Gauls were not capable of defeating the Romans on the battlefield. Instead he used the Gallic cavalry to sabotage the supply trains that kept the Roman army fed, and attempted to destroy farmlands to prevent the legions from living off the land.

But when his cavalry was defeated, Vercingetorix was forced to retreat to the hill fortress of Alesia, where he was promptly besieged by Caesar. For a while it was uncertain who was besieging whom, for strong Gallic reinforcements arrived and in turn surrounded the Roman army. It seemed that Vercingetorix might be able to break out and join the relief force, but Caesar's charismatic leadership carried the day. (Or at least that is what Caesar's memoirs assure us.) Vercingetorix was starved into surrender, and with his capitulation Gaul became a Roman possession. Caesar was not fond of people who defeated him in battle, and Vercingetorix was displayed in Caesar's triumph in Rome, imprisoned and executed six years later.

## Aftermath

The Romans were milder rulers than they were conquerors, and like many other Gallic tribes the Arverni were rather surprised to find that their lands remained under their control and their council of elders was restored to power. In fact, life went on much the same as before, except that the Romans firmly discouraged the intertribal warfare at which the Arverni had once been so adept, and taxes were now paid to the treasury in Rome.

The last we hear of the Arverni is 500 years later, when they struggled against the occupation of their capital (now the city of Clermont-Ferrand) by Visigothic tribes. The details are recorded by the last famous member of the Arverni tribe, St Gregory of Tours – who, despite his name, was born in the Arverni capital.

## Future Echoes

The name of the Arverni survives as that of the Auvergne region of modern France, though Gergovia itself has vanished, perhaps because the Romans were none too keen to preserve the site of their epic defeat.

Vercingetorix is remembered as the father of Gallic nationalism. A monument to his memory stands near the site of Alesia, showing the warrior leader in heroic pose. Perhaps, though, Vercingetorix would be more impressed by the fact that asteroid 52963 in the Minor Planet Catalogue officially bears his name.

An engraving of the statue on the monument to Vercingetorix erected in 1865: the Gallic leader is today revered in France for uniting his nation against a foreign foe.

# *c.* 100 BC – *c.* AD 500
# **The Catuvellauni**
## The Tribe of Caratacus

*Augustus will be considered as a god amongst us when the Britons ... have been added to the Empire.*

Horace, *Odes* 3.5

N

Brigantes

North Sea

•Lindum

Dobunnii

Iceni

Catuvellauni    Trinovantes

Cornovii    Camulodunum•

Moridunum•    Verlamion

Silures

Aquae    Atrebates
Sulis    • Venta Belgarum

Dumnonii    Maiden Castle
•

English Channel

150 km

100 miles

Britannia, that distant island 'against whose shores thunders the monster-filled ocean' – as the poet Horace wrote (*Ode* 4.14) – was originally a place of mystery and fascination for the Romans. After all, they viewed Oceanus, the sea god, as girding the whole world, with the wild land of Britannia lying beyond its boundaries. Therefore, for both Julius Caesar in 55 and 54 BC, and the emperor Claudius in AD 43, it was a matter of great prestige and triumph to venture into this almost mystical island and encounter its inhabitants.

But what was pre-Roman Britain like in reality? One modern writer has argued that the Britons were a peace-loving matriarchal society ruled by wise Druids in harmony with natural forces, whose culture was shattered by the imperialist Roman legions. In truth, archaeology and contemporary texts reveal the Britons to have been as patriarchal, warlike and bloody-minded as most other 'barbarian' tribes.

Hundreds of hillforts dot the landscape of southern Britain, including Danebury near Winchester (Venta Belgarum). Here the ramparts were raised ever higher against foes until one of its gates was eventually burned down about 100 BC, leaving behind a store of thousands of sling stones that could be hurled against the fort's attackers. Further west, the colossal hillfort of Maiden Castle – the largest in Britain – finally fell to the Romans after AD 43.

Certainly at this time there was no sense of a 'British' identity. Britain existed not as a nation but as an island shared between competing tribes, among them the Catuvellauni, Trinovantes and Iceni.


## Caesar's expeditions

In recording his two expeditions to Britain, Caesar makes no mention of the Catuvellauni tribe. It is, though, possible that he did meet them, for the territory of one King Cassivellaunus comes close to that later occupied by the Catuvellauni. If Cassivellaunus was indeed king of the Catuvellauni, then this tribe would already have been well regarded in Britain, for Cassivellaunus led the resistance against Caesar's second incursion in 54 BC.

The alliance against the Roman invader was the first time that Britons had come together as a people, and even then they were far from united. For every tribe that resisted Caesar's legions there were others who enthusiastically welcomed them – and then promptly invited the Romans to take their side in local vendettas with their neighbours.

Overall, Caesar's expeditions to Britain should be viewed more as a reconnaissance in force than a serious attempt at invasion. He discovered that the island was something of a wasps' nest of well-armed and ferocious tribes whose land possessed little that the Romans might covet. Unsurprisingly, after their reaction to Caesar's unwelcome visit, the Catuvellauni and other British tribes were allowed to go their own way for the next century.

### The kingdom of the Catuvellauni

Romans and Britons did not forget about each other, however. Through trade and diplomacy they came into regular contact, and by 20 BC at the latest Catuvellaunian kings were producing their own Roman-style coins. One interesting aspect of these coins is that some were minted at Camulodunum (modern Colchester). Camulodunum had formerly been the principal city of the neighbouring tribe of the Trinovantes, so it would appear that the successors of Cassivellaunus had managed to considerably enlarge their tribal domains.

The British began to use gold coins in the first century BC, both for prestige and to make trade easier with Roman merchants across the Channel.

The peak years of the Catuvellauni came in the reign of King Cunobelin (r. AD 9–40) – who became Shakespeare's Cymbeline. From the scraps of information we can glean, it appears that the true story of Cunobelin was certainly worthy of a drama. Cunobelin had three sons and a brother called Epaticcus. Until his death in around AD 32, Epaticcus was Cunobelin's strong right arm, waging war against another set of neighbours, the Atrebates.

By now the kingdom of the Catuvellauni had expanded from its heartlands around Verlamion (modern St Albans) to encompass much of modern Kent. The area was administered by a son who was then exiled after falling out with his father. This son fled to Rome and offered his submission to the Romans in exchange for his father's kingdom. At this time Rome was ruled by the highly eccentric emperor Caligula. Caligula put together an invasion force too late in the year to cross the stormy English Channel, and relieved his frustration by firing catapults at the ocean and then ordering his soldiers to gather seashells as spoils of his 'triumph over Neptune'.

The actual invasion of Britain had to wait for the accession of the saner if enfeebled Roman emperor Claudius (he may have had cerebral palsy). By now Cunobelin had died, and his successor, Caratacus (or Caractacus; r. c. AD 42–51), had already successfully conquered the Atrebates. The defeated king of the Atrebates appealed to the Romans, who used the pretext of defending a friendly and loyal tribe against aggression to launch an invasion of Britain in AD 43.

A nineteenth-century illustration shows Cassivellaunus, chieftain of the Catuvellauni, making peace with Julius Caesar.

As the Roman legions marched inland, the Catuvellauni again headed the tribal confederation which vainly struggled to halt their advance. First at the Medway and then at the Thames the Britons tried to prevent the Romans from crossing the rivers, and each time they were defeated. Raw courage was not enough against superior Roman tactics, weaponry and experience. The territory of the Catuvellauni was the first major Roman objective, and as a propaganda exercise Claudius himself travelled from Rome to supervise the taking of Camulodunum.

## Guerrilla tactics and defeat

Caratacus and the Catuvellauni were on the run, but not yet finished. Realizing that they could not defeat the Romans in open battle, the king and his men embarked on a hard-fought guerrilla campaign. This was intended to make it impossible for the Romans to settle down in their new conquests. The two sides harried each other for years, with Caratacus being driven far from his homeland and eventually fighting the Roman governor Publius Ostorius Scapula in the mountains of Wales.

Eventually Caratacus was forced to a last stand in AD 51. The Roman historian Tacitus (*Annals* 12.34) takes up the story, explaining how Caratacus

> decided on a further trial of strength.... He rushed to and fro, claiming that this battle would mark the beginning of the restoration of freedom. He named those whose ancestors had driven back the dictator Caesar, and called on them to follow their example in protecting their homes and families.

The Romans attacked and were met with a hail of missiles, but then formed their famous *testudo* formation, with shields overlapped 'tortoise style'. Once they got among the enemy 'the [Britons'] ranks were broken, for they had not the defence of breastplates or helmets', Tacitus reports. The family of Caratacus was captured in the aftermath of the battle, while he himself fled to the territory of the Brigantes tribe in the north. However, as noted, not all British tribes were anti-Roman. Cartimandua, queen of the Brigantes, was happy to put the refugee in chains and hand him over to the Romans.

As a captive in Rome, Caratacus defended himself before Claudius (Tacitus, *Annals* 12.37):

> I was a king descended from glorious ancestors and myself
> a great ruler. I had retainers, horses, treasure and weapons.
> Are you so surprised that I did not want to give them up?
> You want to rule the world, but that does not mean that
> the world will willingly accept slavery.

Impressed by Caratacus' spirited defence, Claudius allowed the captive king to live as an exile in Rome. Rather like their king, the Catuvellauni themselves seem also to have settled down under Roman rule. The tribe became a *civitas*, a recognized civil grouping with their own magistrates. The former capital of Verlamion became a Roman town (*municipium*) called Verulamium, where the first Roman theatre in Britain was later built.

The Catuvellauni seem to have retained their identity as a people long into the Roman occupation, for they are described as a separate group by Ptolemy, a geographer of the second century AD. Ironically, one of the last times we hear from them is in an inscription which proudly testifies that the tribe helped to pay for repairs to Hadrian's

Caratacus defending himself before the emperor in Rome. Prisoners were usually executed after a Roman triumph, but the emperor Claudius was persuaded to spare Caratacus, who seems to have died of old age.

Tombstone of Regina, a Catuvellaunian woman, c. AD 200. Her name and clothing show how Romanized the tribe had become; she was married to a Roman soldier from Palmyra in the Middle East.

Wall. The people once at the forefront of fighting the Roman occupation of Britain were now standing shoulder-to-shoulder with their conquerors in the struggle to keep the 'barbarians' out.

## Future Echoes

Caratacus is probably best known to modern children for his near-namesake Caractacus Pott, created when Ian Fleming took a break from writing the James Bond spy stories to pen a children's tale called *Chitty-Chitty-Bang-Bang*.

The British composer Edward Elgar made Caratacus the subject of a cantata (Opus 35), produced in 1898 and dedicated to Queen Victoria. Though it takes a few liberties with the historical account, the libretto clearly follows the works of Tacitus and Cassius Dio.

# c. 100 BC – AD 63
# **The Iceni**
# Led into Battle by Boudicca

*She was very tall and stern; her look was penetrating; her voice harsh; a mass of auburn hair fell to her hips and around her neck was a heavy torc; she wore a patterned cloak with a thick cape over it fastened with a brooch.*

Boudicca as described by Cassius Dio, 62.2

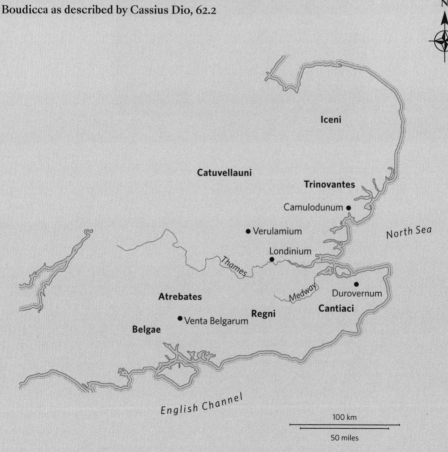

N

Iceni

Catuvellauni

Trinovantes

Camulodunum •

• Verulamium

North Sea

Londinium •

Thames

Medway

Atrebates

Durovernum •

Cantiaci

Regni

• Venta Belgarum

Belgae

English Channel

100 km

50 miles

210    The Coming of Rome

If it were not for Roman greed and misgovernment the Iceni would be as obscure a British tribe as, for example, the wealthier and more numerous Trinovantes. Even today, Roman mistreatment of the Iceni remains an object lesson in how friendly subject people could be turned into fierce enemies so driven by hate that they were prepared to destroy themselves if they could take the Romans down with them.

## Land and life

If any descendants of the Iceni tribe survive, they may well work at Cambridge University, for the ancient borders of the Iceni tribe lay across modern Cambridgeshire and parts of Suffolk, with the tribal heartlands in Norfolk. To the south of the Iceni were the warlike Catuvellauni, and since pre-Roman British tribes tended to be antagonistic to one another, the fact that the Catuvellauni were anti-Roman made the Iceni automatically inclined to side with the invaders.

The first reference to the Iceni may or may not be from Julius Caesar. In the second of his incursions into Britain, in 54 BC, he mentions a people called the Cenimagni who lived north of the Thames. Since 'magnus' means 'great' in Latin, these people were the 'great Ceni', perhaps because an offshoot of the tribe were the lesser (I)ceni.

Archaeology has shown that the Iceni were a well-off people. Their native lands were flat and fertile, and several prosperous homes have been unearthed. Like many tribes in Britain at this period, the Iceni were experiencing a number of violent social changes. Inter-tribal warfare was a regular feature of British life, and if the differences between Caesar's expeditions in the 50s BC and Claudius' invasion of AD 43 are any indication, tribal boundaries could shift dramatically, with new peoples arising and older tribes becoming subjugated or even extinct.

At the same time, trade with Roman-occupied Gaul brought not merely new products such as wine and linen, but also new ideas in everything from social structures to architecture and economic exchange. For example, sometime around 10 BC the Iceni started experimenting with making coins, which traders from over the Channel were fond of using. From the abbreviated script on the coins, it appears the Iceni spelled their tribal name with an 'E'. This has led to considerable speculation among etymologists who have traced the name from everything from a local river to pine cones.

## The Roman conquest

When the Romans arrived on British shores again in AD 43 under Claudius, the Iceni were friendly neutrals. This was fortunate for the Romans, who had their hands more than full with the British tribes who were trying hard to throw them back into the sea. As a result, relations between the Romans and the Iceni were at first amicable.

The situation was doomed not to last, however. The Iceni regarded the Romans as allies who had conquered their troublesome neighbours, whereas the Romans saw the Iceni as a subject people within their empire. These differing perceptions came to a head when the Roman governor Publius Ostorius Scapula decided to embark on a difficult campaign in the western hill country of what is today Wales. To avoid any trouble breaking out behind him, Ostorius ordered the Iceni to give up their weapons.

As a proud and independent people, the Iceni were outraged and rebelled. This was ill-advised, since Ostorius had a large army already assembled, which proceeded to inflict a major defeat on the Iceni. It is probably at this point that the Romans insisted on a change at the top and installed a more compliant ruler, King Prasutagus.

For the next dozen years, life for the Iceni generally went on much as before. The major difference was that with the Pax Romana preventing inter-tribal conflict, their situation was considerably more peaceful, and the Iceni became considerably more prosperous. Yet at the same time, discontent with the Romans was growing.

Far too many Romans regarded the newly conquered lands of Britain as a personal treasure chest to be looted at their convenience. This view extended from the senate in Rome to legionaries on the ground. For example, Seneca, a senior senator and adviser of the then emperor, Nero, was in the habit of forcing the British to accept large loans they did not need, and then charging exorbitant interest. Legionaries who had finished their term of service in Britain sometimes decided to retire and settle there by the simple expedient of ejecting the British from any farms they wanted. Gradually the people of eastern Britain were transformed from reluctant Roman subjects to potential rebels with an abiding

The gold torc of a British warrior found at Snettisham in Norfolk, the territory of the Iceni. Torcs were a way of displaying wealth and status.

A copper alloy head found at Saxmundham in Suffolk, showing the typical protruding ears and strong chin of the Julio-Claudian clan. This is possibly the young future emperor Claudius, who successfully conquered Britain.

dislike of Rome. It seems almost certain that the weapons Ostorius Scapula had ordered destroyed were instead hidden in haylofts and housing thatch, awaiting the moment when they could best be deployed.

That moment came in AD 61 with the conjunction of two events. One was the death of the pro-Roman king Prasutagus. The other was the inexplicable decision of the then governor, Gaius Suetonius Paulinus, to go campaigning in the west at that crucial moment, leaving eastern Britain lightly garrisoned.

Prasutagus had left his kingdom jointly to his daughters and the emperor Nero. Presumably by including the emperor, Prasutagus hoped to secure his daughters' inheritance. This was not to be, mainly because of a man called Catus Decianus. Decianus was the imperial procurator, who was charged with handling the emperor's affairs in Britain. Apparently Decianus independently decided that all royal property in the kingdom now belonged to Nero, and he turned up at the royal palace to collect it.

Not unexpectedly, Prasutagus' widow objected. Decianus responded to her 'insolence' by having her flogged. If this was not criminally stupid and brutal enough, his men also raped the queen's daughters. Both crimes had even greater consequences than might be thought. The widow was not only queen of the Iceni. Her title – Boudicca – indicates that she was also a high-ranking priestess. And the obscenity of raping the daughters was compounded by the fact that in the prevailing culture, that rape meant the daughters were no longer marriageable, thus destroying the royal line.

## The Boudiccan revolt

The east of Britain was already a hotbed of unrest. It seems reasonably certain that some elements were only waiting for Paulinus to take his army west before they caused trouble. The news of the Roman violation of the queen and her daughters spread like wildfire, and within days instead of being a tribe of Roman allies, the Iceni had become a fully equipped hostile army. Most neighbours of the Iceni hated the Romans just as intensely, and swiftly joined the rebellion.

The Roman presence in the area consisted of a detachment of cavalry from the Ninth Legion and a settlement of Roman veterans at Camulodunum (modern Colchester). Neither stood a chance against a tidal wave of well-armed and highly motivated Britons. Rome had lost eastern Britain entirely, and was close to losing the entire province.

In the end Paulinus, hurrying back from the west, had to make a decision – should he stand and fight outside the Roman city of Londinium (London) against Boudicca's vastly more numerous army, or withdraw to somewhere more in his favour and leave the city to its fate? Paulinus opted for the latter. In doing so he probably saved Britain as a province, but at a terrible cost to the first Londoners.

The Iceni and their allies had already pillaged Colchester and Verulamium (St Albans), and their ransacking of London was an orgy of destruction, looting, rape and torture. They left behind smoking ruins and the corpses of impaled men and women – and Paulinus and his legions were their next target.

We do not know today where the final battle was fought. What we do know is that the Romans made their stand on a hillside with impassable sides, so that the British had to advance uphill on a relatively narrow frontage. Courage and passion proved no match for the training and discipline of the legions. Once the Britons were broken, Paulinus hunted them down with methodical fury.

Boudicca vanished. She probably killed herself, and her body was then concealed by her followers, who had also to hide themselves. The vindictive Paulinus appeared intent on exterminating the Iceni as a tribe, and by the time he was replaced (the Roman government wanted taxpayers, not corpses) the Iceni were virtually extinct.

In later years Roman geographers did note a town in eastern Britain called Venta Icenorum (in Norfolk). If the inhabitants were descendants of Boudicca's Iceni they were a vastly diminished tribe whose lands totalled some 14 hectares (35 acres). Nevertheless, the Iceni are remembered today as among the greatest rebels to oppose the power of Rome, and also as a warning to tyrants everywhere that every people, however passive, eventually have a breaking point.

## Future Echoes

The story of Boudicca remained relatively obscure until the late nineteenth century. At that point British historians noted that the name of the queen of the Iceni (whom they called Boadicea) was related to the Celtic word for 'victory'. As the British at that time had a queen called Victoria, the cause of the rebel ruler became celebrated as representing the struggle of free Britons against tyranny.

Today a statue of Boudicca stands on the Thames embankment, proudly celebrated by the city that she burned to the ground. (Beneath London there is still a buried layer of clay baked hard by the fires of Boudicca's pillaging warriors.)

Boudicca commemorated in a modern stained-glass window in Colchester, the city she razed after massacring its inhabitants during her rebellion against the Romans.

# *c.* 12 BC – AD 350
# The Batavi
## Allies and Enemies of Rome

*Agricola ordered four cohorts of Batavi and two of Tungri to close to sword-point for hand-to-hand fighting ... the Batavi began to strike with their shield bosses and to stab [the enemy] in the face. Once they had cut down their opponents on level ground they began to push them back uphill. Other units were inspired by their attack.*

Tacitus, *Agricola* 36.1–2

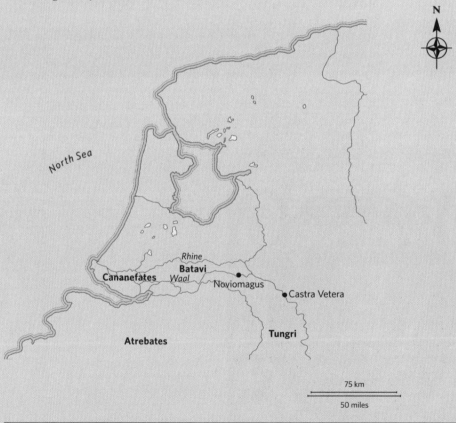

What most impressed the Romans about the Batavi was that they could fight. The Roman historian Tacitus called them 'the most conspicuously heroic of all the German tribes in Gaul', and this was true whether the Batavi were fighting for the Romans or against them. The Batavi were particularly good at mounting attacks across rivers – a skill that was highly prized in an era when rivers often marked the border between different peoples. The Batavi shared with the Iceni of Britain a history of trust betrayed by corrupt Roman officials. For the Batavi, their rebellion had a happier ending – though the same could not be said for many of the Roman legionaries who fought against them.

## Germanic origins

When the Batavi first appear in the historical record they were already established on Batavia, the island which bore their name. This 'island' lies within the modern Netherlands, near the border with Germany. It is created by a split in the River Rhine, with the other branch being the Waal. Part of the island was protected by boggy marshlands, while the fertile river valleys created excellent conditions for agriculture.

According to the Romans, who provide the only textual evidence we have, the Batavi arrived here not long before the Romans who reported their presence. Tacitus thought they were part of the Germanic Chatti tribe, who were forced to emigrate after civil war. Given the fractious nature of German tribal politics this is not unlikely, though Tacitus is certainly wrong in his claim that the island was uninhabited until the Batavi arrived. Archaeology shows that people were living there well before, and given its secure location and excellent agricultural potential it would be surprising if that were not the case.

A reasonable speculation would be that the Batavi were indeed Germans who had split off from their original tribe and moved west. Finding the island a congenial site for a new home, they expelled the original inhabitants and killed those who insisted on staying. It may even be possible to put a rough date on this event. The Batavi were certainly around early in the first century AD. Yet Julius Caesar, who was in the area half a century previously, makes no mention of any such people. Caesar was a careful general who would have noted a well-armed and organized tribe had they been around.

The Batavi were never a numerous people – at their peak they could probably muster some 5,000 warriors. Initially, they had no central city or citadel but were scattered in villages across one end of the island, with some settlements numbering only around a dozen huts. Nor did the Batavi occupy the entire island, for the western end was occupied by a related tribe, the Cananefates. This name means something like 'the leek kings' – a cheerfully derogatory name bestowed on them by their neighbours in recognition of their expertise at growing that vegetable in the light sandy soils which made up most of their farmlands. Both tribes raised cattle and horses.

## Roman allies

Overall the Batavi would have been a perfectly average tribe going about the everyday occupations of a Germanic people on the fringes of the Roman empire, had not the Romans – experts in matters military – noted their potential. One consideration was that the island occupied a strategic site – the two branches of the river made it easier to cross it in relatively easy stages. Indeed the Romans had established a storage base there, Noviomagus (Nijmegen), to serve as a jumping-off point for operations beyond the Rhine. As the Batavi later became more Romanized this developed into their main urban centre. (The strategic advantage was noted by the allies in the Second World War, who tried to take the town of Nijmegen from the Germans in a hard-fought battle in 1944.)

A Roman cavalry helmet of the second century AD discovered in the river near Nijmegen. The name 'Marcianus' is scratched inside it.

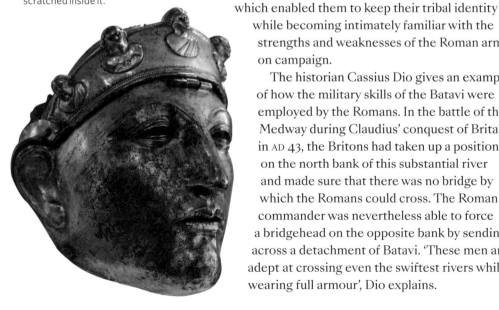

The fighting quality of the Batavi caused the Romans to pay them the rare compliment of allowing them to settle taxes in the form of manpower rather than money. The Batavi served in their own units under their own commanders – something which enabled them to keep their tribal identity while becoming intimately familiar with the strengths and weaknesses of the Roman army on campaign.

The historian Cassius Dio gives an example of how the military skills of the Batavi were employed by the Romans. In the battle of the Medway during Claudius' conquest of Britain in AD 43, the Britons had taken up a position on the north bank of this substantial river and made sure that there was no bridge by which the Romans could cross. The Roman commander was nevertheless able to force a bridgehead on the opposite bank by sending across a detachment of Batavi. 'These men are adept at crossing even the swiftest rivers while wearing full armour', Dio explains.

The Batavians defeating the Romans, by Otto Van Veen. At the time this was painted in the early seventeenth century, the Dutch were resisting occupation by Spain, and found inspiration in the earlier bravery of the Batavians.

With their flank turned, the Britons retreated to the River Thames and once more made a stand on the bank. The Romans were unsuccessful in achieving a crossing until yet again the Batavi got across and overwhelmed the guards on a bridge upstream. The legions then fell upon the Britons before their enemies realized that the Romans had found a way over the river.

This and similar activities made the Batavi valued troops. (When Boudicca rebelled in eastern Britain, the Roman commander Suetonius Paulinus was in the west, deploying Batavian troops as the spearhead of his assault on the island of Anglesey.) As was the Roman way, leaders among the Batavi were given Roman citizenship, and their children were invited to spend time in Rome. The Roman emperor Augustus had already been sufficiently impressed by the size and stature of the Batavi to enrol them as his personal bodyguards, a tradition maintained by his successors. Archaeology shows that at least some Batavi acquired the art of writing in Latin. In short, the Batavi were well on the way to becoming fully assimilated Romans.

## The Batavi as rebels

Despite their lack of numbers as a people, the Batavi were well represented in the Roman army. In AD 69 there were eight serving Batavi cohorts, directly or indirectly under the command of one Gaius Julius Civilis. Though Civilis was a Batavian aristocrat, his name shows that he was also a Roman citizen. The emperor Nero in the last years of his reign was heroically unpopular with both the senate and the army, and this made the commander of elite troops such as the Batavi a man to be feared by the collapsing regime.

Accordingly Civilis was accused of treason. His brother was executed and Civilis was sent to Rome from Germania to face trial. Other plotters brought about Nero's downfall anyway, and the new regime forgave Civilis whatever sins he may have committed and sent him home again. Returning with Civilis were the emperor's Batavian bodyguard, for Galba, the new emperor, had disbanded the unit – something the entire Batavi nation took as a personal affront.

The chaos in Rome escalated into an expanding civil war, and with it came a demand for manpower. Corrupt recruiting officers descended on the Batavi, conscripting not only the able-bodied, but also elderly veterans and the physically infirm, from whom they demanded large ransoms to be excused service. Worse, they also conscripted comely under-age boys whom they took as personal catamites.

The result was an uprising that had a significant effect on Roman history. The Batavi attacked and destroyed two legions at Castra Vetera (modern Xanten), and persuaded two other legions (XIV Gallica and I Germania) to come over to their side. By tying up four legions in the Rhinelands, Civilis and the Batavi crippled the ability of the government in Rome to cope with the usurping Roman general who was to become the emperor Vespasian in AD 69.

Though Civilis had nominally taken the new emperor's side, he continued to fight even after Vespasian had come to power. It was a doomed rebellion. As Vespasian tightened his grip on the empire he was able to bring increasing pressure on the Batavi and eventually he forced Civilis to surrender.

## Later years

Vespasian was no Nero, and he appears to have been sympathetic to the circumstances that led to the Batavian rebellion – not least because this had helped his own cause. The fortress base at Nijmegen was demolished, and the Batavi moved their main settlement to a less defensible position. Thereafter, the process of romanization, which had previously been interrupted by the Batavian revolt of AD 69–70, proceeded smoothly, and the Batavi became apparently contented subjects and soldiers of the empire. They disappeared about the same time that the western Roman empire did. The Salian Franks took over their island, and like the people from whom they had seized it in the first place, the Batavi vanished without trace.

## Future Echoes

In this famous painting by Rembrandt, the one-eyed Civilis and his comrades conspire against the Romans. The painting was originally intended for the town hall in Amsterdam.

The Batavi as rebels against Rome appealed to later Dutchmen of the seventeenth century, sandwiched as they were between the Germans and French. Civilis' revolt was the subject of a huge painting by Rembrandt of 1661–62, commissioned by the leaders of the city of Amsterdam. So strongly did the Dutch identify with the people whom they called 'the first Dutchmen' that when the Netherlands became a colonial power, the main city in the Dutch East Indies, on Java, was called Batavia. This city was a major trading city for hundreds of years until the newly independent state of Indonesia restored the ancient name of Jakarta.

# *c.* 300 BC – AD 275
# **The Dacians**
# On the Edge of Empire

*Domitian made two expeditions against the Dacians.... He suffered many disasters, however ... for the Dacians slew Oppius Sabinus, a person of consular dignity, and Cornelius Fuscus, the prefect of the praetorian cohort, along with several armies.*

Eutropius, *Short History of Rome* 7.23

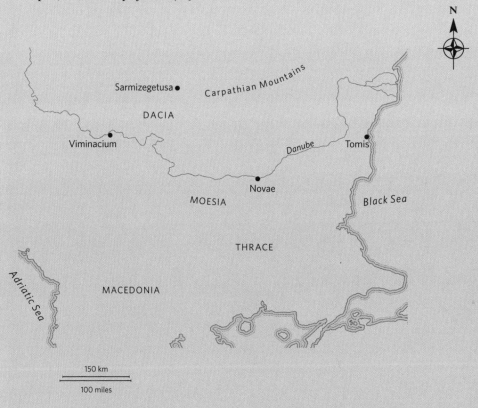

Dacia, in what is now north-central and western Romania, became a Roman province in AD 106. Unusually, this conquest was not driven by a desire to expand Roman frontiers, or for the glory of empire. The major reason was pure exasperation. Almost from the moment Romans and Dacians met, their relationship was defined by violence – mostly, it must be said, on the part of Dacians against the Romans. Eventually, after yet another peace agreement had broken down, the Romans decided to follow retreating Dacian raiders back to their mountain homelands and retrieve a century's worth of booty. It was an odd way for the Dacians to join the empire, but the effects can still be seen today.

## An inaccessible land

The Dacians were basically western Thracians, and shared many of the tribal characteristics of their eastern relatives. They were closest to a Thracian tribal grouping called the Getae, and because few people in the early Classical world had actually met the Dacians, for centuries 'Getae' and 'Dacians' were used interchangeably by Classical writers, leaving a trail of confusion for later ancient historians.

The reason that it was hard for anyone at that time to find actual Dacians was because of the location of their homeland. The land to the south of Dacia was mountainous, and dotted with hillforts occupied by unwelcoming barbarian tribes. The sweeping crescent of the Carpathian mountains made a near impenetrable barrier to the northwest, so the only relatively easy access was through Thrace towards the Euxine (Black) Sea.

It was probably through this route that the first known Dacians were exported as slaves from Greek city-states on the Euxine coast to Athens. Even then it is not certain from the etymology that these slaves were actual Dacians – though the penetration of contemporary Greek coins into the Dacian interior shows that someone or something was being traded at least by the third century BC.

The early Dacians were no more a nation than the rest of the fissiparous Thracians. A large and numerous people, they were divided into fifteen tribes (according to the geographer Ptolemy). The greater part of the warlike energies of these tribes was consumed in feuds with each other, their Thracian relatives and the equally warlike peoples occupying the lands around the Danube. It was only on those occasions when the Dacians united and became a single kingdom that they became a threat to everyone around them.

## Early Dacia

The first such kingdom was allegedly founded by one Rubobostes in the second century BC. It seems the Dacians at that point were finding it hard to fight off Celtic tribes such as the Boii, mainly because at the same time they were also fighting each other. Once Rubobostes had united the Dacians, the Celtic threat was efficiently eliminated.

At least so says the first-century BC historian Trogus Pompeius, as preserved by the later author Justin. Others point out that Rubobostes' story might be a re-imagining of the feats of Burebista, a later king of the first century BC, who did much the same thing, and definitely did exist (see below). There is also confusion about another warrior king called Oroles, who allegedly united the Dacians to defeat the Bastarnae tribe.

Perhaps all that can be said of these somewhat confused accounts is that although they generally fought one another in traditional tribal feuds, the Dacians had a demonstrated ability to come together as a single people if a threat or opportunity of sufficient magnitude presented itself. In the later first century BC the Dacians reckoned they saw one such opportunity and introduced themselves to the Romans with a massive raid into their new province of Macedonia. Since Rome was also extending its grasp along the Danube, such a clash was perhaps inevitable.

As this elaborate Geto-Dacian helmet of the fifth century BC shows, the pre-Roman Dacians were far from mere mountain savages.

With their excellent body armour and a long, scythed pole weapon called the falx, the Dacians were accustomed to being paramount on the battlefield, especially as it has been estimated that they could field around 40,000 warriors and so outnumbered most enemies. This accustomed superiority made the Dacian meeting with the disciplined and even better-armed Romans extremely discouraging, and after the failure of their raid the Dacians largely left Macedonia alone for a generation while they concentrated on fighting and crushing the Celtic Boii and Scordiscii.

The Dacian king at this time was the Burebista mentioned earlier (who is more likely to have crushed the Celts than the fabled Rubobostes). He is the best-documented of the early Dacian kings, and was a contemporary of Julius Caesar. While Caesar was conquering the Gauls in the west, Burebista was mostly focusing on the Celtic tribes and those between his nation and the Euxine Sea. After several ferocious campaigns the Dacians had not only removed this potential threat but had even subjugated some of the Greek cities along the Euxine coast.

In the course of these violent encounters the Dacians, who seem previously to have had a subsistence economy, learned much from the more advanced Celts. About this juncture they developed the potter's wheel and a trading system, and even began minting some tentative coins from their abundant stocks of silver.

## Dacians and Romans

Once Burebista had consolidated his eastern gains, he and the Dacians turned south, causing considerable alarm in Rome. (Caesar contemplated campaigning against them.) However, while the Dacians penetrated as far south as modern Serbia, the threat to Rome faded with the assassination of Burebista – possibly motivated by the judicious payment of Roman gold. Without the powerful personality of the king to hold the tribes together, they collapsed back into internecine warfare.

Unfortunately all written accounts of Trajan's Dacian wars have been lost, so historians have to reconstruct events from the 'comic-strip-style' images on Trajan's commemorative column.

The Romans considered following up this advantage, but once Caesar was also assassinated in 44 BC, Rome had troubles of its own. When Augustus became emperor he contemplated campaigning against the Dacians, but instead settled for driving them out of their southern conquests. In the years that followed, Roman–Dacian relations were wary but largely peaceful. Nevertheless, the Dacians frequently launched minor raids, and they took advantage of the chaos of the Year of the Four Emperors to embark on a major pillaging expedition in AD 69. A number of Roman artefacts have turned up in archaeological excavations from this era, but it remains uncertain whether these arrived through trade or plunder. In any case, Roman patience was wearing thin.

## The Dacian wars

By now, if not earlier, Dacian society had stratified into a warrior aristocracy and priesthood (not much is currently known about Dacian religion), and a peasant class who produced a reasonable agricultural surplus and also mined for silver, iron and gold. All Dacia needed to become a major threat again was another king in the style of Burebista. The Dacians found that king in Decebalus.

Realizing that the best way to unite the Dacian tribes was through warfare against an external enemy, Decebalus began his reign by attacking the Roman province of Moesia in AD 85. The Roman governor was killed, and Rome lost a legion in the subsequent fighting. Rome now took the Dacian threat seriously – they pushed the Dacians back and inflicted heavy casualties. Things might have gone badly for Decebalus if the Roman emperor at the time, Domitian, had not been experiencing political difficulties of his own and needed his army elsewhere. In the end Decebalus accepted nominal Roman overlordship in return for a large payment that everyone carefully avoided calling tribute.

There was no way that the Romans would tolerate this for long, but Decebalus used the opportunity and the Roman bounty to fortify his capital of Sarmizegetusa (established earlier by Burebista). Then, in AD 102, under a new emperor, Trajan, Roman legions stormed across the Danube, defeated the Dacians in battle and forced them to accept peace terms favouring Rome. Decebalus allegedly took advantage of the truce to rebuild his army and plot against Rome, so in AD 105 Trajan returned with 100,000 men, this time with invasion in mind. (The bridge he built over the Danube for his troops to cross lasted until the modern era, when it was blown up as a hazard to navigation.) Details of the campaign are lost, but it is known that Sarmizegetusa fell after an arduous siege. Decebalus fled, later committing suicide to avoid capture. Trajan celebrated his victory with a four-month festival in Rome, financed by gold seized from the Dacians. Some 10,000 gladiators fought in combats. Later, Trajan erected his famous column in Rome, resplendent with carved panels depicting his Dacian campaigns.

## Later Dacia

From AD 106 to 275 the Dacians were Roman subjects, with their rebuilt capital some 40 kilometres (25 miles) from the flattened ruins of its previous incarnation. However, Trajan conquered only part of Dacia. Many Dacians remained outside the empire, forming a group which came to be known as the Carpi. These clashed frequently with the Romans – all the more so as Roman power weakened in the third century. By 273 it was clear that Dacia needed defending against Carpi, Visigoths, Vandals and Sarmatians, and the Romans did not have the manpower for the job. The emperor Aurelian took the decision to abandon the province.

The archaeological record shows a largely peaceful occupation of Dacia. Most of the native Dacian aristocracy had been evacuated and resettled in Roman lands, and the Dacian peasantry gradually merged with the newcomers to lose their distinctive identity.

## Future Echoes

Dacia was never totally de-Romanized in the way that Britain was after AD 410. Even without the apparatus of Roman government, much of Roman language and culture persisted. Today the Romanian language is recognizably Latin, and modern Romania gets its name from the Romans, though this was partly due to later conquests in the Byzantine era.

Decebalus is not forgotten today: a modern rock-carving shows him sternly staring out over the waters of the Danube.

More recently, the Romanians have also taken a greater interest in their Dacian heritage, and anyone wanting to be in one form of Dacia can do so by buying a car. Automobile Dacia has been in business since 1966, and is currently owned by Renault. Regrettably, the number plates are not in Roman numerals.

# Part Four
## The Fall of Rome in the West
### Barbarian Invaders and Settlers

Around the second quarter of the third century AD, the Roman empire changed from being predator to prey. Entire peoples were on the move, sweeping across vast distances and settling far from their original homelands. The cause of these migrations has been hotly debated by academics for the past two centuries.

Plague may have had something to do with it. At the time of the emperor Septimius Severus (r. AD 193–211), troops returning from the east brought with them a new and devastating disease (which was also killing millions in China at the same time). This came immediately after another epidemic that modern historians call the Antonine Plague. Specialists in Late Antiquity argue that by AD 400 Rome had largely recovered from this crisis, but others feel that it was a depopulated empire that collapsed seventy years later.

Other historians point to weaknesses in the imperial system. Despite having had over 150 years to work on it, the Romans had never really agreed on how an emperor should be chosen. The *de facto* solution was to let the army decide which of its commanders should be emperor, and then wait for the Senate's (increasingly irrelevant)

agreement. The problem with this method was that if two different parts of the army could not agree, a messy civil war would ensue.

It was almost of no consequence who became emperor anyway, for almost all of them ended up pursuing the same policies in much the same way. The problem was that some provinces – especially the western ones – felt that the central government was not doing enough to defend them. When that happened the army in those provinces was very likely to pick an emperor whom they thought would work for them.

There are also those who argue that it is pointless debating about what destroyed the Roman empire in the west, because that empire was never sustainable in the first place. The western Roman empire had frontiers that stretched from the mouth of the Rhine all along the Danube to the shores of the Black Sea. That is almost 4,000 kilometres (2,500 miles) of border to defend, even before Africa and Egypt are considered. For the job of maintaining this extensive frontier, Rome had just over 200,000 men – a force about the size of the Belgian army at the start of the First World War.

Yet even that relatively small army was more than the empire could afford. Almost from the beginning, Rome could not pay its soldiers. While Rome was conquering other nations, this mattered little, since conquest had its own momentum and Rome's armies were paid with the loot of conquered countries. Yet when Rome went from predator to prey, what then? The only way Rome could pay its soldiers was to debase the currency. So over the history of the empire, the denarius went from almost pure silver to worthless base metal.

By this argument, the question is not why did the Roman empire in the west eventually fall, but how did it manage to survive for so long?

One thing almost everyone agrees on is that the barbarians did not destroy Rome. They merely pushed over a structure that was already toppling. Certainly, there were repeated barbarian invasions and these caused chaos and widespread suffering. So why did these invasions happen in the first place?

While it seemed to the Romans of the third and fourth centuries AD that the barbarians came at them in wave after unstoppable wave, the fact is that the barbarians had often come up against the Romans, and until the fall of the empire, the Romans had been very good at stopping each incursion in its tracks. In 58 BC Caesar reported that a wave of migrating Helvetii some 300,000 strong had hit the Gallic frontier. Even according to modern lowest-case estimates, Caesar fought off some 50,000 barbarians without asking for reinforcements. A generation before that Rome faced an invasion at least three times larger from the migrant Cimbri. Despite losing over 20,000 men at the battle of Arausio in 105 BC, Rome eventually turned back the invaders, killing or capturing around 180,000 of them.

Yet when we reach the tail-end of the empire, Alaric and his Visigothic barbarians were able to march unopposed through Italy and sack Rome in AD 410 with an army of some 30,000 men at most. Other barbarian 'hordes' were almost as meagre – yet Rome was virtually defenceless against them. Clearly, barbarian invaders may have triggered the final collapse, but they were merely the last, decisive element in an already fatally weakened system of empire.

Yet if the barbarians were not *the* problem, they certainly were *a* problem. During the era AD 250–550 the disruption recorded by Roman historians within the empire only hints at the even greater chaos beyond the borders. We now know that the migration of the Goths began over a century before that people reached Rome's frontiers. Pressure from the Huns split the Goths into **Visigoths** and **Ostrogoths** and each tribe reached Italy at separate times. German tribes such as the **Alamanni** were also forced for the same reason into crossing the Roman frontiers in a series of devastating raids which were made all the easier by war and disruption within the provinces the barbarians attacked.

The result was that tribes that had started in one part of the continent, such as the **Alans** of the Black Sea region, ended up somewhere totally different. (In the case of some of the Alans this was Brittany in what is now France.) The Visigoths migrated from Rome's northeast frontier to merge with the population of Spain. The **Vandals** went one better by starting somewhere in Scandinavia and finishing in Africa. Another migrant tribe from modern Denmark, the **Jutes**, joined the Angles and the Saxons in driving back the Romano-Britons and settling in the land which became England.

One of the distinguishing features of all these invaders, of whichever tribe, is that none were violently opposed to Roman civilization. Nor did the Romans violently object to them. Even the Visigoths, who arguably did more harm to the Romans than any other tribe, were essential allies in the climactic showdown with the Huns. Like the Visigoths, other invaders were just as happy fighting with the Romans against other barbarians, or in the case of the Alans to join both Roman and barbarian armies to fight against each other as mercenaries.

Very often, barbarian tribes settled in unoccupied lands within the Roman frontiers and displaced the local administration. They and the Roman population lived well enough side-by-side, with the main difference being that taxes paid by the local Romans now went to the barbarian leaders. These leaders were often markedly less corrupt than the Roman administrators who had preceded them, and unlike the overstretched Romans, their armies actually did provide a degree of protection for the residents.

As a result, barbarian settlement within the empire could vary from invasions which almost wiped out the local culture (as in Britain) to other situations where the barbarians left the local culture intact. Nowhere was this latter phenomenon more noticeable than in Italy, where the Ostrogoths took over from the Romans so smoothly that life in Rome itself went on as normal.

The 'Fall of the Roman Empire' was so un-momentous an event that few at the time would have noticed that it had happened. Europe had to wait for historians of the early modern era to discover that Rome fell after all. In any case, the empire in the east, based in Constantinople, survived ultimately until 1453, when it was put out of its misery by the Ottomans. These Byzantines (named by later historians after Byzantium, as Constantinople was previously known) actually thought of themselves as 'Romans', and called themselves such.

This is not to deny that the era saw momentous changes. Wherever new tribes tried to settle within the confines of the empire, they themselves had to deal with later invaders. In subsequent centuries Lombards, Slavs, Franks, Suebi and Gepids came pouring in from the north and east to eventually give modern Europe the form it has today. Yet what we see now as a seething cauldron of displaced humanity looked rather different on the ground. Thirty years is a short time to a historian, but it is a generation to the people living through those years, and humans are remarkably adaptable, given a few decades in which to adapt.

Nor was it not only western Europe which had to cope with tribes of warlike migrants. It seems appropriate that the last people in this book are the **Hephthalites**, the mysterious tribe sometimes called the 'White Huns'. These were but one of the tribes that crashed against northern India and caused chaos within the borders of the Sasanian Persian empire, including in the ancient cities of Mesopotamia, where our story began.

# 1st century BC – AD 1230
# **The Alans**
# Westwards Through a Falling Empire

*They dwell in wagons covered with rounded canopies of bark, and in these they roam over the endless wastes … in the wagons their babes are born and raised; the wagons form their permanent dwellings.*

Ammianus Marcellinus, 31.2,17

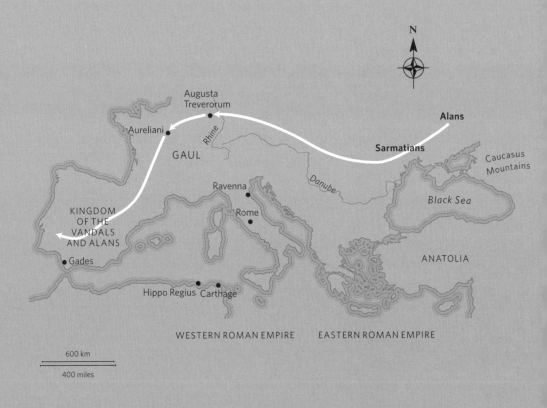

The fifth century AD was a disaster for the western Roman empire, which began it largely intact and had vanished by the century's end. Yet the convulsion which brought down Rome was just one part of the massive changes reshaping western Europe. Other nations were also caught up in the chaos, to cope as best they could. One such were the Alans. They began the same century in the lands east and north of the Black Sea and were then scattered across the continent and beyond, finding homes in Brittany, Spain, Africa, Italy, southern Russia and possibly even China.

## Origins

The Alans were an Aryan people: in fact it is sometimes argued that the word 'Alan' is a corruption of the word 'Aryan'. And even before they became dispersed across the western world, they were already accustomed to moving. In the first century BC they were in Central Asia travelling west. They arrived in the lands north of the Black Sea in the first century AD, and came as an unpleasant shock to the Sarmatians living there. Until the arrival of the Alans, the Sarmatians had considered themselves the supreme horse warriors of the ancient world.

Like the Sarmatians, the Alans were heavily armoured horsemen, and one of their favoured weapons was the lariat (a long lasso with a loose slip knot). This might seem an odd weapon to use against men armed with lances and swords, yet the lariat was just the means to bring the real weapon to bear – gravity. Any horseman will attest that being pulled to the ground from a galloping horse is extremely dangerous. When the force of that fall is exacerbated by the weight of around 23 kilos (50 lbs) of weapons and armour, it becomes exponentially more dangerous. That's even before considering that the victim cannot properly break his fall because his arms are pinned by the lasso, and will probably then be dragged along the ground thereafter. Typically, the Alans also disdained shields, to allow them the greater aggressive potential of two-handed broadswords.

The inscription accompanying the lance-bearing cavalryman on this relief tells us he was the son of a courtier in the kingdom of the Crimea. Rather inappropriately, his name is Tryphon which means 'soft' or 'delicate'.

## A (temporary) home

The Sarmatians had little choice but to shift grudgingly southwards and westwards to make space for the new arrivals, and the Alans settled in the vast plains north of the Black Sea. While they were a single nation, it is doubtful that at this stage the Alans were a single people. The fourth-century AD Roman historian Ammianus Marcellinus commented that the Alans tended to absorb others whom they conquered, 'united under a single name, because of their similarly barbaric habits and shared culture and weaponry' (31.2).

Ammianus has given us a further description:

> They are almost all tall and handsome, and tend to have blond hair.... They delight in combat and danger, and regard it best to die in battle. A man who passes away from old age they consider a degenerate coward, and send him to the next world with bitter insults.... They are proud of nothing so much as those whom they have personally killed, and to make trophies of the slain they tear off the heads and use the skins as trappings on their warhorses.

Archaeology has confirmed other aspects of Ammianus' account. The early Alans were a nomadic people who lived largely from wagons, and if they did stop to cultivate crops they moved on after a season. Young men despised farming and indeed were not keen on any task that could not be performed from horseback. Raiding was a favourite occupation, and that is how they introduced themselves to the settled peoples of the West. In AD 72 a horde of Alans tore through Armenia, plundering as they went. When the Armenian king met them in battle his army was shattered, as he would have been himself had he not been quick enough to cut through the lariat pulling him from the saddle.

The Parthians came in support of their Armenian ally, but the Alans savaged them also. The Alans then 'laid waste the country, and took a huge quantity of booty and slaves from both kingdoms with them as they withdrew' (Josephus, *Jewish Wars* 7.7).

While largely insulated from the Roman empire by the Sarmatians, the Alans were certainly not unknown to the Romans. First- and second-century writers as diverse as the philosopher Seneca, the satiric poet Martial and the geographer Ptolemy all expected their audience to be familiar with the Alans. This is probably because the Alans were happy to hire themselves out as mercenaries to both the Romans and Parthians, who were engaged in a long series of wars.

An ornate necklace probably worn by a high-ranking Alan lady of the first century AD. It is part of a huge hoard of treasure found at Tilya Tepe in Afghanistan.

In AD 135 the Alans attempted to take a larger bite out of the Roman empire. Since at this point the empire was near the height of its strength, this was probably unwise. The Romans fought back hard and defeated the Alans in Anatolia. The report of the governor whose legions did most of the fighting has been preserved in a memoir called 'Order of Battle against the Alans', which remains a key text on Roman army formations. The Sasanian Persians, successor state to the Parthians in the early third century BC, evidently had the same problem with the Alans, for they built a substantial wall along their northern border. Though also like the Parthians, the Sasanians were equally happy to make use of their services as mercenaries.

## Catastrophe

The Alans might have continued indefinitely with what for them was an ideal lifestyle, but they were by no means the last wanderers to come from the east to push against Mediterranean lands. By the late second century AD the Goths had transformed from easily massacred wandering bands into a tidal wave of well-armed humanity that threatened to sweep everything from its path. Alans, Sarmatians and Romans – all peoples with little regard for each other – found themselves reluctant collaborators against this threat. Fighting the

An ancient Alanian necropolis in Ossetia in the Caucasus Mountains, where some of this wandering people eventually found a home.

Goths, the Alans were stretched, but they hung on grimly until AD 375 when they were struck by the hammer-blow of the Huns.

This impact split the Alan nation apart. One group retreated north into the Caucasus, where they formed a kingdom called Alania that existed well into the medieval period. Others took service with the Huns and survived as a subject people. (They might have taken some satisfaction in serving under Hun commanders in successful campaigns against the Goths.) Meanwhile other Alans joined the Goths in their flight to the west. On 31 December AD 406, perhaps 100,000 barbarians (of whom some 30,000 were warriors), made up principally of Vandals, Alans and Suebi, crossed the Rhine into Roman Gaul. This marked one of the critical moments in the breakdown of the western Roman empire.

## Alans abroad

As ever, the opportunistic Alans took whichever side would serve them best, and since the armies of the day were all desperate for manpower, there was no shortage of offers. We hear of Alans fighting for the Romans, against the Romans and with and against the Goths.

Subsequently, in the early fifth century, Alans in Gaul fought with the Vandals against the Franks, and with the Romans against the Burgundians. Later Franks and Alans buried their differences to combine against the Visigoths, and some Alans settled down in Brittany as subjects of the Frankish Merovingian kingdom.

Other Alans kept moving and had founded a kingdom across central Spain by AD 411, though they eventually lost this to the Vandals, with whom they partly merged in 415. Some eleven years later, as members of the allied 'Kingdom of the Vandals and Alans', the tribe joined in the assault which wrested North Africa from the Romans. A minority in this new confederation, these Alans quickly lost their identity and became part of the Vandal population.

Back in the Caucasus, the Alans had settled down and taken up agriculture, which they had once so despised. They became rather good at it and their kingdom flourished until it fell under the domination of the Khazars. They then became wealthy through the trade which flowed along the Silk Road until in 1230 they were hit by yet another wave of invaders. These were the Mongols of Genghis Khan, who were the final blow. As ever, the Alans rode out the storm as best they could – some took service with the Mongols and are last recorded as imperial guards in Beijing. Others merged with the population of Hungary and yet others took refuge deeper in the Caucasus mountains.

## Future Echoes

Traces of the Alans remain scattered across Europe, from the hunting dogs called Alano Español in Spain, to the pass called the 'Alan Gate' (the Darial Gorge) in the Caucasus, to the name 'Alain' in Brittany, which some etymologists argue is the origin of the name 'Alan' in Britain and elsewhere. (There are other possibilities.)

The last remnants of the Alans survive today in their retreat in the Caucasus mountains, where they make up the bulk of the people known as the Ossetians. After spending much of the twentieth century as part of the Soviet Union, the Ossetians took advantage of the post-Soviet era to again become autonomous as a breakaway state from the Republic of Georgia. Tensions in the region remain high, and yet again these, the last of the Alans, live in uncertain times.

# AD 200 – AD 533
# The Vandals
# An Unfair Reputation?

*Till Goths and Vandals, a rude northern race,*
*Did all the matchless monuments deface.*
*Then all the Muses in one ruin lay,*
*And rhyme began t' enervate poetry.*

John Dryden, 1694

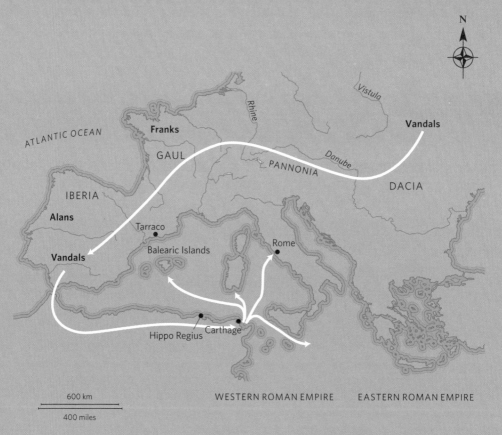

If asked for an archetypal tribe that rampaged around the late Roman empire like a barbarian wrecking ball, the Vandals would be many people's first choice – surely the name says it all? Like those who are called this today, they specialized in mindless destruction for its own sake – and the pinnacle of their misdeeds was looting and defacing the Eternal City of Rome.

But have we misjudged the Vandals? It now seems that far from being bent on destroying Roman culture, the Vandals respected it. Their progress through the Roman empire was not a tour of wanton destruction but an attempt to find a home while being chivvied and persecuted by stronger peoples.

## On the move

The first time the Vandals appear in the historical record, they had just moved out of southern Poland. The sixth-century AD Gothic historian Jordanes reports that the Vandals briefly established considerable domains between the Vistula and Danube rivers. Today it is commonly believed that the Vandals originated even further north, possibly in the district formerly called 'Vaendil' in Sweden. Other etymological theories suggest that the name 'Vandal' comes from the Germanic word 'Wandel', or 'wander'. If the latter is correct, then the Vandals are rightly named, for few peoples have wandered as long or as far.

The Roman writer Cassius Dio recorded the first contact between the Vandals and the Roman empire. This was in the second century AD, when Vandal tribesmen made an incursion into Rome's new province of Dacia (now mostly modern Romania). After tense negotiations, the Romans and Vandals came to an equitable arrangement by which the Vandals agreed to stop raiding the Roman settlements in exchange for land. Later, in the third century, the Vandals took advantage of Roman weakness to expand west into Pannonia, where they skirmished with both Romans and the rival tribe of the Goths. (The Vandal settlement in Pannonia was eventually given official sanction after the Vandals petitioned the emperor Constantine I for permission to live in the area.)

Thereafter Roman and Vandal had little to do with each other until the early fifth century, when Attila the Hun and his hordes were sweeping westwards and the Vandals were desperate to get out of their way. In 406, they fled from the Huns into Gaul. At this time, northern Gaul was occupied by the Franks, who did their utmost to make the new arrivals feel unwelcome – tens of thousands of Vandals died in battle. Within a year the Vandals made a second attempt to enter the territory, allying themselves with the Alans. After they crossed the frozen Rhine, they treated both Gauls and Franks as hostile peoples, burning and plundering their way through the province.

By 409, the Vandals and their allies faced stiffer resistance in Gaul and retreated south across the Pyrenees to a new home in Iberia. By and large they travelled peacefully, and were welcomed as allies by both the local peoples and Roman authorities. The Alans settled in the centre and west of the peninsula, and the Vandals mainly in the south and northwest. But the peace broke down with the arrival of yet another barbarian tribe, the Visigoths.

Harried by the Romans and the Visigoths, the Vandals fought back, winning some battles and losing others. Eventually they reverted to full barbarian mode and stormed through southern Spain, sacking and looting the cities of Tarraco (Tarragona) and Hispalis (Seville). The capture of the port of Tarraco gave the Vandals possession of a fleet, and they took to the water with remarkable aptitude for a people who had until then barely seen the ocean.

## A Swedish tribe in Africa

After sacking the Balearic Islands, the Vandals put their newfound maritime skills to good use by ferrying their people across the Strait of Gibraltar – eventually all 80,000 of them. Thus in AD 429 these Swedish migrants became an African tribe. North Africa was at this time one of the last remaining prosperous provinces of the Roman empire, and the source of the grain with which the authorities fed the people of Rome. Under their most successful leader, Geiseric (r. AD 428–77), the Vandals besieged the Roman governor in Hippo Regius (modern-day Annaba in Algeria) in 430. St Augustine, church father of Hippo Regius, died during the siege.

The Romans fought hard to retain control of the province, but were deceived by a peace treaty in 435 in which the Vandals promised that they would not attack Carthage. It was a catastrophic error, and one that was to lead to the economic ruin of the western empire. In 439 the Vandals took Carthage itself.

The Romans recognized that they had lost Africa and made peace. So powerful had the Vandals become that a daughter of a Roman emperor was pledged to a Vandal prince in marriage. Then that Roman emperor, Valentinian III, was murdered (a common occurrence), and the new emperor reneged on the wedding. The infuriated Geiseric gathered his army and sailed to Rome in 455.

This Vandal-era mosaic from Bord-Djedid, near Carthage, Tunisia, shows a horseman in front of a Roman-style villa. So Romanized had the Vandals become at this point that it is impossible to tell if the rider is a Roman or a 'barbarian'.

So weakened was Rome by this time that the entire force the empire sent against the invading barbarian army consisted of one man – Pope Leo I. The Vandals subscribed to a now extinct form of Christianity called Arianism, and Leo seems to have persuaded them at least to pillage Rome in an orderly fashion. The resentful Romans opened the gates and watched as the Vandals helped themselves to whatever caught their eye and sailed off in ships burdened with plunder.

Contemporary accounts – all written by Catholics – created the enduring image of the invaders 'vandalizing' the imperial city. Yet ironically, at home in Carthage, Vandals behaved in very Roman ways. They spoke Latin, wore silk, built grand townhouses and churches and enjoyed chariot races. And they administered their territories much as the Romans had done, collecting taxes in a similar way.

Even so, the Vandals remained lethal opponents of the Roman empire. When in 468 the western and eastern Roman emperors together sent an armada of 1,100 ships – the largest ever assembled in late antiquity – to recapture Carthage, Geiseric, through low cunning and the use of fireships, annihilated them. This finally broke the economic spine of the western empire. In the following century the population of the city of Rome fell by 80 per cent.

Eventually the Vandals got their comeuppance. By the sixth century, the western Roman empire had collapsed, but the eastern empire under Justinian I (the Great; r. AD 527–65) was determined to regain Rome's former glory. Squabbles over succession had weakened the Vandals, and they were unable to mount sufficient resistance against a large-scale Byzantine invasion which retook Carthage in 533. The last Vandal king, Gelimer (r. AD 530–34), was given estates in Galatia, where he died. His people slowly merged with and disappeared into the native population of North Africa.

While the Vandals share some of the blame for the downfall of Rome, few realize that no one came closer to saving it than a 'barbarian' with a Vandal father. Flavius Stilicho, born in Germania in AD 359, became a Roman general and fought off the Goths and other barbarian tribes. He was for a time the most powerful man in the western empire. But in AD 408 the emperor Honorius succumbed to jealousy and xenophobic pressure and had his empire's best defender executed.

A famous portrait carved from ivory of Stilicho, the general who was among the last great defenders of Rome. Though he led Roman armies, Stilicho was of half-Vandal parentage.

## Future Echoes

Apart from lending their name to mindless destruction ever since, the Vandals have also inspired an opera. *Sieg der Schönheit* ('The Triumph of Beauty') is the German composer Georg Philipp Telemann's take on the Vandal sack of Rome, focused chiefly on the romantic involvements of the principal protagonists. It has enjoyed periodic revivals since its premiere in 1722.

The Vandals plunder Rome – a popular artistic theme during the Enlightenment and early modern era. This example is a nineteenth-century engraving by Heinrich Leutemann.

# AD 376 – AD 800
# **The Visigoths**
## The Tribe that Broke Rome

*Alaric [King of the Visigoths] said he would not give
up the siege of Rome unless he was given all the city's
gold, silver, barbarian slaves and movable assets.
When one of the ambassadors asked with what that
would leave the Romans when so much was taken,
Alaric replied 'their lives'.*

Zosimus, *New History* 5.40

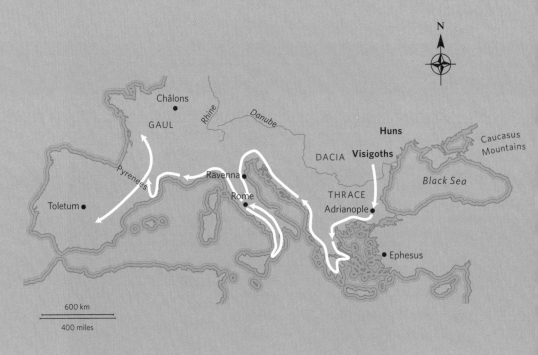

While the Vandals are somewhat unfairly blamed for the fall of Rome, the tribe that had already done more than any other to bring down the Roman empire has largely escaped widespread condemnation. Not only did the Visigoths destroy Rome's last field army on the battlefield, but a generation later it was the Visigoths who shook the foundations of the Western world by capturing and (in a rather respectful way) sacking Rome.

## Mass migration

Until the late third century AD, the Visigoths (literally 'West Goths') were just 'Goths'. With the withdrawal of the Romans from their former possessions in Dacia the Goths moved in. Where they had moved from is a matter of considerable debate. According to the legends of the Goths themselves (helpfully recorded by the Gothic historian Jordanes in his *History of the Goths*), they were originally from somewhere in southern Scandinavia before they migrated south and east, settling in different places, sometimes for generations.

Eventually the Goths met the Huns, who were forcing their way westwards, and they retreated before the threat. It is uncertain whether it was pressure from the Huns that had pushed the Goths into Dacia in the first place, but this was certainly what pushed them out. In 376 a huge mass of Goths appeared on the Danube frontier, appealing for sanctuary within the borders of the empire.

The Romans, however, had little reason to love the Goths. Over a century before, the Goths had plundered those same provinces where they were now seeking sanctuary. Worse still, the Goths had also later discovered the attractions of the Mediterranean and on different occasions their fleets had sailed down the coast to pillage promising locations, including the famous temple of Artemis in Ephesus.

Visigothic belt buckles were elaborately decorated and were symbols of rank and status. This example from the Metropolitan Museum, New York, includes rare lapis lazuli.

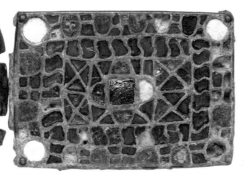

Despite this disreputable history, the eastern Roman emperor Valens (r. AD 364–78) decided to allow the Goths into the empire, on the basis that Rome needed the manpower. It is the Goths of this mass migration, led by a king called Fritigern, who were to become the Visigoths, though no one was calling them that yet.

## The beginning of the end of Rome

It has to be said that the Romans brought catastrophe on their own heads. The Goths, having migrated in a hurry, were willing but unable to settle back into the rural agrarian lifestyle they had enjoyed in Dacia. They lacked grain for seed and in fact they lacked food altogether. Corrupt Roman officials used starvation to squeeze every last bit of revenue from the Goths (it was said that at one point a child could be purchased for a loaf of bread). The stupidity of so mistreating a proud, well-armed people with considerable military experience was made plain when the Goths rose in revolt.

Valens was outraged by Gothic 'ingratitude' and by the damage done to Thrace by Gothic plunderers. Accordingly he gathered together a field army (which was not easy, as Rome was desperately short of soldiers) and set out to quash the upstart enemy. On 9 August 378 that field army – the last Roman military force of any substance – was utterly destroyed by the Goths. The Romans lost some 20,000 men, whom they were never able to replace. Valens had no time to regret his mistake, because he was among the dead. The battle of Adrianople, where this catastrophe occurred, marks what many historians regard as the beginning of the fall of the Roman empire.

## The sack of Rome

It took a while, but without fighting another major battle the Romans were able to force the Goths to come to terms. Under the last ruler of a united Roman empire, Theodosius I (r. AD 379–95), the Goths agreed to submit to the original conditions of their entry into the empire. They became Roman subjects, but were allowed to fight with their own weapons and leaders instead of joining the legions. At a later point people started calling these 'Roman' Goths the 'Visigoths' to differentiate them from their eastern cousins, the Ostrogoths. It seems the Visigoths approved of the name and readily adopted it for themselves.

The peace survived as long as Theodosius did. On his death in 395 the empire was divided between his two young sons, with the somewhat incompetent Arcadius becoming emperor in the East, and the wholly incompetent Honorius ruling in the West. Assisted by a coterie of inept advisers, Honorius decided to execute the last man capable of holding the western empire together – a general of Vandal parentage called Stilicho. To compound this catastrophic error, Honorius' counsellors permitted a pogrom of the families of the Gothic warriors who made up the backbone of what might loosely be called the 'Roman' army.

Unsurprisingly, most of the Visigoths who had previously thought of themselves as Roman now defected to the Visigothic king Alaric I (r. AD 395–410). Alaric had a storied history with Rome, having sometimes fought for the Romans and at other times against them. Now, with Italy suddenly defenceless, he decided to march on Rome. On 24 August 410, close to 800 years since barbarians had last sacked Rome (and 45 years before the next occasion), Alaric and his Visigoths plundered the city. Admittedly, Alaric did his best to keep loss of life and damage to property to a minimum. As Christians, the Visigoths spared many of Rome's holiest places, including the two main basilicas, Old St Peter's and St Paul's. Nevertheless centuries of treasure were stripped from the city, while news of the sack sent a shockwave around the civilized world.

## The Visigothic kingdoms

Alaric died soon afterwards, and his successors abandoned his plan to move the Visigoths to Africa. Instead, they settled in southern Gaul, where the emperor Honorius granted them land. In their new home the Visigoths repaid the favour to Rome, for it was they who won the day when their old nemesis, the Huns, followed them as far as Gaul.

This victory was at the battle of Châlons in AD 451 (also known as the battle of the Catalaunian Plains), where a coalition of the armies of the west managed to throw back the Huns of Attila. The critical moment came when the Visigothic king, Theodoric, led a cavalry charge which broke the enemy as they attempted to take a crucial ridge. Theodoric died in the charge.

Subsequently, in 507 the Visigoths clashed with the Franks and were driven south over the Pyrenees. (This unification of Gaul under the Frankish king Clovis is generally seen as the birth of modern France.) The final move of the Visigoths as a people saw them migrate first from the region around modern Barcelona ultimately to establish their capital in Toletum (Toledo). In the mid-sixth century, the Visigoths came into conflict with Rome

A Visigothic memorial from a basilica in Cordoba, Spain. The subject was Christian (XPI is a Greek abbreviation for ChRi[st]), but the age was uncertain: 'vixit annos plus minus LXXV' or 'lived for more or less 75 years'.

Dating from AD 661 the Visigothic Basilica of St John the Baptist is considered the oldest Christian church in Spain.

once again, as Justinian I struggled to re-establish the Roman empire in the west. (It is impossible to know how far he might have got with this ambitious and highly expensive project, as a devastating plague intervened, wiping out a good proportion of the peoples of the eastern empire.)

The Visigoths held on to most of Spain, despite the initial resentment of their subjects there. Like most peoples of the West, the Spanish were Nicene Christians (roughly equivalent to Catholics), while the Visigoths had converted to Arian Christianity several centuries previously. A central belief of the Arians was that Christ was a separate being from the Father and subordinate to him. Over the following years it became plain that the Visigoths could hold on to their Arian beliefs or their Spanish kingdom, but not both. By AD 600 the Visigothic kings, at least, had abandoned Arianism.

A hundred years later, such fine points of Christian theology became somewhat irrelevant, as the Visigothic kingdom came under attack from the armies of another religion. Though the Visigoths fought bravely, they were unable to prevent most of Spain from becoming a Muslim Caliphate under the Ummayads, who invaded from North Africa. By AD 800, those Visigoths who remained in Spain were subjects of the Caliphs. They merged with and vanished into the general population. Other fragments of the tribe survived in France, or hung on in the far north of Spain, but the Visigoths were doomed as a separate people.

## Future Echoes

Many blamed the Visigothic sack of Rome on the Christians, claiming that the old pagan gods would never have permitted such a desecration. This prompted the early Christian writer St Augustine of Hippo to write his seminal text *The City of God*. In this Augustine argued that man should look for the City of God in heaven and disdain the distractions of earthly cities – embodied by Rome. Other ideas key to later theology such as that of Original Sin and the notion of evil were also expounded.

The Visigoths held advanced views on the property rights of married women. These were enshrined in their legal system which was codified while the Visigoths were in Spain. Much of this code survived to be incorporated into later European legal systems. The basic concept now known as 'community of property' remains a central issue in many modern divorces.

The Visigothic Code was one of the most advanced legal documents of its day. This elaborate seventh-century copy is from the National Library, Madrid.

# The Ostrogoths
## Heirs to Rome

*We delight to live after the law of the Romans ...
and we are as much interested in the maintenance
of morality as we can possibly be in war....
Let other kings desire the glory of battles won,
of cities taken, of ruins made; our purpose is,
God helping us, so to rule that our subjects should
grieve that they did not earlier acquire the blessings
of our domain.*

King Theodoric of the Ostrogoths,
quoted in the *Letters of Cassiodorus*

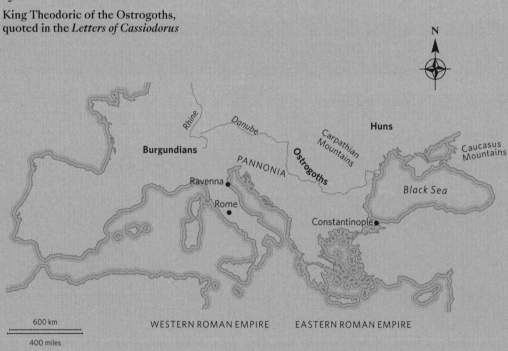

It is the start of the year in Rome. The new consuls have been appointed, and have assured the city that the subsidized food distribution to the plebs will continue. The people are looking forward to chariot races at the Circus Maximus and the usual round of religious and civic festivals. The scholar Flavius Cassiodorus and the Roman senator and philosopher Boethius are working on texts which will later become classics.

If in the late fifth century you had asked a Roman about the 'fall of Rome' almost a generation previously, the response would have been a blank look of incomprehension. Under the Ostrogoths, Rome was doing very well. It is one of the ironies of history that Roman civilization in the West was first preserved by the 'barbarian' Ostrogoths and then crushed by the Romans of the East.

## Breaking free from the Huns

With the westward migration of part of the Gothic people into the Roman empire, the Goths were split into two nations: the Visigoths of the west and the Ostrogoths of the east. The eastern Goths had already acquired many of the trappings of civilization by the year AD 370. At least some were literate, they were Christian and they traded extensively with the Romans. Then a few years later the Huns arrived.

Given that the western Goths who fled the Huns were systematically starved and exploited by the Romans, it seems that the eastern Goths felt that surrender to the Huns was the better option. Over the following decades, the Ostrogoths remained under Hunnic suzerainty, but were largely left to get on with their own affairs. Then in 453 came the death of Attila, leader of the Huns, the man known in the West as the 'Scourge of God' (a title Attila rather liked). The sons of Attila immediately began squabbling over his legacy, which gave the Ostrogoths and other subject peoples the chance to regain their independence. This was confirmed when the Ostrogoths led a tribal alliance which broke the power of the Huns at the battle of Nedao in Pannonia in 454.

As this illustrated manuscript demonstrates, the Ostrogoths were far from illiterate barbarians. Two Visigothic kings are portrayed, plus Theodoric the Ostrogoth.

## Ostrogoths and Romans

The Ostrogoths now became a power in the lands lying between the fading hegemony of Rome in the West and the still intact empire of the East. At this point a young Ostrogothic prince called Theodoric (AD 454–526) was sent as a diplomatic hostage to Constantinople. Over the years, as Romans and Ostrogoths constantly switched from being allies to enemies and various shades in between, young Theodoric received a master-class education in the arts of politics, diplomacy and palace intrigue. His natural aptitude for these subjects led to his appointment as Consul in the eastern empire before he returned home to become king of the Ostrogoths. In 489 he led perhaps 100,000 of his people, including some 25,000 fighting men, into northern Italy from the Balkans.

At the time the remnants of the western empire were under the control of a warlord called Odoacer. Though technically subject to the emperor in the East, Zeno, Odoacer was becoming increasingly erratic and hostile and causing trouble. Theodoric put his earlier training to use and after several battles finally resolved the issue in 493 by inviting Odoacer to a banquet in Ravenna and there killing the upstart warlord with his own hands.

By this simple but drastic solution Theodoric was thus simultaneously the 'barbarian' king of the Ostrogoths and top Roman government official, with his capital in Ravenna. Thereafter Rome and Italy enjoyed a generation of peace. During the reign of Theodoric life in Italy under the Ostrogoths continued in many ways as it had under the Roman emperors. After thirty years of rule, Theodoric made a major state visit to Rome in celebration, distributing grain to the poor as the emperors had done and reconstructing the city walls. Yet he also maintained a separate legal and religious Ostrogothic identity, which ultimately meant that his successors could not fully count on the support of the native population.

A small Ostrogothic eagle worn as jewellery. That the eagle closely resembles Roman depictions of this bird is probably not coincidental.

## Ostrogoths and barbarians

The main difference between Italy ruled by Ostrogoths and Italy under the last emperors was that Ostrogothic Italy was much more peaceful. Now that the 'barbarians' were in charge, other barbarians were strongly discouraged from invading or pillaging. When the Vandals tried, they were firmly crushed. An alliance with the Vandals thereafter was secured by marrying the Vandal king to Theodoric's sister. In this way Theodoric used his female relatives

as political pawns to secure marriage alliances with the Visigoths and Burgundians. When it came to the most dangerous of barbarian tribes – the Franks – Theodoric himself married a Frankish princess.

With the Visigoths content to accept the Ostrogoths as senior partners in their relationship, Theodoric could consider himself master of a substantial tract of Rome's former empire. This included much of Visigothic Spain, all of Italy and Sicily and lands in Pannonia stretching to the frontiers of the eastern empire. The current eastern emperor Zeno had problems of his own. A stable bulwark to the west suited him, not least because Zeno and Theodoric got on well at a personal level. Sadly, neither Zeno nor Theodoric were immortal and when these two died this happy arrangement collapsed.

## The Gothic War

Theodoric's successors lacked his abilities and the Ostrogothic kingdom had multiple rulers in the six years after his death. This presented an opportunity for the predatory

This painting of around 1520 of Theodoric's mausoleum by Giovanni Maria Falconetto is an accurate depiction of the building, which still stands in Ravenna today.

Justinian I, successor to Zeno in the east.

In 535 the Romans of the East declared war on the Ostrogoths and set about reclaiming Italy for the empire. The Roman general Belisarius conducted a quick, efficient campaign which so impressed the Ostrogoths that they offered to make him king in place of their own incompetent royal clan. Belisarius pretended to agree, but instead annexed the Ostrogothic kingdom for the eastern Roman empire.

There were two problems with this opportunistic act. The first was that the people of Italy – both 'Roman' and Goth – had on the whole been quite happy as Ostrogothic subjects. They were reluctant to return to the embrace of the empire, which they

associated with corrupt government and high taxes. The second problem was that Justinian had no desire to let Belisarius establish himself as virtual co-emperor in the West. His aim was to reunite the empire under his sole rule, and not share it with a potential usurper. Belisarius was recalled and dispatched to fight the Persians, and a less capable but loyal administrator was sent to rule the highly restive Ostrogoths and Italians.

By 545 the situation in Italy had deteriorated so badly that Justinian was forced to order Belisarius back. Yet he still feared the general as a possible rival. For the Ostrogoths and Italy as a whole this was the worst of all possible worlds, as Justinian allowed Belisarius just enough money and supplies to keep the war going but not enough to win it. Rome was captured, lost and recaptured, and with each siege and change of overlord the once-great city became more dilapidated and depopulated. By 548, the last great Ostrogothic

Romans and Goths meet in battle on the Ludovisi sarcophagus of the mid-third century AD, a time when the tribe had not fully differentiated into Visigoths and Ostrogoths.

general, Totila, had fought Belisarius to a standstill. Belisarius was recalled to Constantinople and never returned west.

The long war had sapped the Ostrogoths' strength, and with their reputation fading, other opportunistic tribes began raiding and seizing Ostrogothic lands. Totila died in battle and the Ostrogothic nation more or less died with him. The Lombards moved into north Italy (and have been there ever since) and the Romans kept a tenuous grip on the south. By 565 the dream of an integrated Romano-Ostrogothic kingdom had completely evaporated, and the Ostrogoths as a people had vanished also.

## Future Echoes

The Goths have given their name to the Gothic style of architecture which emerged in the twelfth century. Medieval buildings in the style abound in Europe, from the Duomo in Milan, to Notre-Dame in Paris and the dreaming spires of Oxford. The term was introduced in the sixteenth century to indicate the then view of the style as barbaric. So it is ironic that by the nineteenth century it should have become so admired that it gave rise to the Gothic Revival style of architecture.

Gothic buildings proved ideal settings for a literary genre of Gothic stories, which combined blood, horror and gruesome death, often with hapless heroines. Classics of the genre include Mary Shelley's *Frankenstein*, Bram Stoker's *Dracula* and the works of Edgar Allan Poe.

This Gothic church interior would have seemed familiar to Alaric or Theodoric, but was in fact designed in 1899 for Christ Church, Bedford Avenue, Brooklyn, New York.

# 1st century AD – AD 510
# The Alamanni
## A Long Feud with Rome

*The Suebi, that is, Alamanni, seized Gallicia. Not long after a quarrel arose [with the Vandals] ... when they were about to give battle, the king of the Alamanni said: '...Let us avoid mutual massacre in battle, and instead let two of our warriors take the field in arms and fight. Then he whose champion wins shall hold the region without more conflict.'... And the champion of the Vandals was slain.*

Gregory of Tours, *History of the Franks* 30.2

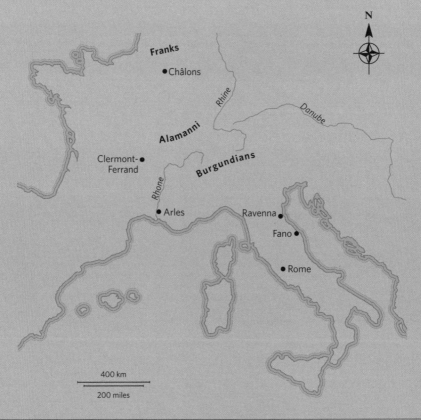

We do not hear of the Alamanni until AD 213, though they had been around a long time before then. History often overlooks people who quietly tend their fields and avoid battle and massacre. That was the story of the Alamanni until the glory-seeking Roman emperor Caracalla (r. AD 211–17) decided to boost his reputation with the army by attacking the tribe. Up to that point the Alamanni had considered themselves friends and allies of the Romans. But henceforth, the Alamanni were implacable enemies of Rome.

## Peaceful beginnings

It is generally thought that the nucleus of the Alamanni were the Germanic Suebi, a people described in the first century AD by the historian Tacitus. This particular offshoot of the numerous Suebi settled on the banks of the Main, the river which flows through the German city of Frankfurt today. The name Alamanni probably comes from old German and means 'All Men' – 'men' in the sense of 'mankind', as it would appear that many others apart from the Suebi joined and merged with this people over time.

The Romans may themselves have helped to swell the number of the Alamanni, for they are known to have resettled a number of displaced German peoples in the region. While later Romans called the Alamanni savages ('barbari'), this savagery had more to do with their fury against the Romans than their lifestyle. The Alamanni were in fact very Romanized. They were largely urbanized (as far as any third-century people were urbanized), literate and traded extensively with the Romans across the river. By some reports the women wore Roman-style clothing.

Lodhanri, king of the Alamanni, confers with high-ranking councillors in this illustrated manuscript, the so-called 'Breviary of Alaric'.

## How to turn friends into enemies

The Alamanni were in fact a model of a peaceable German tribe – until Caracalla. He 'treated them, the very people he claimed to help, as though they were the most bitter enemies', remarks the historian Cassius Dio. 'He summoned the men of military age on the pretext that his army needed them to serve as mercenaries. Then he had them surrounded, and when he gave the signal by raising his shield, he had them cut down. Then he sent cavalry after the rest' (Dio, *History* 78.13).

Dio also makes little secret of his contempt for Caracalla. 'The German people ... denied him any false claims to wisdom or bravery. They showed him up as a treacherous fool and outright coward.' The Alamanni heartily agreed; now that their trust in Rome had been destroyed, it proved impossible to win back, even after Caracalla had been assassinated. This was unfortunate, because in the third century AD, the Romans had far more enemies than they could handle, and the last thing they needed was to add to that number.

## The Alamanni vs Rome

It took a generation for the Alamanni to recover from the massacre of their menfolk, but by AD 250 they were ready for revenge. The king of the Alamanni was a man named Chrocus, and his mother may well have lost family to Caracalla, for the historian Gregory of Tours describes her as inculcating her son with her hatred of the Romans. In 256 the Alamanni burst into Gaul from across the Rhine in a savage tide, pillaging and burning towns and indiscriminately slaughtering everyone they came across. The city of Clermont-Ferrand was roughly mauled and largely ruined. By one report Chrocus was then defeated at Arles, captured and executed. By other accounts (at this point matters are highly confused and our sources unreliable) the Alamanni were merely rebuffed and turned their vengeful attention upon Italy itself.

Certainly, the Alamanni were in Italy by 259, because the harassed emperor Gallienus had to pause in his efforts to stem the Gothic tide in order to stop the Alamanni in their advance near modern Milan. It was Gallienus' successor, Claudius Gothicus, who finally drove out the invaders when he inflicted a decisive

The Aurelian Walls of Rome were built in the third century AD when, after many years free from barbarian invasion, Rome finally had to be defended once more. Though built in haste, the emperor Aurelian did an excellent job, and much of the fortifications survives today.

defeat on the Alamanni on the shores of Lake Garda in north Italy. It is highly probable that the future emperor Aurelian (r. AD 270–75) was also present at this Roman victory. The defeated Alamanni withdrew to the forests of Germany to plot their next move, while Claudius would die during a campaign against the Goths in 270.

The death of Claudius and Aurelian's problems in securing the succession brought the Alamanni back. They were still recovering from their beating at Lake Garda, and so in this invasion were junior partners to another tribe called the Juthungi. The invasion caught Aurelian by surprise, and for a while it looked as though the combined tribes might fall upon the lightly defended city of Rome itself. Aurelian averted disaster and defeated the Alamanni and Juthungi at the battle of Fano in 271. Nevertheless, the emperor had received enough of a scare to begin the urgent construction of defensive walls around Rome. (These 'Aurelian Walls' still partly surround the old city.)

A warrior is embossed near the hilt of this magnificent seventh-century AD sword sheath from an Alamannic grave in Sigmaringen, Germany.

## A continuing threat

A pattern had become established that was to last for the remainder of the history of the western empire. At least once every generation the Alamanni would take up their weapons, study which part of the crumbling Roman empire was weakest, and come pouring over the border at that point. This happened twice in 298, and again in 356. On this last occasion the Alamanni won an initial victory and devastated much of the Rhinelands before they were expelled the following year by the emperor Julian.

No one expected that this would keep the Alamanni at bay for long, and they were right. In 367 the emperor Valentinian had it all to do again. This time he took the fight to the Alamanni and defeated them at the battle of Solicinium (in Germany, though the actual location is unknown). This major reversal subdued the Alamanni until 406, when an irresistible opportunity to strike a blow against Rome presented itself. A bitter winter froze the Rhine, and as soon as this natural barrier was removed, a horde of barbarian tribes swarmed across. The ecclesiastical writer Jerome lists over a dozen tribes, including Vandals, Sarmatians, Alans, Saxons and, naturally, the Alamanni.

This crossing of the Rhine marked a major point in the fall of the Roman empire in the west. Rome began that winter with frontiers largely intact and as they had been for centuries; by spring it had lost huge tracts of land, the empire's western armies were exhausted and swathes of territory had been devastated. The empire never recovered.

The Alamanni remained a threat for the following decades, but are largely absent from the historical record because all attention was focused on the even greater threat posed by Attila the Hun. Then in 450 Attila's horde broke into Gaul. If there was pillaging to be done west of the Rhine the Alamanni were certainly not going to miss out and they became enthusiastic allies of the Huns.

In 451 Attila's career of conquest was brought to an end at the battle of Châlons, or Catalaunian Plains. The Hunnic army was forced to retreat, and the indomitable Alamanni were close to being finally broken. They attempted a spirited comeback with the remnants of their army in 457, but were repulsed from Italy.

## The later Alamanni

After 470 the Alamanni gave up their attacks against Rome. Their centuries-long feud came to an end when the Roman empire in the west was no longer there to feud with. Instead of Romans, the

The Alamanni finally met their match in the Frankish king Clovis, as depicted here in an imaginatively inaccurate nineteenth-century painting by Paul-Joseph Blanc.

Alamanni now had to contend with the fierce Frankish tribesmen who had taken over Gaul. The Franks under their king Clovis I (r. 509–11) were able to do what the Romans could not – beat the Alamanni in battle and keep them subdued. In part the Alamanni accepted Frankish rule because it was largely nominal. The Alamanni occupied an area covering part of what is now eastern France, Liechtenstein and much of Switzerland and northern Italy, and by and large the Franks left them to it.

The Alamanni gradually became Christian during the eighth century, and their leaders suffered during the upheavals of the Carolingian empire and later the Holy Roman Empire. Nevertheless, the Alamanni never really disappeared as a people. Nor did the name drop out of use. To the Franks the Alamanni became synonymous with Germans as a whole, and Allemagne is the modern French name for Germany. Today the version of German spoken in former Alamanni lands is descended from their dialect.

## Future Echoes

For much of the Middle Ages 'Alamannia' was a recognized state which gradually evolved into the Duchy of Swabia. The Hohenstaufen dynasty of Swabia also dominated the Holy Roman Empire through the eleventh and twelfth centuries.

The Alamanni also survive as a family name, Alemanni. Aristocratic Alemanni from Germany adopted the name of their people as a surname when they moved to Italy. Later Alemanni family members were involved in Italian politics from Florence to Naples. There are still Alemanni today – as exemplified by, for instance, the American actress Alexa Alemanni (who is fluent in Italian).

# 5th century AD – 7th century AD
# **The Jutes**
## Forgotten Invaders of Britain

*From the Jutes are descended the people of Kent, and of the Isle of Wight, and those also in the province of the West Saxons who are to this day called Jutes.*
Bede, *Ecclesiastical History of the English People* 15.2

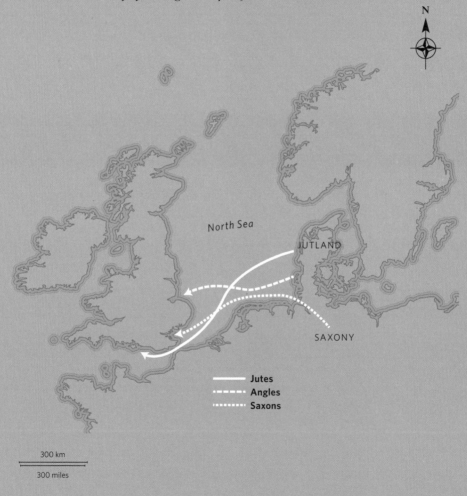

N

North Sea

JUTLAND

SAXONY

——— Jutes
- - - - Angles
········· Saxons

300 km

300 miles

Many modern English people may be able to name the Angles and the Saxons as two of the Germanic peoples who settled in the island after the Roman legions left, but there was also another one they may not recall so readily. That 'other one' is the Jutes. Yet while the descendants of those German settlers are called Anglo-Saxons, and the country is called England from 'Angles' Land', the Jutes have vanished without much trace. So who were they, and why has memory of them been lost?

## Invaders from across the sea

The Angles, the Saxons and the Jutes all came from the same area – basically modern Denmark plus the part of Germany immediately adjacent. Indeed, the modern Jutland peninsula takes its name from the Jutes, known as the 'Iutae' by the Romans. While later British history neatly divides the people of this whole region into three distinct tribes, modern archaeological evidence suggests that the overall picture was a lot less tidy. There was much intermarriage between aristocrats of the three peoples at the top of the social pile, and between peasants in adjoining lands at the bottom. It would help immensely to know if the tribes spoke different dialects of German, but as all were similarly illiterate not much trace of their languages survives in the original form.

As with so many other peoples, something set the population of the Danish peninsula on the move in the fifth century. For once the Huns may not have been to blame, because they were busy driving the Goths westwards across the Eurasian landmass half a continent away. It may simply be that Britain, after centuries of Roman settlement, was economically and agriculturally wealthy and the Jutes and their fellow tribesmen found that irresistible.

Sadly, at this time British records are also somewhat lacking. (The Dark Ages were particularly dark in post-Roman Britain.) Almost all the texts we have are ecclesiastical records kept by monks, and they were not greatly interested in politics, warfare or ethnography, so most non-religious reports of any value tend to be almost incidental. Furthermore, the new arrivals were worshippers of Woden and the Germanic gods, so they generally regarded monasteries as well-stocked treasure houses to be plundered. Those monks with direct experience of the early invaders often did not live to tell the tale.

The best accounts are from monks living in Wales, who thought of themselves not as Welsh, but as the original Britons. It seems from their reports that the earliest invaders of the island were

An illumination from a twelfth-century manuscript, the 'Miscellany on the Life of Saint Edmund' by the Alexis Master, shows armed Angles, Saxons and Jutes swarming across the English Channel.

the Angles. The Jutes soon followed, encouraged by reports from those returning to their homeland, and they began settling in large numbers on the British east coast. The records, though little better than legends, tell of two Jutes, Hengist and Horsa, tribal leaders who landed in Britain in 449–50. They and their warriors were originally mercenaries, but after Horsa died in battle, Hengist founded a kingdom in what is today Kent. This he held against both the more numerous Angles and the indignant British.

## Saxons and Jutes

Gildas, a British cleric writing in the late fifth or sixth century and perhaps the most reliable of the post-Roman historians, suggests that the then ruler of the Britons (Vortigern) called on the Saxons for help in repelling the Angles. (Even at this early stage it would appear that the Jutes tended to be overlooked. Britons lumped the early

Germanic invaders together under the name of 'Angles' whether they were Angles or Jutes. And not just the Britons – in a letter in the late sixth century, Pope Gregory addressed King Æthelberht – who was almost certainly a Jute – as 'King of the Angles'.)

Inviting in the Saxons was a remarkably ill-advised move, whatever the reason. Already in late Roman times there was in Britain an official called 'Count of the Saxon Shore', whose job was to maintain coastal forts and signal fires to warn of Saxon raids. Asking the Saxons to deal with the Angles and Jutes was rather akin to inviting a fox into the hen house.

The Saxons quickly established that the Jutes were better fighters than the Britons, and so bypassed them to take lands from the Britons further to the south and west. These lands later became Sussex ('South Saxons') and Wessex ('West Saxons') respectively.

Not only did the Jutes hold their own, but by around 700 they were considered as perhaps the dominant Germanic tribe in Britain (though this did not prevent the Britons from still calling them 'Angles'). One of the few who got it right was an eighth-century monk from Northumbria called the Venerable Bede, whose *Ecclesiastical History of the English People*, completed in 731, provides a substantial amount of what is known of the first three hundred years of post-Roman Britain.

The Venerable Bede at work in an illustration from a manuscript now in the British Library.

'Warriors from the three most formidable German nations, the Saxons, Angles and Jutes were given lands by the Britons. They were allowed to settle there on condition that they maintain the peace and security of the island' Bede reports (1.15).

Just before Bede's time King Æthelberht, the Jutish king of what is now Kent, converted to Christianity. It is not known if the Jutes of the 'Isle of Wihtwara' (the Isle of Wight) or the related people of 'Haestingas' (Hastings) immediately followed suit, but the conversion of the Kentish Jutes made their capital of Cantwaraburg a religious centre, as it continued to be in later centuries as the city of Canterbury. According to Bede, this Æthelberht was the great-great-grandson of Hengist, the founding king of the Jutes. After Æthelberht's death, which Bede says came after a – suspiciously – long reign of over half a century, the Jutes briefly returned to paganism.

## Assimilation and demise

The Jutes were the English people closest to France and they had settled in a very Romanized part of Britain. For both these reasons they are considered as having been somewhat more cultured than their Germanic kin. In fact, many of the non-British inhabitants in the region may have been imported during the final years of Roman rule and settled there by the Roman authorities. Therefore when the Jutes arrived a 'barbarian' people was already in the region, who acted as a semi-romanized buffer and allowed for some degree of integration.

Archaeology has also clearly shown that there was considerable interaction between the Jutes and the Franks. More Frankish artefacts have been found in lands occupied by the Jutes than in the more extensive lands of the Angles and the Saxons combined. The text of the Laws of Æthelberht (*c.* 600) is the oldest document surviving in Old English and this suggests that the later Jutes may also have been more literate than their English contemporaries.

Around the seventh century Kent faced dynastic problems. Exactly what went on is now lost in the mists of time, but it is clear that kings and usurpers in the royal line spent so much time fighting each other that they failed to take care of business. The River Thames was a trade route reaching deep into the British interior and tolls and tariffs were a valuable source of income. This slipped out of Kentish control as the Saxon kingdoms of Mercia and Wessex started to take a predatory interest in Kentish affairs.

By now it is uncertain to what extent Kent was exclusively inhabited by the Jutes. As mentioned, the Jutes, Angles and Saxons were never well-differentiated peoples, and intermarriage between the tribes and the Romano-British population was rapidly diluting any distinctively Jutish elements. The final blow destroying the Jutes as a people was delivered by the Vikings, who swarmed over Kent in the tenth century, attracted by that region's wealth. By the time of the Norman invasion of 1066, the Angles had merged with the Saxons to become a single, hyphenated people, and the Jutes had altogether vanished.

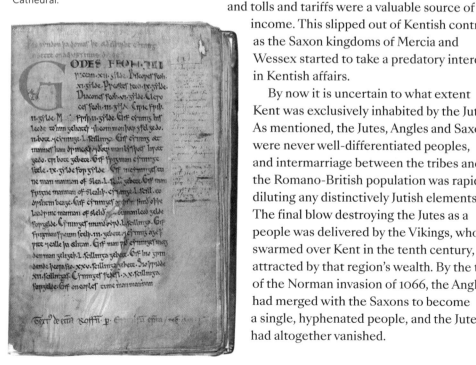

Among King Æthelberht of Kent's contributions to posterity was this law code, now held in the library of Rochester Cathedral.

## Future Echoes

Canterbury's reputation as a religious centre was considerably enhanced by the later martyrdom in 1170 of the 'turbulent priest' Thomas Becket. The city became a place of pilgrimage, as shown by the *Canterbury Tales* of Chaucer (*c.* 1400), one of the earliest English literary works. It was possible to get to Canterbury reasonably rapidly from London by keeping a horse at a pace somewhere between a trot and a gentle gallop. This became known as a 'Canter'.

Because the Jutes were somewhat friendlier to the Romano-British population, and because their lands were closest to more Romanized Gaul, many aristocratic Romano-British families, their householders and retainers chose to abandon Britain via Jutish lands and settle in the Armorican peninsula on the mainland of Europe. So many Britons settled in Armorica that the peninsula became known as 'Little Britain' (Brittany). By way of distinction, the actual island might be referred to as 'Great Britain', a designation that has been in use ever since.

A rider, sometimes said to be Chaucer himself, cantering to Canterbury in a detail from a facsimile of the early fifteenth-century Ellesmere Manuscript of the *Canterbury Tales*.

# Mid-5th century AD – 6th century AD
# **The Hephthalites**
# The Mysterious 'White Huns'

*The Ephthalitae are of the stock of the Huns in fact as well as in name; however they do not mingle with any of the Huns known to us, for they occupy a land neither adjoining nor even very near to them.... They are the only Huns who have white bodies and facial features which are not ugly.*

Procopius, *History of the Wars* 1.3.1

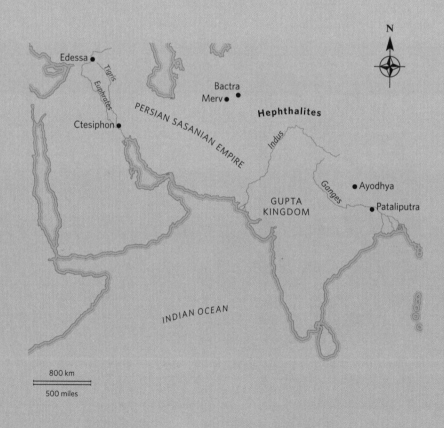

Procopius, who was writing about the Hephthalites in the sixth century AD, also says that they lived a sedentary life under a single king (apart from when unified under Attila, the Huns proper tended to form loose tribal confederations) and had a code of laws. Consequently, it seems fair to question whether the people he is describing were Huns at all. Yet Procopius is very firm on this point, even though all the details he lists seem contrary to his original statement. According to Procopius, they were Huns, and the Hephthalites have been known as 'White Huns' ever since.

## Disputed origins

Some scholarly studies claim that the White Huns were originally a Chinese tribe. Driven from their homeland, this people attached themselves to the Huns in their westward migration. Others disagree: the White Huns were not Huns at all, no matter what Procopius might say. Their name has Persian roots, and Indian texts report that the Hephthalites were fire-worshippers. This leads to the suggestion that the Hephthalites were an Aryan tribe of Kushans from Bactria who happened to attack the Persian Sasanian empire at the same time that the Huns attacked the west. Contemporary writers gave all invaders the generic name of 'Hunas', so this Bactrian people came to be inextricably confused with the Huns. When the Hephthalites started minting coins they used a Bactrian script, which further strengthens the Aryan hypothesis.

Nevertheless, yet a third school of thought informs us that despite the above arguments, the Hephthalites were indeed Huns. Hunnic tribes had each a distinctive colour by which their tribe affiliation might be recognized – there were tribes of Red, Green and Blue Huns. That the complexions of the Hephthalites were paler than their fellow tribesmen may have given them a claim to the colour white, but the very fact that they did so within the Hunnic tribal system proves that they were Huns, and were actually behaving as Huns in this at least.

A final opinion might be offered, namely that despite all the many scholarly debates and theories, no one really knows who the Hephthalites were, or where they actually came from.

Hephthalite coins show an eclectic mixture of Indian, Greek and Persian influences.

## First appearance

Whatever their origins, the White Huns appeared on the northeastern borders of the Persian empire in the mid-fifth century AD and immediately became a headache for both the Sasanian Persians and the Gupta empire of northern India. To the Romans in their collapsing empire, the Sasanians had always seemed an inexorable and relentless enemy, so they took a certain satisfaction from seeing their eastern rivals having to cope with barbarian invaders themselves.

There is no doubt that the Hephthalites were nomadic, for otherwise they would not have arrived where they did at all. Yet once they had inserted themselves into a vast wedge of land between India and the Persians, the Hephthalites showed little inclination to continue their wandering ways. It helped that the lands they had chosen were fertile and offered great potential for trade with both India and Persia. Also the new kingdom of the Hephthalites sat squarely across the Silk Road, and allowed Hephthalite aristocrats to become wealthy by doing little more than taxing caravans *en route* from China to the west.

As might be expected, the Persians were less than happy about the new arrivals, and between 435 and 450 they tried unsuccessfully to dislodge them from the lands they had seized. However, different

Pale faces predominate in this picture of a wedding procession from Samarkand, now in the Museum of Afrasiab, Uzbekistan.

as they were in many ways from other Huns, the White Huns shared the trait of being ferocious fighters. The Sasanian Persians were no mean fighters themselves, as the Romans had discovered the hard way, but eventually it became plain to them that they were not going to shift the Hephthalites very easily.

There were even times when the presence of a numerous and warlike people on their borders was useful to the Sasanians. When another tribe of Hunas (who may or may not have been Huns) swept in from the east, Indians, Persians and Hephthalites put aside their differences to fight off the new arrivals. Thereafter a Persian royal called Peroz used his recently established contacts with the Hephthalites to enlist their aid in Sasanian dynastic struggles. This Hephthalite intervention proved decisive, and Peroz ascended the throne in 458.

## Hephthalites and Persians

Given his debt to the Hephthalites, it seems rather ungrateful that as soon as Peroz became king the first thing he did was to gather an army and march against them. Peroz might have chosen to strike in 459 because he knew that the Hephthalite forces were committed to campaigns on the other side of their lands in a series of wars against the Indian Gupta empire. At this time the Gupta empire, rather like the Roman empire to the west, was in precipitate decline and the Hephthalites were certainly not helping the situation.

Exactly what happened next is unclear, but it is certain that, even though they were fighting on two fronts, the Hephthalites came out as victors. According to later a Islamic text (the *Shahnameh – The Book of Kings*), Peroz tried hard to close with what he thought was the Hephthalite army. It was in fact a cavalry screen which led the Sasanian king and his army ever deeper into the desert. Heat and thirst did the work of fighting for the Hephthalites and Peroz was forced to surrender. Meanwhile, on the other side of their lands, the Hephthalites were pummelling the Indians so successfully that they had taken over a large part of the Gupta empire. Uttar Pradesh, Punjab and Kashmir were at least partly occupied.

Peroz was nothing if not persistent. According to one source, his hatred of the Hephthalites stemmed from the extensive practice of homosexuality. Certainly, the Hephthalites formed what were at the least very deep friendships. Procopius (*History of the Wars* 1.3.8) reports that 'Groups of up to twenty become extremely attached to one another, and they become permanent banqueting-companions. They even have a share in each other's property, as though it is held in common. Then, upon the death of the man who founded this company, it is the custom that all these men to go alive into the tomb with him.'

Whatever the source of Peroz's deep animosity, it had a high price. Following the loss of his first army in the desert, Peroz returned with a second. This was defeated and Peroz was captured. After he had ransomed himself and returned to Persia, he raised yet another army, apparently determined to defeat the Hephthalites or die in the attempt. If so, he got his wish, because in 484 Peroz, together with his army, perished in battle.

These multiple defeats decimated the manpower of the Persians and consequently Sasanian aggression against the Romans practically ceased, giving the Roman empire in the east valuable breathing space to reorganize after the loss of the western Roman empire. In fact the Romans so appreciated the feud between Sasanians and Hephthalites that they paid part of Peroz's ransom so he could return to the field.

Central Asia was to be ruled by the Hephthalites for the next century. Both Indian kings and the Persians paid them tribute. Hephthalite arms sponsored the man who succeeded Peroz, and the next time Hephthalites and Persians took to the field it was in a combined attack on Edessa in the eastern Roman empire in 503 in the so-called Anastasian War.

## Decline and fall

The same migratory pressures that may have brought the Hephthalites to the borders of the Persian empire later brought the Turks. The Sasanians eventually recovered from the disastrous rule of Peroz, and became aggressively restive. In India, Hephthalite misgovernment and religious intolerance had sapped the support of the native population. With the Turks pressing from the north, the Hephthalites found themselves under attack from all sides, and they buckled under the strain.

By the end of the sixth century the Indian empire of the Hephthalites had fragmented and a Turkish-Persian alliance had conquered Central Asia. The Hephthalites held on to some principalities in Afghanistan, but by then they were of little interest to the Persian and Indian sources upon which we rely for information. As mysteriously as they had appeared, the Hephthalites faded away once more.

The end of the Hephthalites as the Persian hero Sukhra crushes them in battle somewhere in Khorasan (between modern Iran and Afghanistan).

## Future Echoes

The Hephthalites vanished, but not completely without trace. Their presence long affected the culture of the Bactrian people, while those Hephthalites who remained in India rapidly merged with the population. Even today some Indian towns and villages bear the names which were allocated to them by the Hephthalites during their brief and often brutal rule.

# Epilogue

*Cities and Thrones and Powers,*
  *Stand in Time's eye,*
*Almost as long as flowers,*
  *Which daily die:*
*But, as new buds put forth*
  *To glad new men,*
*Out of the spent and unconsidered Earth,*
  *The Cities rise again.*

Rudyard Kipling, *Cities and Thrones and Powers*, 1922

It is hard to read of the peoples described in this book without thinking of one's own 'tribe', whosoever they may be, and wondering what the future holds for them. Of the dozens of tribes and peoples described here, few have endured and many that have are much diminished. Does the same fate await your people and culture? Almost certainly.

Consider the non-indigenous peoples who have migrated to North America. They have been a presence on the continent for three hundred years. Few, looking at their mighty cities and crowded thoroughfares can imagine them as anything but permanent – and yet? The Akkadian people became established in Sumeria around forty-three centuries ago. They quickly became the dominant power in the region, and their laws and language were adopted by their neighbours. Their king, Sargon, was rightly known as 'the Great' for his achievements. Few Akkadians, looking at their own mighty cities and crowded thoroughfares could imagine them as anything but permanent. And yet, today only a handful of historians know of the Akkadians; the capital city of Akkad, which gave this people their name, is lost so comprehensively that no one today knows where it once stood.

Consider also an archaeologist called Nabonidus. He is famous for an expedition to the oasis city of Tayma in Saudi Arabia. There he discovered a ruined temple to the sun god Samas, and nearby a ruined temple established by an Akkadian king called Naram-Sin. Both temples were painstakingly excavated and the artefacts dated. Yet the most interesting thing about Nabonidus as an archaeologist is that he was a Babylonian who lived around two and a half thousand years ago. That puts his excavations at the mid-point between the time that those temples were built in 2200 BC and today. Human history has lasted a very long time, and what we term 'modern history' is a laughably small fraction of that period. Ask most people to describe 'the most important' people and events in history, however, and almost all their choices will be from the modern era.

So this history of lost and forgotten peoples is a reminder that our time and culture is ephemeral. Even if we do not vanish as have so many peoples before, within a few generations of change our descendants would regard us as distant strangers. The people and events filling our mental horizons will eventually become footnotes in obscure texts. That sense of permanence and importance we enjoy today was once also felt by the Akkadians.

# Further Reading

## Part One: The First Civilizations
### The Akkadians
Grayson, A. K., 'The Empire of Sargon of Akkad', *Archiv für Orientforschung* 25 (1974), pp. 56–64.

Levin, Y., 'Nimrod the Mighty, King of Kish, King of Sumer and Akkad', *Vetus Testamentum* 52 (2002), pp. 350–66.

Speiser, E. A., 'Some Factors in the Collapse of Akkad', *Journal of the American Oriental Society* 72 (1952), pp. 97–101.

### The Amorites
Homsher, R. S. and Cradic, M. S., 'Rethinking Amorites', in O. Lipschitz et al. (eds), *Rethinking Israel: Studies in the History and Archaeology of Ancient Israel in Honor of Israel Finkelstein* (Winona Lake, IN, 2017), pp. 131–50.

Kenyon, K., *Amorites and Canaanites* (Oxford, 1966).

Van Seters, J., 'The Terms "Amorite" and "Hittite" in the Old Testament', *Vetus Testamentum* 22 (1972), pp. 64–81.

### The Canaanites
Gray, J., *The Canaanites*. Ancient Peoples and Places (London, 1964).

Lemche, N. P., *The Canaanites and Their Land: The Tradition of the Canaanites* (Sheffield, 1991).

Tubb, J. N., *Canaanites*. Peoples of the Past. Rev. ed. (London, 2006).

### The Elamites
Bridey, F., 'Susa and the Kingdom of Elam in the Neo-Elamite Period', in G. Brereton (ed.), *I Am Ashurbanipal: King of the World, King of Assyria* (London and New York, 2018), pp. 166–79.

Cameron, G. G., *History of Early Iran* (Chicago, 1936).

Pittman, H., 'The Proto-Elamite Period', in P. O. Harper et al. (eds), *The Royal City of Susa. Ancient Near Eastern Treasures in the Louvre* (New York, 1992), pp. 68–70.

Potts, D. T., *The Archaeology of Elam: Formation and Transformation of an Ancient Iranian State* (Cambridge, 1999).

### The Hittites
Bryce, T., *The Kingdom of the Hittites* (Oxford and New York, 2005).

Collins, B., *The Hittites and Their World* (Atlanta, 2007).

Gurney, O. R., *The Hittites* (Baltimore, 1952).

### The Hyksos
Booth, C., *The Hyksos Period in Egypt* (Princes Risborough, 2005).

Redford, D. B., 'The Hyksos Invasion in History and Tradition', *Orientalia* 39 (1970), pp. 1–51.

Van Seters, J., *The Hyksos: A New Investigation* (New Haven, 1966).

### The Sea Peoples
Dickinson, O., 'The Collapse at the End of the Bronze Age', in E. H. Cline (ed.), *The Oxford Handbook of the Bronze Age Aegean ca. 3000-1000 BC* (Oxford, 2010), pp. 483–90.

Oren, E. D. (ed.), *The Sea Peoples and Their World. A Reassessment* (Philadelphia, 2000).

Sandars N. K., *The Sea Peoples: Warriors of the Ancient Mediterranean, 1250–1150 BC*. Ancient Peoples and Places (London, 1978).

## Part Two: From Assyria to Alexander
### The Lost Tribes of Israel
Ben-Dor Benite, Z., *The Ten Lost Tribes: A World History* (Oxford and New York, 2013).

Parfitt, T., *Journey to the Vanished City: The Search for a Lost Tribe of Israel* (New York, 2000).

Shtull-Trauring, S. (ed.), *Letters from Beyond the Sambatyon: The Myth of the Ten Lost Tribes* (New York, 1997).

### The Arameans
Bryce, T., *The World of the Neo-Hittite Kingdoms: A Political and Military History* (Oxford, 2012).

Lipiński, E., *The Arameans: Their Ancient History, Culture, Religion* (Leuven, 2000).

Tubb, J. T., 'The Levant and Assryia' in G. Brereton (ed.), *I Am Ashurbanipal: King of the World, King of Assyria* (London and New York, 2018), pp. 118–37.

## The Philistines

Ben-Dor Evian, S., 'Ramesses III and the "Sea-Peoples": Towards a New Philistine Paradigm', *Oxford Journal of Archaeology* 36 (2017), pp. 267–85.

Dothan, T. and M., *People of the Sea: the Search for the Philistines* (New York, 1992).

Litani, G., *The World of the Philistines: The Rise and Fall of the Philistine Culture; Beginning of the 12th Century BCE–End of the 7th Century BCE,* trans. Z. Gal (Ashdod, 2013).

## The Dorians

Alty, J., 'Dorians and Ionians', *Journal of Hellenic Studies* 102 (1982), pp. 1–14.

Hall, J. M., *Ethnic Identity in Greek Antiquity* (Cambridge and New York, 2000).

Thomas, C., 'Found: The Dorians', *Expedition Magazine* (1978), pp. 21–23.

## The Phrygians

Roller, L. E,. *In Search of God the Mother: The Cult of Anatolian Cybele* (Berkeley, 1999).

Sivas, T. and Sivas, H. (eds), *Phrygians: In the Land of Midas, In the Shadow of Monuments* (Istanbul, 2012).

Thonemann, P. (ed.), *Roman Phrygia: Culture and Society.* Greek Culture in the Roman World (Cambridge, 2013).

## The Illyrians

Appian, *Illyrica,* Loeb Classical Library (Cambridge, MA, 1912).

Matijašić, I. '"Shrieking Like Illyrians", Historical Geography and the Greek Perspective of the Illyrian World in the 5th century BC' *Arheološki vestnik* 62 (2011), pp. 289–316.

Wilkes, J., *The Illyrians* (Oxford, 1996).

## The Lydians

Hanfmann, G. M. (ed.), *Sardis from Prehistoric to Roman Times* (Cambridge, MA, 1983).

Laflı, E. (ed.), *Archaeology and History of Lydia from the Early Lydian Period to Late Antiquity (8th Century B.C.–6th Century A.D.)* (Izmir, 2017).

Payne, A. and Wintjes, J., *Lords of Asia Minor: An Introduction to the Lydians.* Philippika 93 (Wiesbaden, 2016).

## The Sicels

De Angelis, F., *Archaic and Classical Greek Sicily: A Social and Economic History* (Oxford, 2016).

Leighton, R., *Sicily Before History. An Archaeological Survey from the Palaeolithic to the Iron Age* (London and Ithaca, NY, 1999).

Sjöqvist, E., *Sicily and the Greeks: Studies in the Interrelationship Between the Indigenous Populations and the Greek Colonists* (Michigan, 1973).

## The Medes

Dandamaev, M. A. et al., *The Culture and Social Institutions of Ancient Iran* (Cambridge and New York, 2004).

Diakonoff, I. M., 'Media', in I. Gershevitch (ed.), *The Cambridge History of Iran* 2 (Cambridge, 1985), pp. 36–148.

Driscoll, J. F., 'Media and Medes', *The Catholic Encyclopedia* 10 (New York, 1911).

## The Chaldeans

Brinkman, J. A., *Political History of Post-Kassite Babylonia 1158–722 B.C.* (Rome, 1968).

Brinkman, J. A., 'Notes on Arameans and Chaldeans in Southern Babylonia in the Early Seventh Century B.C.', *Orientalia* 46 (1977), pp. 304–25.

Oates, J., *Babylon.* Ancient Peoples and Places. Rev. ed. (London, 1986).

## The Kushites

Dunham, D., 'Notes on the History of Kush 850 B.C.–A.D. 350', *American Journal of Archaeology* 50:3 (1946), pp. 378–88.

Edwards, D. N., *The Nubian Past* (London, 2004).

Welsby, D. A., *The Kingdom of Kush: The Napatan and Meroitic Empires* (London and Princeton, 1996).

## The Bactrians

Holt, F., *Thundering Zeus, The Making of Hellenistic Bactria* (Berkeley, 1999).

Sherwin-White, S. and Kuhrt, A., *From Samarkhand to Sardis: A New Approach to the Seleucid Empire.* Hellenistic Culture and Society 13 (Berkeley and London, 1993).

Tarn, W. W., *The Greeks in Bactria and India* (Cambridge, 1966).

## Part Three: The Coming of Rome

### The Thracians

Fol, A., *Thrace and the Thracians* (London and New York, 1977).

Venedikov, I., 'Thrace', *The Metropolitan Museum of Art Bulletin* 35 (1977), pp. 73–80.

Webber, C., *The Thracians* 700 BC–AD 46 (Oxford, 2001).

### The Epirots

Champion, J., *Pyrrhus of Epirus* (Barnsley, 2017).

Greenwalt, W. S., 'Macedonia, Illyria, and Epirus', in J. Roisman and I. Worthington (eds), *A Companion to Ancient Macedonia* (Oxford, 2010), pp. 279–305.

Hammond, N. G. L., 'The Ethne in Epirus and Upper Macedonia', *Annual of the British School at Athens* 95 (2000), pp. 345–52.

### The Sabines

Brown, R., 'Livy's Sabine Women and the Ideal of Concordia', *Transactions of the American Philological Association* 125 (1995) pp. 291–319.

Husband, R. W., 'Race Mixture in Early Rome', *Transactions and Proceedings of the American Philological Association* 40 (1917), pp. 63–81.

Plutarch, 'Romulus', *Lives* Vol. 1, trans. J. Dryden, ed. A. H. Clough (New York, 2001).

### The Samaritans

Knoppers, G. N., *Jews and Samaritans: The Origins and History of Their Early Relations* (Oxford, 2013).

Pummer, R. *The Samaritans* (Leiden, 1987).

Tappy, R. E., *The Archaeology of Israelite Samaria, Vol. 1: Early Iron Age through the Ninth Century* BCE (Leiden, 1992).

### The Garamantes and Numidians

Balmaceda, C. M. and Comber, M., *Sallust: The War Against Jugurtha* (Liverpool, 2008).

Daniels, C., *The Garamantes of Southern Libya* (Cambridge and New York, 1970).

Walsh, P. G., 'Massinissa', *Journal of Roman Studies* 55 (1965), pp. 149–60.

### The Sarmatians

Brzezinski, R. and Mielczarek, M., *The Sarmatians* 600 BC–AD 450 (Oxford, 2002).

Melyukova, A. and Julia, C., 'The Scythians and Sarmatians', in D. Sinor (ed.), *The Cambridge History of Early Inner Asia* (Cambridge, 1990), pp. 97–117.

Sulimirski, T. *The Sarmatians*. Ancient Peoples and Places (London, 1970).

### The Nabataeans

Graf, D., *Rome and the Arabian Frontier: From the Nabataeans to the Saracens* (Aldershot and Brookfield, VT, 1997).

Starcky, J., 'The Nabataeans: A Historical Sketch', *The Biblical Archaeologist* 18, no. 4 (1955), pp. 81–106.

Taylor, J., *Petra and the Lost Kingdom of the Nabataeans* (London, 2001; Cambridge, MA, 2002).

### The Celtiberians

Alberro, M., 'Celtic Heritage in the Northwest of the Iberian Peninsula', *Emania* 19 (2002), pp. 75–84.

Almagro-Gorbea, M., 'The Celts of the Iberian Peninsula', in V. Kruta et al. (eds), *The Celts* (London, 1991), pp. 389–405.

Matyszak, P., *Sertorius and the Struggle for Spain* (Barnsley, 2013).

### The Galatians

Chisholm, H., 'Galatia', *Encyclopedia Britannica* 11 (Cambridge, 1911), pp. 393–94.

Krentz, E., *Galatians* (Minneapolis, 1985).

Strobel, K., 'State Formation by the Galatians of Asia Minor', *Anatolica* 28 (2002), pp. 1–46.

Strobel, K., 'Central Anatolia' in D. M. Master (ed.), *The Oxford Encyclopedia of the Bible and Archaeology* (Oxford, 2013).

### The Arverni

Caesar, C. J., *Caesar's Gallic Wars*, trans. W. A. McDevitte and H. G. Bohn (New York, 1869).

Ebel, C., *Transalpine Gaul: The Emergence of a Roman Province* (Leiden, 1976).

Malleson, G., 'Vercingetorix', *Transactions of the Royal Historical Society* 4 (1889), pp. 1–40.

### The Catuvellauni

Bédoyère, G. de la, *Roman Britain: A New History* (London, rev. ed., 2013).

Branigan, K., *The Catuvellauni,* Peoples of Roman Britain (Gloucester, 1985).

Braund, D. *Ruling Roman Britain: Kings, Queens, Governors, and Emperors from Julius Caesar to Agricola* (London, 1996).

Cottrell, L., *The Roman Invasion of Britain* (New York, 1992).

### The Iceni

Bulst, C. M., 'The Revolt of Queen Boudicca in AD 60', *Historia* 10 (1961), pp. 496–509.

Collingridge, V., *Boudica* (London, 2006).

Johnson, M., *Boudicca* (London, 2012).

Laycock, S. *Britannia – The Failed State: Ethnic Conflict and the End of Roman Britain* (Stroud, 2012).

### The Batavi

Matyszak, P., *Imperial General: The Remarkable Career of Petellius Cerialis* (Barnsley, 2012).

Pierce, W. M., *History of the Batavi: The Ancestor of the Dutch and the Boers of South Africa* (1996).

Roymans, N., *Ethnic Identity and Imperial Power: The Batavians in the Early Roman Empire* (Amsterdam, 2004).

### The Dacians

MacKendrick, P. L., *The Dacian Stones Speak* (Chapel Hill, 2000).

Rossi, L., *Trajan's Column and the Dacian Wars* (London and Ithaca, NY, 1971).

Wilcox, P., *Rome's Enemies (1): Germanics and Dacians* (London, 1982).

## Part Four: The Fall of Rome in the West
### The Alans

Alemany, A., *Sources on the Alans: A Critical Compilation* (Leiden, 2000).

Bachrach, B. S., 'The Alans in Gaul', *Traditio* 23 (1967), pp. 476–89.

Bachrach, B. S., *A History of the Alans in the West* (Minneapolis, 1973).

### The Vandals

Clover, F. M., *The Late Roman West and the Vandals* (Aldershot and Brookfield, VT, 1993).

Hughes, I., *Gaiseric: The Vandal Who Destroyed Rome* (Barnsley, 2017).

MacDowall, S., *The Vandals: Conquerors of the Roman Empire* (Barnsley, 2016).

### The Visigoths

Gwynn, D., *The Goths. Lost Civilizations* (London, 2018).

Heather, P. (ed.), *The Visigoths from the Migration Period to the Seventh Century: An Ethnographic Perspective,* Studies in Historical Archaeoethnology (Woodbridge, 2003).

MacDowall, S., *The Goths: Conquerors of the Roman Empire:* (Barnsley, 2017)

### The Ostrogoths

Barnish, S. and Federico Marazzi, F., 'The Ostrogoths from the Migration Period to the Sixth Century: An Ethnographic Perspective', *The English Historical Review* 124 (2009), pp. 1448–50.

Burns, T. S., *A History of the Ostrogoths* (Bloomington, IN, 1984).

Hodgkin, T., *Theodoric the Goth: The Barbarian Champion of Civilization* (London and New York, 1891).

### The Alamanni

Chisholm, H. (ed.), 'Alamanni' *Encyclopedia Britannica* (Cambridge, 1911), p. 468.

Drinkwater, J. F., *The Alamanni and Rome, 213–496* (Oxford and New York, 2007).

Wood, I. (ed.), *Franks and Alamanni in the Merovingian Period: An Ethnographic Perspective.* Studies in Historical Archaeoethnology (Woodbridge, 2003).

### The Jutes

Chadwick, M., *The Origin of the English Nation* (Cambridge, 2010).

Starcke, V., 'The Jutes' in V. Starcke, *Denmark in World History: The External History of Denmark from the Stone Age to the Middle Ages* (Philadelphia, 1962), pp. 88–98.

Welch, M., *Discovering Anglo-Saxon England* (London and Philadelphia, 1992).

### The Hephthalites

Frantz Grenet, F., 'Regional Interaction in Central Asia and Northwest India in the Kidarite and Hephthalite Periods', *Proceedings of the British Academy* 116 (2002), pp. 203–24.

Litvinsky, B. A. 'The Hephthalite Empire', in *History of the Civilizations of Central Asia, III: The Crossroads of Civilizations: A.D. 250–750* (Paris, 1996), pp. 135–62.

Stein, M. A. (ed.), 'White Huns and Kindred Tribes in the History of the Indian North West Frontier', *Indian Antiquary* 34 (1905), pp. 74–85.

# Sources of Illustrations

Images are listed by page number
**a**=above, **b**=below, **l**=left, **r**=right

# Index

First published in the United Kingdom
in 2020 by Thames & Hudson Ltd,
181A High Holborn, London WC1V 7QX

First published in the United States of
America in 2020 by Thames & Hudson
Inc., 500 Fifth Avenue, New York,
New York 10110

First paperback edition published 2022

*Forgotten Peoples of the Ancient World*
© 2020 Thames & Hudson Ltd, London

Text © 2020 Philip Matyszak

Maps by Martin Lubikowski,
ML Design, London

British Library Cataloguing-in-
Publication Data
A catalogue record for this book is
available from the British Library

Library of Congress Control Number
2019949040

ISBN 978-0-500-29694-3

Printed and bound in China
by RR Donnelley

MIX
Paper from
responsible sources
FSC® C144853
www.fsc.org

Be the first to know about our new
releases, exclusive content and author
events by visiting
**thamesandhudson.com**
**thamesandhudsonusa.com**
**thamesandhudson.com.au**